MY LIFE IN FOOTBALL

ROBBIE FOWLER

MY LIFE IN FOOTBALL

BLINK
bringing you closer

Published by Blink Publishing
2.25, The Plaza,
535 Kings Road,
Chelsea Harbour,
London, SW10 0SZ

www.blinkpublishing.co.uk

facebook.com/blinkpublishing
twitter.com/blinkpublishing

Hardback – 978-1-788-701-10-5
Trade paperback – 978-1-788-701-11-2
Ebook – 978-1-788-701-12-9

A CIP catalogue of this book is available from the British Library.

Typeset by seagulls.net
Printed and bound in Great Britain by Clays Ltd, Elcograf S.p.A.

1 3 5 7 9 10 8 6 4 2

Blink Publishing is an imprint of Bonnier Books UK
www.bonnierbooks.co.uk

This book is dedicated to my incredible family, without whose love and support I would be nothing.

My wonderful mother Marie, who gave me everything. My Dad Bobby, who I miss every day. My sister Lisa, who was always there for me. My brothers, Anthony and Scott, who kept my feet on the ground.

Special thanks to my fantastic children Madison, Jaya, Mackenzie and Jacob, who I love more than anything in the world. You four are my pride and joy and you make me smile every single day.

Thanks don't go near to expressing the love and gratitude I have for my amazing wife Kerrie – my rock, my refuge and, quite simply, the love of my life; but thank you for saying 'Yes'. I might be far away but you're all right here in my heart.

CONTENTS

24TH MARCH 1997

It's Liverpool against Arsenal in a live game at Highbury. We're both still just about involved in the title race, third and fourth respectively. It was being billed as a clash of the purists as the country's two most attacking teams came up against each other.

We're 1–0 up and Mark Wright sends a speculative ball for me to chase after – and I find myself leaving Tony Adams in my wake, with only David Seaman to beat. I slightly overrun the ball, giving Seaman a sniff of a chance, and he rushes out to try to smother it. I get there first, nick the ball past him, but in doing so, my momentum (and the change of direction) sends me sprawling in the box. Seaman hadn't touched me and had no intention of doing so. The referee was chasing the play from behind and from his point of view, it probably looked a stone-cold foul by the keeper.

The ref caught up with us and immediately pointed to the spot. Straight away, I jumped up and went over to him, waving my hands to say, 'No contact, no contact.' I assured him that Seaman hadn't touched me, but he'd already made his decision.

Two days later, the club received a fax addressed to me from Sepp Blatter – the President of FIFA. He told me how refreshing it was that I'd tried to get the penalty decision overturned.

The very next day I received a letter from UEFA, telling me they were fining me £1,000 for displaying a political slogan on my T-shirt at a previous game.

Talk about hero to zero.

This is a footballer's life.

1

LIVERPOOL (HOME)

To this day people ask whether Toxteth was the making of me. I'm not sure what to make of that. Up until I got my first flat in the Albert Dock I never lived anywhere else, so it's not like I can compare my childhood home with another place. I grew up in a maisonette on one of the main through roads, Windsor Street, and when I was about ten or so we moved to Hughson Street, off Park Road. There was me, my older sister, Lisa, our Anthony, who was a few years younger than me, and, later on, our Scott came along.

Our Lisa was the best big sister you could wish for (and still is). She wasn't one of those bossy older siblings who's always telling you off and putting you down. Lisa was more of a mate when we were growing up, then, as we got older, she was someone I could always talk to, full of good advice. And, as much as I loved Everton, our Anthony was Liverpool mad. Born in 1980, he was getting into footy just as King Kenny was building that incredible, all-conquering team of John Barnes, Ray Houghton, Peter Beardsley and John Aldridge (and soon Anthony would soon have someone closer to home to cheer for, too!).

The world of my childhood spanned from the recreation ground on Upper Warwick Street to the youth club on Park Road. That was me, right from the first whistle – a normal, outdoorsy, football-loving Toxteth lad. All my family lived in and around Liverpool 8 and I loved growing up there.

Toxteth of course became world-famous (or infamous) after the riots of July 1981 and, like a lot of inner-city areas, it has had its problems over the years. Scousers often describe themselves as 'North Enders' or 'South Enders'. Jamie Carragher and Steve McManaman are pure North End, but I'm from the sophisticated South End of the city. Toxteth and Dingle, known to locals as Granby or Liverpool 8, is the area that stretches from the Maternity Hospital on Upper Parliament Street down past the Anglican Cathedral, all the way to the River Mersey and along as far as Princes Park. The river and the sea played a huge part in developing Toxteth as an area and as a community. From the grand old merchants' villas around Belvedere Road and Princes Drive to the dense terraced streets of the Dingle, Liverpool 8 always had a mix of housing and the broadest mix of peoples – Irish, Jamaican, Filipino, Ghanaian, Welsh, Nigerian, Somali ... All of these nations and many, many more made Liverpool 8 their home, adding a certain something to the local flavour.

The Toxteth I grew up in was a tough, busy, multi-cultural community – tight-knit and, I suppose, a bit suspicious of outsiders. But 'community' is what it was and is, and this is where I'm from. I think what interviewers are driving at when they ask me about Liverpool 8 is this assumption that the place was so rough and so poor that I must have been desperate to get out. Far from it! I had a dead normal, happy childhood. At no stage did I feel impoverished or neglected, or whatever. I always had the best footy boots, always had a smile on my face, and in every way I can think of, I was just another normal kid who lived for football. But where those reporters *are* spot on is that the streets I grew up on, and their equivalent in London, in Manchester, in Belfast, Newcastle or Glasgow – time and time again, these are the streets that breed footballers. You look at Raheem Sterling or Dele Alli today; Steven Gerrard and Wayne Rooney; Gazza, Paul Ince, Alan Shearer from my time; Kenny Dalglish, Ian Rush, going all the way back to Jimmy Johnstone and Georgie Best … There's a pattern there, isn't there? These are all working-class boys from the inner-city streets or sprawling new towns and council estates and they all badly, badly want to be footballers. There's no Plan B to fall back on. They want it, and they want it like mad.

That was me, too: inner city born and bred, and football mad. I don't know if there's such a thing as a born footballer, but footy was pretty much all I ever thought about and the only thing I did from the day I could walk. Some might say

I never got much faster than those toddling days, but boy, did I want to play! As it happens, I did have a bit of trouble with my mobility as a kid. It's a common enough thing, but I was born with a 'clicky' hip, which is just a minor design flaw that, these days, would be spotted at birth and treated with a correctional brace. Mum took me to see various doctors and consultants over it, but the consensus was that nature has a way of righting these things. I actually grew up walking with a slightly uneven gait for those first few years, though it sorted itself out before primary school. I also had asthma as a kid but neither that, nor my hip, could keep me indoors. There was the Rec, a patch of land right opposite our maisonettes – it was turned into an all-weather pitch when I was about eight and I used to be out there with a ball, morning, noon and night. I truly believe that everything that happened later can be traced back to that little scrap of green (or brown, when the rain came down in the winter) turf. Over the years, I've spoken to a lot of players who come from a similar background and they all have a similar tale to tell. Each and every one of us was out until all hours with a ball glued to our feet, playing wherever and whenever we could, until there was no one left to play against or with. I remember this feeling of sadness, almost akin to betrayal, when the last of my pals said they had to go home. I lived right opposite the rec, so there was always my mum or my sister or someone to keep an eye on me – but I never wanted to come in.

Over the years people have asked, how do you manage to strike a ball so cleanly, so hard, with so little back-lift? I think the answer is out there on that scruffy patch of land, day in, day out, trying little things. I would punch through the ball in different ways, transmitting the power from different parts of my legs. None of it was scientifically thought through, it was more a case of trying to entertain myself, seeing what would happen if I hit the ball on its side, or with the side of my foot instead of my instep. I remember thinking, 'Wow, look at the way it swerves when you hit it like that!' And, over time, if you do something often enough, it definitely gets easier – it becomes another arrow in your quiver. So, when there was no one else to play with, I'd be just as happy practising all these things by myself, doing turns against imaginary opponents, knocking the ball against the wall, trapping it, slotting it, chipping it, and so on. Even when I was eight or nine, I'd be playing against lads of 14, 15, 16 and I could always hold my own. I was very small and nippy, and even though they were all bigger and stronger, it was hard for them to get the ball off me. I mean, I was never lightning quick – certainly not over 20, 30 yards – but I was fast in and around the goal area. Over five or ten yards, I was quick in my head as well as with my feet, and that is key to scoring goals. And, for as long as I can remember going way, way back, I always, *always* scored goals.

Right from those days playing scratch games, I would be 'first pick'. When you all line up – whether it's a game during break at school or one of those long, hot games in your summer holidays – I was always the first to be picked. That's not me being big-headed; the other captain, whichever team didn't get me, used to have a weed on, like – 'We've got no chance, now.' So, I had an idea I was a good player, right from an early age. I'd also be on the receiving end of some rough treatment, which is another litmus test of whether you're starting to get a name for yourself – kind of a back-handed compliment. Most of the time I'd just bounce off the tackle or, if they got me, I'd jump back up and carry on. Nothing really bothered me. Over time I learned to anticipate the wild tackles and either ride the challenge, jump it or change direction. After a while that just becomes another part of your armament as a player – knowing what's coming and how to avoid it or absorb it.

Years later, as part of my pro licence I did a thesis on the question of *Nature or Nurture*: are the very best players born with exceptional natural talent, or can we coach players to an elite standard? My argument was, whereas a degree of natural ability gives a player a head start, it is practice, practice, practice that takes you to the very highest level. Messi aged seven, dribbling a tennis ball in and out, left foot, right foot, in and out. Beckham staying behind after training solely to practise free kicks. And there was me and my dad, Bobby, out on that field on Upper Warwick Street, doing routines. Everyone used to tell me (and Dad told me enough times!) that he was a very good player himself. He played in midfield for Nicosia in the South Liverpool league and came up against some cracking teams and some very good players. My dad never had any ambitions other than enjoying the game, playing and watching, but he knew his football inside out. He could see from a very early age that I had talent and he, more than anyone, made sure that I put in the hours and worked like mad, honing that natural ability.

In the summer months there used to be these big games of footy where everyone from all around our area, all ages and sizes, mucked in. There was a big Somali community by ours and the Somali lads loved a game – so much so that they'd often come straight from prayer, still wearing their formal dress and their best shoes. I would be playing in these games that seemed to go on all day, 20-a-side, and even at that level I would score some unbelievable goals. Dad saw, right from the start, that I might just have what it takes to be a player. He saw that I could accelerate from a standing start and weave in and out of players and get a shot away, so he'd work with me, again and again, concentrating on my strengths but also any weak points. For example, I was quite small in those days, so he'd make sure that I'd practise my headers – 'Just because you're small doesn't mean you won't get chances with your head, so let's make sure they count,' he'd say. And I'd run in from the left, then the right, with him chucking the ball in at different speeds and angles, forcing me to adjust my body shape, or my starting position, or just to react quickly to a half-chance.

One thing my dad was adamant about was that I had to be comfortable on both feet. I was a natural left-footer, I would dribble, shoot, pass – everything was on my left foot, which was always seen as a big advantage in those days, but Dad had me out on that field working on my right peg. It's not like he had to force me, by the way – I wanted to do it, I wanted to be as good as I possibly could be. But, at first, I was that walking cliché of the player whose other foot is just for standing on. It felt really uncomfortable to me, even the basics of trying to kick with my right foot at all – let alone hit it with any power, direct the ball or even score! The best way I can describe it is that it was exactly like a right-hander trying to write their name with their left hand – completely awkward and alien. But my old fella knew full well that, with work, with practice, with routine I would start to 'feel' the ball with my right boot as well as my left.

We'd start first of all by just doing volleys and loopers with a smaller, heavier practice ball. I'd bounce the ball in front of me and then either clip it on the half-volley or clear it as far and as hard as I could. That's what I mean by looping the ball – it was a clean strike, like a goalkeeper's clearance, hitting the ball from underneath, getting the best contact and as much distance as I could. This technique was just a very effective way of getting a good, strong connection and a more natural kind of instinctive feel for the ball with my right foot. Over time, with practice, it began to feel much more natural until, eventually, I didn't think twice about using my right boot.

With everything we know today about sports science and so on, we're much more aware that the brain responds to repetitive behaviour patterns. If we do the same thing again and again, the brain will eventually absorb that routine, almost like a bar code if you like, processing the info so that eventually a function becomes 'second nature'. That was the basis of my *Nature or Nurture* paper, and that was me, day after day, night after night, out on that field with my dad, hammering that training ball – left foot, right foot, right foot, left. Neighbours walking past must have thought, 'There he is again, little Robert Ryder – same old drills, over and over. Give the poor kid a break!'

But it never felt like that to me. For me it was never a chore, it was something I wanted to do in order to get better. It just seemed obvious: if you want to improve and take that next step, you have to work at it. So many of the goals I scored over the years, honestly, I scored them in miniature out on the recreation ground – in fact, my first ever goal in an England shirt was a direct replica of one of those right-footed 'loopers'! I'll tell you about that one later, but there was a different sort of loop through the Schools and Youth football system to navigate first, before the limelight started to flicker …

2

ROBERT RYDER

Long before I became 'God' – before Growler, before The Toxteth Terrier/Terror, before I was even Robbie Fowler – I started to make a name for myself as a goal-scorer, and my name was Robert Ryder. Not Robbie – Robert. I don't know whether that's a Liverpool thing or a Catholic thing, or whether it's a 'thing' at all, but whereas *Coronation Street* was 'Corrie' and your electricity was 'the lecky', everyone was known by their full names. Anthony (with the 'th' fully enunciated!) Gerard. Thomas. Robert. My mam and my old fella were never the most conventional of folks and, best mates though they were, they never really got around to the 'living together' part of being a couple. To me and my big sister Lisa, there was nothing unusual about Mum and Dad living apart – that was just how it was, and maybe that's the secret to how they stayed the best of mates! Anyway, the fact is that they never really lived under the same roof but, to us, that was often the best of both worlds. When we lived in Windsor Street, Dad was literally just over the road in Upper Warwick, so I'd go down the pitches with him, do my training, maybe watch a bit of footy at his, then come back to ours at bedtime. I never felt anything other than complete love and protection from both of my parents, and my grandparents, right from my first steps and I'm grateful for the upbringing I had.

I went to St Patrick's Primary, just around the corner from our maisonette, and everyone knew me as Robert Ryder. It was only when I went to secondary school – Nugent, in Wavertree – then later when I first started training with Liverpool, that I had to take my birth certificate along. From that point on I began using my dad's name: Fowler. I don't know, maybe I had this vague thought that Fowler sounded more like a footballer's name, a goal-scorer's name. There was a cricketer, Graeme Fowler, who was known as Foxy. On some level, I might have been thinking 'Fox in The Box', but there really wasn't any big reason behind the change. I was Robert Ryder all the way through primary school and then, when I went to big school, I was Robert Fowler.

Fowler or Ryder, I'd scored goals from the off and as young as seven or eight, I started trying to perfect my finishing. I'd be looking for that sweet spot just inside the post, where not even the best keepers could keep it out. When we moved on to playing with nets, I'd hit the inside net, time and again. Maybe that's a result of playing with a smaller ball in my earlier years, maybe there's some instinctive

eye-to-foot co-ordination, but what's for sure is that I practised, day after day, aiming for those far corners where not
even the best goalies stood a chance of getting up or down to
the ball. Another thing that might have been a factor in the
way I was able to clip or bend the ball into those unreachable
spots was that, from a young age, I played snooker and pool.

A gang of us would go down to St John's Youth Club next
to the big Park Road sports centre in the Dingle and, for our
20p entry fee, we could play footy, pool, snooker or just hang
out. This is where I first met my lifelong pal, Ste Calvey. It
was one of those situations where we'd been hearing about
each other for a while and I think everyone expected us to
be big rivals, even enemies. But we just hit it off, right from
the start. It was partly that we both had similar, daft senses
of humour and partly that he was only one who could give
me a decent game of pool! It's not like I've analysed it to any
great degree, but I do think that games like pool and snooker,
even golf, can perhaps help your accuracy when you're using
a lot of side edge and spin and aiming for a very small target.
Like I say, it's not a scientific theory, but I'm sure, over time,
you must absorb little things like clipping a ball on its side to
make it swerve and so on. And when you move from a small
ball and a small target to a bigger ball with more to aim at,
it can only help your accuracy. So St John's is where I first
met my lifetime bezzy mate, Ste Calvey, who has accompa-
nied me on many an adventure – including some very early
forays into culinary heaven. As a seasoned athlete my body

has always been a temple, so me, Calvey and the gang used to round off our nights at St John's with the original *haute cuisine* – a dirty great tray of chips and gravy, sometimes with a side order of crisps. I'd like to think the svelte figure I've carried into early middle age is living testament to that nutritious and delicious F-Plan Diet!

When I was nine, I started playing Under 11 football against the best teams in the South Liverpool area. My first team was Singleton and I used to get the bus down to Jericho Lane to train and play. As much as you go on to achieve in the game, there's nothing to touch that feeling, the moment when you put your kit on for your first competitive side. It's magic, pulling your shirt over your head and being a part of something: being in a team. The colours of your shirt seem brighter and more vivid than normal colours – the whole ritual is electric. Singleton had this beautiful Argentina-style kit and I'll never, ever forget the feeling, pulling that top on for the first time to go out and play in a proper, competitive game. Sometimes I still feel that same shiver of excitement – it's half anticipation, half nerves or nervous energy – when I drive past the Jericho pitches; it takes me right back to those very early days with Singleton.

That first year we went the entire season unbeaten, League and Cup. Maybe it was our Argentina kit that inspired us, but we played some lovely one-touch, give-and-go football. In our Cup final we came up against Dove & Olive from Speke, who were the other really strong team in South Liverpool at the time. The final was at the Metal Box sports club down Garston way. Metal Box was one of the big factories back then and their pitch was just beautiful. For us kids, who were used to playing week in, week out on boggy fields with no drainage and trying to make the best of it, it was a pleasure running out onto a surface like that – it was as close as any of us had come to a proper, pro-standard pitch.

Dove & Olive had a lad called Kevin Keegan playing for them, whose reputation went before him – and not just because his name was Kevin Keegan, either. Even at that age, the best players are already starting to get a name for themselves around the Junior scene and this Keegan lad had been scoring for fun all season. So, with me scoring a few too, this final between Singleton and Dove & Olive was being billed as the shoot-out at the O.K. Corral. They started really strongly and Keegan scored a first-half hat-trick, but I scored five in the second half and we won the Cup 5–4! I'll never forget the referee, Mr Daley, congratulating both sides and saying it was the best game he had ever officiated at.

The big thing about winning that first cup is that it gave me a feeling, a deep sense of satisfaction, that we'd achieved something together as a team and I'd more than played my part in it. That basic feeling never left me, as long as I played. The urge to repeat that sensation – a gang of you, made up, all hugging and congratulating each other as you hold a silver trophy up in the air – honestly, there's nothing like it. The drive to keep on winning and experiencing that same 'champions' feeling drove me on for the rest of my career. Today, there's a certain sense of achievement for finishing fourth or qualifying as Best Behaved or whatever and, I don't know, don't get me wrong, I understand the knock-on effect of qualifying for the UEFA Champions League and everything that comes with it, but all I can say is that none of it comes close to holding a cup aloft – just ask Jordan Henderson how that feels!

I got the taste for it that day at Metal Box and it drove me on and inspired me, just wanting to do it again and again. For me, personally, I want to be judged on what I've won rather than what I nearly did. A club's directors, sponsors and owners may well celebrate fourth place in the League, but I can tell you most players would rather hold up the FA Cup or the League Cup or any other cup that gives them a moment, plus a medal they can celebrate together on the day and cherish forever, long after they've hung up their boots.

* * *

After Singleton, I moved on to Thorvald in the Edge Hill Junior League. Again, Thorvald was a strong team all round – we used to rattle up some eye-popping scorelines. One game, we beat Hazelton 21–0 and I had a penalty saved, but I still scored 12 in that one, anyway. We even managed to beat that score, winning 23–1 against Durning – I racked up a measly 17 in that one! Both Singleton and Thorvald played in the Sunday League, which left my Saturdays free, so when I could get the money together, I would go up to watch Everton if they were playing at home.

Most Division One football (which was what the top division was called, before the Premier League) was still played at 3pm on a Saturday afternoon in the 80s, so that would be my aim – get the money together and get to the game. It's well known now that I grew up supporting Everton. I used to idolise Graeme Sharp and Tricky Trev – Trevor Steven, completely different types of player who were just dynamite together. Graeme Sharp was the complete striker's striker, not just for the goals he scored but his all-round game, the way he brought other players into an attack – he was much more technically gifted than he's really been given credit for. Maybe that's because he had Trevor Steven alongside him, providing his supply-line – anyone would look cumbersome next to Tricky Trev. He was so clever and inventive, he could go past defenders with ease and get these inch-perfect, pinpoint crosses into the box, time and again. Looking back, I think I wanted to be both of them. I wanted to make goals, score goals, go past players, slide killer passes in – but, top of the list ahead of everything, I just loved sticking the ball in the net.

As much as I idolised Graeme Sharp, I also admired Ian Rush a lot. Obviously, I wasn't there in the flesh at the Liverpool matches back then, but I still picked up a lot from Rushy, just watching him on *Match of the Day* or *The Big Match*. It's funny, because one of the great tactical revolutions in modern football is the High Press: asking your strikers to close down the opposition defence, forcing them into a hurried clearance or nicking possession from them, high up the pitch. Roberto Firmino does that brilliantly for Liverpool, Tottenham play that way, lots of the top teams these days try to harry defenders in their own box – but it's no different to what Rushy was doing in the 80s. He was magnificent at that basic attack as the first line of defence philosophy. If you gave him the merest sniff of the ball, he was so fast, he'd be on to the defender in a flash and take the ball off him. I would sit right in front of the telly and watch him close up, trying to pick little things up.

But that Everton team around the mid-80s was every bit as good as Rushy's Liverpool team of the day. Between 1984 and 1987, the two sides shared just about every prize going. I would try anything – literally anything – to get along to Goodison as often as I could, to see my heroes close up. It sounds mad saying this now I've got a young lad myself. I don't think I'd be happy with him even walking to the shops, but I quite often used to walk to Everton all the way from Liverpool 8, often on my own. It wasn't a big deal at all then. Obviously, I'd get the bus if I had money, but unemployment was at its peak in the city around 1984/85 so whatever cash I could get together would be spent getting into the ground. I knew what pubs my dad and my uncles would be in, so I'd do the rounds, scrounging ten bob here, a pound there, until I had enough – I think it was about £2.50 to get in – and I saw some fantastic games.

Just as I was saying about pulling on your first kit for your first team, there's nothing quite like those first few visits to a proper football stadium to see *your* team play. Your first glimpse of the stands as you approach the ground, the noise and the smells, the people in the streets, all excited – the scarves and hats and footy shirts. Then going through the turnstiles and up the steps; your first sight of the pitch – a different shade of green to anything you've ever seen! All I could think was: I want to do that, I want to play in games like this, on a pitch like that, in front of a crowd this big.

Yet it was always Liverpool who were after me! The goals I scored for Thorvald and Singleton led to an invitation from Liverpool Schoolboys to come for trials at Penny Lane. A lot of people who only know Penny Lane from The Beatles' song think it's an imaginary, fantasy street, but, to me, it looms large in my development as a player. Whether you're going past there today on a Beatles Tour or the 86 bus, the Penny Lane pitches are still there, just about visible behind Liverpool College and the big Tesco superstore. Bearing in mind how diddy I was back then, I suppose I was a little bit intimidated by the set-up. It wasn't just that everyone seemed huge, but that first trial was the one and only time I can remember when I thought my boots were a bit crap, compared to every else's. I must have done okay in my old-school 'Billy's Boots' anyway, because I was invited into the squad. The very next day, Dad went out and bought me a boss pair of Nike Rio to celebrate this big moment in my development as a football player.

Playing at Liverpool Schoolboys level was a big step up in standard and intensity; it was as close to the real thing as anything I'd known up until then. You're talking about top, top players, even at that age. Our captain back then, and one of my very best mates to this day, was Tony Grant. Granty had everything – he was a good size, he was athletic, he was good on the ball and, even at that age, he had a bit of grace about him. The very best midfielders – the ones who dictate play like Jan Molby did for us – always seem to have time on the ball. They're unflappable, their head is always up, looking for the best option, and that was Granty – he was the type of player that gives you confidence, just by having him on your side.

I played a lot of games up front with a lad called Paul Flaherty from Tuebrook – he was a good player too; him and Granty ended up going to Everton – and another Toxteth lad, Dele Adebola, who joined Crewe Alexandra and went on to have a good career at Birmingham City. Between the three main attacking players we had a good mix of pace, brawn and skill and we all knew where the goal was – plus, we had Tony Grant conducting the orchestra.

Right from that time, age 11 onwards, LFC's main youth scout, Jim Aspinall, was on the scene, too, giving myself and my dad the soft sell about joining Liverpool. At first, it was nothing too intense. It must be a fine line for the scouts – or it was in those days – not to put you under too much pressure. Jim would come over, have a little chat with me and Dad, keep on reminding us how much they rated me, and then leave it at that. He'd leave us his calling card, which was one of those Prontaprint jobs with ornate swirly writing at the top:

Jim Aspinall – Area Representative Scout
to Liverpool FC

You half expected it to say: 'Reasonable rates, music to suit all ages' underneath! I've kept all the calling cards from the scouts who showed an interest and the one that always makes me smile is the Everton rep, who wrote: 'Sorry, no Comps for Dad.'

The scouts at Everton knew I was a Blue. I think they, and Granty, just assumed I would automatically sign for Everton, so they didn't go over the top trying to woo me, at first. Yet, in spite of being brought up a Toffee, there was always something about Liverpool that got under my skin and made me want to play for them over Everton. This was all happening towards the end of the 1985–86 season, as Liverpool and Everton were going toe-to-toe in the race for The Double – in an era when winning the League and the FA Cup in the same season really did count as something special.

Everton were the reigning champions and top of the League; Liverpool and West Ham were chasing them. It was Kenny Dalglish's first season as player-manager – and Kenny was soon to have a direct impact in my signing for the Reds. As the famous Liverpool terrace song says, it was Kenny's goal at Stamford Bridge that brought the League title back to

Anfield on the final day of the season, then the Reds went on
to beat Everton at Wembley to clinch the Double.

At the same time, things were hotting up for me. There'd
be times when scouts from all over the country would come
to watch me play. It was exciting, starting to think that you
might actually make it as a footballer – but it was hard to
concentrate on your game. I'd do something good – or something I thought was good – and I'd find myself looking over
to see if the scout had clocked it! Sometimes I'd catch sight of
Jim Aspinall on the touchline, trying to look calm but clearly
starting to get anxious. He'd put in so much spadework, it
would have been a shame for his efforts not to bear fruit. Yet
Jim would never overdo it – he seemed to understand that
too much pressure might have an adverse effect. That wasn't
me or my dad being difficult – quite the opposite, really. It's
such a huge decision and you want to be sure you get it right.

So, it's fair to say that Jim's patient, paternal approach
paid off in the end because, in September 1986, aged 11, I
took up Liverpool's offer to train there as part of the club's
Youth Development Scheme. That was another thing that
always seemed larger than life – getting an official letter with
a club crest at the top. My first ever Liverpool 'deal' was a
letter of invitation, asking me to go and train with the club
for the next 12 months. There was nothing contractual and
no obligation to renew after that initial year, but nevertheless, I had an official offer on official Liverpool F.C. (and
Athletic Grounds!) notepaper and I was over the moon.

Before Liverpool had an academy, Mal Cook ran what was then called The Centre of Excellence, with training taking place every Tuesday and Thursday. We did a lot up at Melwood (LFC's main training facility) to give the trainees a sense that they really were now on a pathway to being part of the Liverpool set-up. Most of the Liverpool First Team players would have finished for the day by the time our sessions started at 5pm, but occasionally, you'd see one of the big players who'd stayed behind for physio or whatever.

I remember standing there on one of the training pitches just staring at John Barnes one time, when he was recovering from a long-term injury. You know that these players are real, they're human, but there's something mad about being a few yards from the actual person himself – they're superhuman. You can't help staring and you're thinking, maybe, *maybe* one day, you'll be pulling on the shirt and playing alongside players like these. When the weather was bad or Melwood wasn't available to us, we'd train at the Vernon Sangster Centre – an all-sports venue in Stanley Park, just over the road from Anfield.

I started off going down the Centre of Excellence twice a week, training under Frank Skelly, Dave Shannon and Hughie Macauley, and this is where I sometimes think that, for all the skill you might have, for all the ability and opportunity, the big thing you just can't legislate for is a slice of luck. Thinking of me and Granty, who most people involved with Liverpool Schoolboys football would have said were the two standout players from that crop of 86, I honestly think I made not just a good choice but a very *lucky* choice when I opted to train with Liverpool. Tony Grant comes from a long line of Evertonians and it never entered his, or their, head for him to play for anyone but the Blues. But if you stand back and look at the type of player he was – this elegant, cultured midfielder who could play a slide rule pass – he was coming into an Everton set-up that was going through difficult times.

Going into the mid-90s when Tony broke into the First Team, they had this *Dogs of War* self-image. You might argue that that mentality was what saved the club from relegation, but for Granty, I'm not so sure that that kind of backs-to-the-wall siege mentality was the ideal environment for his unique talent to flourish. When the chips are down and you're staring relegation in the face, a nervous crowd won't give you the luxury of an extra touch, or a moment's hesitation as you pick the right pass. It would take unreal self-belief to carry on playing your natural game in those circumstances. Yet, when you look at the way players like Dom Matteo, Jamie Redknapp, Steve McManaman, Don Hutchison and myself came into a Liverpool team who tried to play a certain style of football, I can't help thinking Granty would have thrived in our squad at that time. Like I say, you can't predict what's going to happen and you can't personally influence whether your own luck will turn out to be good or bad … it's just that I think I was pretty bloody lucky choosing Liverpool!

3

TRAINING DAYS

That first year of training flew by. I was at secondary school by then, Nugent in Edge Hill, and I'd take two buses, straight after school, to train at LFC, then another two buses back home again. I didn't know him well at this point, but all the talk among the trainees was about a local lad, Steve McManaman, who had made the step up into the main squad. Steve Heighway took over from Mal Cook as head of youth development and Liverpool were starting to talk to Dad about another 12-month deal. As much as I was keen to renew the agreement, Dad wanted to keep things informal while I was still a schoolkid. He never said as much, but maybe he was still harbouring dreams of Everton coming in for me. More likely, he was just looking out for me, as he always did.

That summer of 1987, Granty and I both got the letter inviting us to come down to Nottingham for trials with England Schoolboys. It was to be a week of training, five-a-side and full games, with the 100 or so who had been invited ultimately being whittled down to a core squad of 25. These lads would then go on to Lilleshall, which was the FA's newly opened Centre of Excellence, near Telford. In theory, that squad of young players would stay together right throughout the age groups, growing and gelling as a squad until they eventually became the basis of the main England team for years to come. Before the trials, I got a letter from Steve Heighway:

> *Dear Robbie,*
>
> *A quick note to wish you all the best at the England trials next week. All the staff here are very proud of you and wish you well. If you need any 'kit' to take with you that your parents cannot provide, just give me a call.*
>
> *Robbie, I promised we would not pester you and we have not. It was great to see you on Tuesday. This place is an open door for you in your school holidays. When you get back from trials, come and see us. Perhaps you would like to watch the first team train or, better still, train with us for a couple of mornings – you choose!*
>
> *See you when you get back. Very best of luck,*
> *Steve*

Granty and I were put on a train to Nottingham and we were met at the other end by an FA official. The training camp should have been a lot of fun, but I found it daunting right from the start.

There are two versions of me. Most of the time I'm outgoing and, I suppose, quite loud and perky when I'm in my comfort zone, around people I know. But I can be quite shy as well, and I'm never at my best in those early moments when you're meeting new people for the first time. We got out onto the training pitches and I don't know, it just didn't happen for me in the way I'd become used to. Everyone out there on those pitches seemed really big, for one thing – and they were all really fucking brilliant, too! In my mind, they were all at least as good as me, many of them loads better. I had never doubted myself up until then, but I found myself afflicted by a sudden lack of self-confidence and, as the week went on, I just couldn't break free of it. Maybe it was being away from home for the first time, maybe it was because I was still very slight, but things just didn't work out at all. It was no surprise to me when I wasn't invited to join the Lilleshall set-up, but I was shocked that they didn't pick Tony Grant, either. I thought he'd done well out there, yet neither of us got the nod. It was the first time I had ever tasted rejection or disappointment as a young footballer and the train journey back to Liverpool was mired in self-doubt. Up until then I had just taken it as read that I was well on a pathway that would lead to me becoming a successful professional footballer. Now I was being told I wasn't quite up to it. What if they were right? What would I do if I couldn't make it as a player? I really did not have a Plan B!

The best way to deal with rejection is to channel it into a positive force. 'I'll show them!' is one of the greatest forms of human motivation and after the initial disappointment subsided a little, that raw desire to prove the FA wrong is what picked me up and kicked me on. I took Steve Heighway up on his offer, spent the remainder of my summer holiday up at Melwood and gradually got my confidence back. By the time the rest of the schoolkids returned for training, I was flying again. What really helped was that I loved training and genuinely loved coming into Melwood and all that it entailed. The curriculum at LFC was always more technical than tactical – in fact, I don't remember playing in a 'proper' game there until I was about 14 or 15. It was all small pitch drills (sometimes just the corner of a small pitch), pass and move, control, technique, making sure that whatever position you played in, you were comfortable on the ball – basically, the same things I'd been doing with my dad since I could walk.

If you look at the big soccer academies now, there'll be at least two specialist coaches for every position, at every level and age group. But, back when I started training with Dave Shannon and Hughie Macauley and then Steve Heighway, they were with you all the time doing little manoeuvres, turns, step-overs, different ways of using set plays, corners, free-kicks – the real basics of elite-level football. Whatever the special aspect of the game we looked at, the focus was always 100 per cent on the technical side of it. So, whereas the FA and England might have wanted bigger, more physically imposing players at Lilleshall and the accent there was on athleticism, I don't remember ever doing anything at Liverpool that wasn't grounded in skill, expertise and technique. We'd work in the smallest, most confined spaces and try to use speed of thought, physical speed, skill and ingenuity to get ourselves free and carve out a shooting opportunity.

The Sweat Box was an adaptable mini pitch surrounded by wooden walls (some of them marked out with circles, A, B, C, etc.). For one session, you might chip the ball against one wall, turn and 'pass' it against the next wall, then your coach would shout, 'C!' and you'd have to try to spin and hit that circle with the ball. Everything you learned in the Sweat Box or on the five-a-side pitch was what you'd take onto the bigger stage. The idea is that you learn to see the smaller picture as part of the bigger picture but, again, it's the basic one-touch, two-touch, pass and move. You'd learn everything – spins, peeling off a player, shooting from ridiculous angles and aiming for the most acute spot because the miniature goals are so tight, the keeper looks massive. It shouldn't come as any big thunderbolt to anyone that I loved scoring goals but, more than anything, I loved sticking the ball away into the bottom corner. It might look brilliant, slamming it high into the top corner – and I've had my share of those, too – but you're half-giving the keeper a chance if your shot is aimed high. The majority of goalkeepers are right-handed, so if you try to keep the ball low and hard to their left-hand corner, it's almost impossible for them to get down, let alone keep it out.

GOAL!!!

When training was at the Vernon Sangster Centre, it was all indoors. Obviously, there weren't touchlines in the traditional sense, so we integrated the walls into a lot of our drills. Hughie or Dave would designate a corner of the pitch, 10 x 10 feet or 15 x 15, and the idea was that, using one touch only, you had to work your way out of the corner, up and back again, just playing one-twos or using the walls. If there wasn't an obvious pass on, you had to use your imagination, nutmeg your opponent, whatever – but you could never stand still. It was far from easy but those short, sharp spaces are what eventually made you into a player – and I loved it. And we did *loads* of five-a-side. Anyone who follows football will know that, going right back to Bill Shankly's day, five-a-side is a huge part of the Liverpool philosophy. I don't think five-a-side is used as widely in the modern game, but it's something I will definitely incorporate into my own training and coaching regime as I make my big move into management.

For me, five-a-side's core ingredients of speedy, one-touch play are the ideal platform for a young player to learn the fundamentals of the game; like a bridge from Youth football into the professional game. If you think about your peripheral vision in a five-a-side game, it's very narrow and your options are always quite restricted. It's up to you to find solutions. But take those basic principles onto a bigger pitch, where your peripheral vision is wider, and with 11-a-side, you obviously have more options.

I'm not saying it comes easier, necessarily, but after the monotony and repetition of all that practice and training, it starts to become second nature and you do everything faster, instinctively and a lot more clinically – the one and two touch give and go, little spins around corners, that quick look over your shoulder to see who's on you, who's with you. Even the basics like following up when someone's taken a shot, just in case the keeper spills it. That's what makes you a player – those quick, instinctive plays in short, sharp spaces. And that was the basic journey for me, from Sunday League to Liverpool Boys, to the LFC Centre of Excellence, a strange progression from 20-a-side to 11-a-side to five-a-side.

All of this of course pre-dates the highly organised world of Academy Football that we see today, where most top clubs have representative squads and teams from Under 8s all the way to the Under 21s, coached to pursue that club's philosophy and brand of football right from the very start. Back in my days at the Centre of Excellence, LFC didn't have Under-13 or Under-14 teams, so my main outlet for competitive football was with Granty and Dele Adebola with Liverpool Schoolboys. Our head coach was Bob Lynch, who I admired and respected so much that I only ever referred to him as 'Mr Lynch'. Even when he came along to see me make my England debut, I spotted him during the warm-up, trotted over and said, 'Thanks for coming, Mr Lynch!'

With one or two exceptions, the basically schoolboy squad stayed together right through to Under 16s. That Under-16 team was brilliant, the optimum blend of tough, robust defence with a creative midfield and a lethal attack. But, not for the first time, Granty and I were to taste disappointment when Sheffield beat us 1–0 via a horrible, deflected own goal in the replayed final of the English Schools Trophy at Anfield. Nevertheless, that team was a big leg-up for me, emotionally and practically, at a time when I was starting to question my own ability. The camaraderie, the wins, the goals and the near-misses, along with Mr Lynch's astute tactical analysis and the sheer confidence he gave you going out to do battle, were a major factor in my development over a notoriously difficult period.

That age, around 14 or 15, is critical in the life of a young footballer. There is so much to distract you and knock you off balance in your teenage years. Time and again, you see the best young players you've grown up with start to fall away around that age.

That didn't happen with me; I had a great set of mates who understood how much my football meant to me. Even on Saturday nights, when most teenagers are getting on with what most teenagers do, my pals would stay close to home with me, knowing that I would usually have to be up bright and early for training, or for a match. And on those odd occasions when they did lead me astray (I was always completely wide-eyed and naïve, as you'd imagine), there were my dad and the rest of my family to remind me where my priorities lay. On top of all that support from family and friends though, I really do believe that run with Liverpool Schoolboys was exactly what I needed at exactly the right time. I felt what it was like to be part of a team again, what it was like to get to a final. And I felt what it was like to run out onto that beautiful pitch in front of a big crowd at Anfield.

* * *

I was going to turn 14 in April 1989, which meant it was time for Liverpool to start making their mind up about who among that year's trialists was to be offered Associate Schoolboy terms. The pathway to your first full contract as a pro footballer would typically be a year or two on Associate Schoolboy terms then, once you left school, a year or two on YTS terms – that was the Youth Training Scheme which had replaced the traditional Apprenticeship system for school-leavers in the 80s – before signing full professional terms. Within that basic framework, there's room for negotiation.

Steve McManaman was another boyhood Blue, but one of the key things that steered him towards Liverpool was the club's willingness to take a longer-term view. Macca was small and skinny and there was a feeling that he would need more time to develop and grow. LFC was prepared to offer the security of a three-year deal (Everton would only offer one-year firm) and I was hoping the club would offer me something similar.

I knew I was doing okay. Steve Heighway had started talking in a general sense about the challenges and pitfalls of being a professional footballer. Some of the behind-scenes people like Tom Saunders started coming down to take a proper look at me. Tom was a lovely man, a club director who was highly respected among the LFC establishment, but known and loved by everyone at the club, too. The *Liverpool Echo* used to refer to him as 'Crack Euro Spy Tom Saunders' but his role at Liverpool went way beyond checking out the opposition ahead of big European games. Tom was a scout, a confidant, a diplomat and way before it became common-place for clubs to have them, he was an Ambassador for LFC, travelling all over the world to represent the club – and he started coming along to watch me play.

I had an inkling my dream might be about to come true when I was standing at the bus stop after training one freezing February night in 1989. It was one of those evenings that's so cold, you can see your breath in the night air. I'm hunched up, flapping my arms to keep the cold out like a penguin, just praying a bus will come along soon. Next thing, Kenny Dalglish pulls up in this big Mercedes. He was the manager by then, obviously, as well as being probably the greatest player ever to pull on a Liverpool shirt, and he's pulling up at my bus stop, sliding down the window of his Merc.

'Jump in!' he goes. 'I'm headed your way.' Oh aye, I'm thinking, you live up in Southport and I'm in Toxteth, it's not exactly on your way, Kenny! But of course, firstly, I respected him too much – in fact, I was probably too scared of him – to say anything back to him. On top of that, a part of me realised he wouldn't be giving me the time of day if he didn't know that Liverpool were interested in signing me. And an even bigger part just wanted a ride in his supercar. The final factor was I was desperate to get out the fucking freezing cold! So, in I jumped, tongue-tied and wide-eyed at all the buttons and lights on the Merc's dashboard – the padded leather gear stick, the smell of luxury. If this was what you could get from being a good footballer, by God I wanted it!

I managed to mumble and point the way back towards Liverpool 8 and Kenny kept the conversation flowing about how he used to walk to training at Celtic when he was kid and how hard work was at the root of everything good in life. As we turned left by The Rialto, I started smiling inside at the thought of this Liverpool F.C. legend pulling up outside ours in this big posh car and me getting out, giving it the Big I Am. If I could've got Kenny to beep his horn as he went up our street, I swear I would have had no problem with that – I wanted everyone to see me getting dropped off by King Kenny. Goes without saying, as sod's law would have it, it was so Baltic cold, no one was out on the street.

Kenny Dalglish dropped me off and the entire neighbour-hood was buttoned-up indoors! Not even my dad saw him.

A few weeks after my 14th birthday, a letter arrived at my dad's place. He made a big thing of opening it dead slowly, telling me it was just another red arrears bill. I was

leaning over his shoulder and even though the LIVERPOOL
FOOTBALL CLUB letterhead was laid out in huge block
capitals in those days, all my eyes could focus on was the
little Candy logo underneath – they were the sponsor on the
Liverpool shirt worn by Ian Rush and John Barnes and our
latest Scouse goal-scoring machine, John Aldridge. I wanted,
more than anything else in the world, to wear that shirt with
that logo. Dad was holding the letter away from me, playing
out the moment for as long as he could. Eventually, he read
it out:

> *Dear Mr Fowler,*
>
> *As we have suggested to you for some time, we
> have been impressed with Robbie's performance and
> we have come to the time when we would like Robbie
> to sign as an Associated Schoolboy with the club...*

That was it! I didn't need to hear the rest – I was off down
the street, not exactly sure where I was going or who I was
going to tell, just this big, mad grin all over my face as the
message began to sink in. I was on my way, I was going to be
a professional footballer!

4

BREAK ON THROUGH

In my first year as an LFC Associated Schoolboy, Liverpool won the League with two games to spare. Even though John Aldridge had left earlier that season for a new challenge with Real Sociedad, the club wasn't quite beating a path to my door to step into his boots just yet. We signed Ronny Rosenthal from Standard Liège, plus there was a fella called Ian Rush playing up front. I did, however, sign on for a second year on Associated Schoolboy terms, resulting in a letter from King Kenny on 14th May 1990.

Dear Robbie,

I am delighted that you have taken the important step of renewing your Associated Schoolboy terms with Liverpool Football Club. We hope you will have another enjoyable and successful year with the club.

We do expect high standards of behaviour and commitment while you are with us. I would also remind you of your continued commitment to, firstly, your school athletic activities and, most important, your academic studies.

Yours sincerely,

K. Dalglish (Manager)

I was obviously chuffed to bits that Kenny Dalglish was even aware of me but after everything he'd done for the families and the wider Liverpool community that past year, since the Hillsborough disaster, I was amazed and touched that he found the time and the headspace to write. He is a truly remarkable man and it's completely right and fitting that he's had the Kemlyn Road stand at Anfield named in his honour.

I settled in quickly at Melwood, loving every second as a player on a pathway. Each time I did well, Steve Heighway would dish out the praise but then, just as quickly, remind me how far there was still to go before I was ready to run out at Anfield for the First Team. Steve had a monthly column in the LFC magazine, where he would round up all the news and results from the Youth team. It became a regular thing for him to write words to the effect of 'another great goal from young Robbie Fowler. Robbie is a sensible lad who knows the First Team is still a stride or two away in terms of standard.' But, for as long as I was only at LFC on Associated Schoolboy terms, any other team could have come in for me. Everton, having taken it as read that I'd sign for them eventually, finally woke up and started their charm offensive. Suddenly there *were* 'Comps for Dad!'

Wolves, who had an excellent Youth set-up back then, made a firm offer. But I'm a simple, loyal sort of fella and it had been Liverpool who had shown the love, right from the start. In my heart of hearts, it had been LFC for me from the summer of the England Schoolboys' rejection at Nottingham. Having the reassurance of being able to just go back to Liverpool and hang around at Melwood, doing odd jobs, but mainly just watching the stars going about their pre-season training and their day-to-day routines cemented a deep and lasting bond with me. I just loved the feel of the place – it was down to earth, yet there was a real sense of history and greatness.

As soon as I turned 16 on 9th April 1991, I signed YTS terms as an LFC Apprentice on an eye-popping £29.50 a week, with the guarantee of a full professional contract on my 18th birthday (terms to be agreed in good faith). I got my head down, with the immediate goal of trying to cement a place in the legendary Liverpool Reserves team, managed by Phil Thompson. I say 'legendary' because going back to the days of Bill Shankly, Liverpool Reserves had been built up to become an almost mythical, unbeatable force – winning their own division, the Central League, season after season and acting as a hothouse for a whole succession of future LFC talents. Phil Thompson himself came through the Reserves system and this was to be another major step in my football education. Up until now, with all my coaches from Mr Lynch to Dave Shannon, Hughie MacAuley and Steve Heighway, I had only ever known a supportive, nurturing, educational approach. Man management had not come into the equation so far, but I was about to find out about a whole new method of leadership.

Let me get one thing straight, right from the start: I like Phil Thompson. I've met him on numerous occasions since we both went our separate ways, and it's clear as can be that his one big lifelong passion is Liverpool F.C. The club is the love of his life and everything he did as an employee of LFC was to further the team's aims rather than his own. I realise that now, even if it was a bitter pill to swallow sometimes, but by God, did Phil have a special way of motivating you! Right from my first few days reporting to Melwood as an Apprentice, the older Reserves and YTS players advised me to keep out of his way. He was the archetypal drill sergeant – you could hear him a mile off, berating some poor sod for failing to track back or closing his eyes for a header or letting one of his socks slide down … Honestly, you could be bollocked by Phil Thompson for almost anything at all!

It didn't take too long for me to find myself on the wrong side of his attentions. One of our jobs as apprentices was to bundle the kit for the First Team players. Remember, this was still in the days of us young lads cleaning the boots and so on, and we'd hang each player's shirt on their individual peg. I was quite a bubbly character, I got along with everyone (at least I hope I did), but I was particularly good mates with Phil Charnock – who is a physio at the club, these days. One day, us YTS lads were laying out the First Team kit and I was standing there with Ian Rush's Number 9 shirt, holding it up, staring at it and telling Phil Charnock that one day, I was going to wear that shirt. I was just a kid, starstruck. It wasn't like I was saying, 'I am the great Robert Bernard Fowler. This shirt is mine, it is only a matter of time!' I was just daydreaming out loud, thinking, 'One day …', 'Imagine how it must feel …', that sort of thing. Next thing, Phil's gone quiet and this shadow falls over the dressing room and there's Phil Thompson, letting me know in very robust terms that I wasn't fit to lace Rushy's boots and I would never, ever be good enough to wear the shirt!

I knew not to even try to explain myself. It had already been instilled in us not to try to answer back to Thommo and I think I was more amazed than crushed. I just stood there gaping at him. Looking back, I think all the shouting and so on was just his way of trying to get the best out of the kids. By goading us and challenging us and berating us to breaking point, I think he was testing us all to see who had the spirit to withstand the brutal reality of big-time football. Even though it worked well for me, it still seems an odd way of motivating a young player – and I doubt it'll be one I'll take into my own management career.

Sadly, the after-effects of Hillsborough took their toll on Kenny Dalglish to the point where he simply couldn't carry on. In January 1991, he left the club after an epic 4–4 draw at Goodison in the FA Cup replay, before I ever had a chance to play for him. Graeme Souness came in and, ultimately, he would be the manager who gave me my chance. But, in the short term, there was a time-served path of progression that every home-grown player had to follow: B Team, A Team, Reserves, First Team, and I was no different. So I carried on scoring at a meteoric rate and made my way through the gears quite quickly. I was a regular in the Reserves under Sammy Lee by the time I was 17, even though I was still professionally and emotionally an Apprentice. But I played alongside some fantastic pros in that team, picking up priceless tips and tricks and insights into the game. Depending on who was coming back from injury or who had suffered a dip in form and been dropped from the First Team, I found myself lining up alongside players like Jan Molby, John Barnes, Mark Wright, Glenn Hysén, Mark Walters, even the great Ronnie Whelan. How can you not learn from talent like that?

Yet, with every seeming stride forward there'd be a snag waiting to bring you back down to earth. Before the start of the new season, Graeme Souness brought Dean Saunders in to partner Ian Rush up front. I'll be honest about it, even though I was still only 16, in my own mind I was definitely starting to eye that second striker role. Soon after Souey came in, he started to break up Kenny's team. Peter Beardsley left for Everton and even though we had players like Paul Stewart, Ronny Rosenthal and Mark Walters, there wasn't another natural striker in the squad. I'm not embarrassed to admit that I'd looked up the stats on Liverpool's youngest ever player and was holding out vague thoughts that I still had plenty of time to beat Max Thompson's record.

Then, in April 1992, with the Reds in an FA Cup semi-final against Portsmouth and me starting to imagine myself being out there at Wembley, one day, scoring the winning goal in a Cup final, Liverpool went and signed a young teenage striking sensation – paying Wrexham £250,000 for 18-year-old Lee Jones. Lee was a year older than me and had already been knocking them in on a regular basis at a much higher level than I had ever played. But, we're only human and for me, signing Lee Jones was a very bad sign. Even I could accept the logic of Souness wanting to reunite Rushy with his international partner, Dean Saunders – two seasoned professionals, off-the-peg and ready to go. But that partner-ship had not really gelled in the way Souey had banked on and I was allowing myself to think that this could be my way in. Maybe I might start by getting a place on the bench? Maybe, if things were going really well – or really badly – I might even get a minute or two on the pitch? That's what I was starting to dream about, then we went out and signed another young striker. I was gutted. In my heart of hearts, I had to believe I was a better prospect than Lee Jones, but what can you do? Back to the drawing board, back to work.

In fairness to Graeme Souness (who, as manager, doesn't have to explain himself to anybody, let alone snotty-nosed

16-year-old apprentices), he called me in to reassure me that he, and everybody at Melwood, had the highest of hopes for me and the greatest of faith I would make it. He just didn't think I was ready, yet – that old thing about me being too slight to withstand the physical rigours of the Premier League. I wanted to say to him, if I'd have known it was a matter of body size, I could have just doubled-up on the chippy dinners and crisp butties! Seriously, though, it meant the world to me at that point in a career that hadn't even taken a run-up, let alone got off the ground, to hear from the manager's own lips that he rated me and my chance was going to come.

It came in November 1992 at Vale Park – of all places – and after that painful rejection all those years ago, my breakthrough came with England Under 18s, rather than Liverpool. In the 1992–93 season, there was more focus than usual on the nation's new crop of Under 18s as the UEFA Youth tournament was due to be held in England at the end of the season. I was behind some of the young strikers like Julian Joachim, Jamie Forrester and Paul Scholes, who had come through the Lilleshall system, but I was handed my first ever international cap for a game against Switzerland. The mad thing is I didn't get that many chances – but I managed to get a hat-trick anyway, and we won 7–2. Mr Lynch was there as always, and Steve Heighway came along to support me too, with a gang from the Liverpool Youth set-up. But, more so than for anyone, my first ever International goal must have been pretty special for my dad. I ran over to where he was standing, with a great big grin on my face, punching the air with both fists. I know he was made up – he was hugging everyone in sight, pointing and shouting, 'That's me lad, that is!' – but nobody was more made up than me. It wasn't so much a two-fingers to the suits at the FA who I thought had held me back, more the sheer joy that goal-scorers always feel, no matter how scruffy or sublime a goal is, when the ball hits the back of the net. I was over the moon and came home clutching the match ball to convince myself it wasn't all a dream.

My goal-scoring feats for England didn't go unnoticed. Graeme Souness called me in again and congratulated me on the hat-trick. He said that scoring in a game like that was definitely another step in the right direction for me; I was doing everything right, everyone knew sooner or later I'd break into the First Team. For now, so long as I just kept my head down and kept on working hard, it was bound to be sooner. I think I floated out of his office on a cloud of self-esteem!

On 13th January 1993, I thought the day had finally arrived. We were playing Bolton of the Second Division – two leagues below us – in the replay of our third round FA Cup game. We weren't great at all in the original game at their place, but managed to come back from 2–0 down to level things up. Everybody, including Bolton's manager, Bruce Rioch, thought they'd let their chance slip now the game was going to a replay at Anfield. Liverpool were expected to batter them and, in my head, I was thinking I might get on for the last 10 or 15 minutes if we were winning comfortably. This is how footballers think – especially at that age. We're selfish, it's normal. I wanted to get on that pitch, score my first goal for Liverpool and hear the crowd chant my name. I even had a song for myself in my head! I couldn't wait to tell everyone I knew that I might at last be about to get a game for the Reds.

I was on the bench with Don Hutchison, who we'd signed from Hartlepool that season – another exceptionally talented young player. It was a bitterly cold night and I spent a lot of the time trotting up and down the touchline, mainly just to stay warm. Unfortunately, it was the Trotters from Bolton who took the game by the scruff of the neck. They scored very early on and went in 1–0 up at half-time, our attack barely troubling them. Anyone in the crowd could see there was no chemistry among the Liverpool front three or four – and that was a big part of the problem. With Mark Walters, Paul Stewart and Ronny Rosenthal as our attacking three, there was no out-and-out striker there, no real goal threat at all.

Things got worse in the second half when Michael Thomas suffered a nasty tendon snap. This meant Hutch was on for the last half-hour or so, while I carried on patrolling the sidelines. As I jogged past, I could hear individual voices in the crowd shouting out to me:

'Go on, Robbie, lad. Get on there and sort this shambles out!'

Bolton got a second goal with about 15 minutes or so remaining and those individual shouts were turning into angry demands from the crowd.

'Get the kid on! He can't be any worse than this shite!'

It was unfair on my teammates, who were trying like mad to stave off this looming Cup Upset, but it just wasn't clicking for them. In my head and in my heart, I could not for the life of me understand why Graeme Souness didn't just take a gamble and throw me on for the last ten minutes. Firstly, the crowd is always massively supportive of any player making their debut – especially a local lad, one of their own, who has come through the ranks. Secondly, there'd be the element of surprise. In cases like these, even experienced defenders are liable to underestimate an untried young kid. Most rugged centre-halves think a bit of the rough stuff during your first duel will put the rookie back in his box. But a lot of 'kids' are streetwise enough to take a kick from The Bruise Brothers and give one back while they're at it – I certainly was. But the main thought running through my head as the clock ran down and the Reds faced a humiliating FA Cup exit was that the gaffer should just throw me on because nothing else was working! That team out there wasn't going to score if the ref added another 90 minutes' injury time so, with the alternative almost certain defeat, why not just go for it? There was no downside.

Years later, Souey told me that he rated me so highly, he didn't want to taint my name by association with this all-time low. He didn't want it on his conscience that a player he expected to go on to great heights would have 'defeat against lower-league Bolton' next to his 'Debut' statistics. And he was worried that such a negative start would affect my natural game – I might over-think things, become cautious, safety-first rather than following my instincts. Don't get me wrong, I appreciate the thought, but I still wish he'd thrown me on – I defo would have scored!

I felt I was edging ever closer though, so much so that I decided to make a statement purchase that would mark me out as a serious player among this group of top-class pros. Right throughout my association with Liverpool F.C. up to this point, I had travelled everywhere by bus. My dad didn't drive, but I had not long passed my test. I'd always been into my cars, as a fantasy thing, going back way before the time Sir Kenny ran me home in his Merc. It's one of the things you grow up dreaming about, isn't it? What car would you buy if money was no object? John Barnes and Rushie had BMWs, Razor Ruddock had a Porsche, so I felt the time had come to make my own announcement. I threw my hat into the ring and let anyone who was in any doubt know that Robbie Fowler was the new kid in town.

It was with great pride, therefore, that I arrived for training in the spring of 1993 in the lovingly preserved 1983-plate beige Ford Escort I had purchased with my bulging footballer's pay packet. The tsunami of respect and love I felt from my admiring teammates as I parked up for training that Monday morning still lives large to this day among my fondest memories: I had definitely arrived.

My first game for Liverpool did not arrive, however. Once again, I found myself on the bench for a dead-rubber last game of the season versus Tottenham, though this one was starting to feel more promising. We blew Spurs away in the first half, going into a 3–0 lead, when the boss uttered those five immortal words: 'Go and warm up, Robbie.' Out there on the green, green grass of Anfield was my former Everton hero, Pat 'Psycho' Van Den Hauwe. Psycho was notorious for being one of the hardest tacklers in hard-tackle history, but I didn't care who I was up against, I fancied myself to beat *anyone* and score *anywhere*.

Standing there, looking out onto the pitch, I had a combination of goose bumps, shivers, cold sweats and a thumping heart, but above all, I was grinning inside like a lunatic. The moment had come, I was going on! I was about to make my debut for Liverpool Football Club.

I stripped off and did as Souey said, trotting gently but meaningfully up and down, my eyes never once leaving the action. By that time, I had built up a minor but growing reputation from scoring so many goals for the Reserves and the various youth teams on my way up through the system. There were ripples of recognition and applause as I jogged along the touchline – then Tottenham went and scored. The bastards! Souness immediately jumped up and started waving me back to the bench. Instead of throwing the Boy Wonder on, he decided to shore things up and make sure we ended this wretched season with a win. He sent Torben Piechnik on; they scored another: 3–2. Then Spurs got a penalty, which Bruce Grobbelaar saved – a rare miss for Teddy Sheringham. I was looking down at the back of Souness's head, trying to transmit thought suggestions to him:

'Play Robbie Fowler! Put the kid on! Robbie will put this game to bed, Souey! Give Fowler a chance!'

But the call didn't come. It was only in the last five minutes that we got a penalty ourselves. Mark Walters slotted that one very coolly and Tottenham threw the towel in. Before the end, both Rushy and John Barnes chipped in with goals and we ran out easy enough, 6–2 winners. As I joined in with the low-key walk around Anfield to applaud the crowd for their unstinting support, none of it felt particularly real to me. I was gutted, in all honesty. I'd been *that* close, but ultimately hadn't got onto the pitch, and I was now seriously beginning to wonder whether I ever would. The club kept telling me how much they rated me, yet I was still on the same terms of that first basic contract, treading water. Making the big time felt a million miles away.

5

LONDON CALLING

It was the same story with England Under 18s, too. Even after my hat-trick against Switzerland, I was back on the subs bench for the next few International games. By the time the UEFA tournament kicked off for real, in July of 1993, I was nowhere near first- or second-choice striker. England had been drawn in a horrible group, along with France, Holland and Spain. Portugal and Turkey were both tough opponents in the other side of the draw, but ours truly was the Group of Death.

Our opening game, against France at Stoke City's ground, saw two strong teams cancelling each other out for 70 minutes. It was as though not losing was the big priority so early on in the tournament. If you lost Game One, it would be doubly hard to claw yourself back into contention, so the game was a risk-free stalemate, with France more than happy just to keep possession and move the ball sideways and backwards.

With a quarter of an hour left to go, our manager Ted Powell sent on me and Kevin Gallen, the brilliant young QPR striker. Kev was only 16, but he was already being talked about as the new Clive Allen. Me and him struck up a great rapport in training, and I always felt comfortable playing alongside Kev. Ted's gamble paid off almost immediately. Kevin slotted a rebound home on 80 minutes and, a couple of minutes later, I put the game to bed with a goal that was a direct throwback to those early days on the rec in Upper Warwick Street when Dad used to make me practise, over and over, on my right foot.

With France pushing for an equaliser, our defence was fighting a rearguard action, happy to just clear the ball long. One of these clearances was nodded back and the ball just dropped nicely, a foot or two in front of me, sitting up and crying out to be hit. A quick glance up and I saw that their keeper was a pace or two off his line, so I just did what came naturally: I leaned back very slightly, got a great connection with my right foot and 'looped' it over his head, smack into the net from 25 yards! I ran over to where my dad was standing, with a great big grin on my face, punching the air with both fists.

We were up and running and, in fairness to Ted Powell, he ran with Kev Gallen and I from that point onwards. Next up, we were playing a strong Holland team captained by Clarence Seedorf and also featuring up-and-coming stars like Giovanni van Bronckhorst and Patrick Kluivert. We put up a truly brilliant first-half performance though – once again, Kev Gallen and I got one each, and we were 3–1 up at half-time. Our defence, which included Sol Campbell and Gary Neville, soaked up everything Holland could throw at us in the second half, then we finally broke them with a genius goal from Julian Joachim – a flick-and-volley that was a bit like Gazza's famous 1996 goal against Scotland at Wembley (more of that one later, too).

That saw us through to our final group game – a winner-takes-all decider against the glamour team of the group, Spain, at the glamour venue of the tournament, Walsall. Neither team had dropped a point. Whoever won this one was going through to the final against Turkey or Portugal. It was a mad, unexpectedly feisty game, with us taking an early lead, Javi Moreno getting sent off for a studs-up tackle on Gary Neville then, with 20 minutes left, Spain getting an equaliser out of the blue. I think we'd been coasting a bit up to this point, thinking we could just keep hold of the ball and wear Spain out. If anything, they became tighter and more energetic after Moreno went off and, for a spell at least, we were rattled.

Then Julian Joachim went on a run down the left, cut the ball back at a lovely pace for me to run onto and I just hit an absolute screamer past their keeper. The scenes! A hugging masterclass only surpassed after Xabi Alonso's equaliser in Istanbul. We all ran to the corner and went into this massive pile-on, with yours truly at the bottom of the stack, and it was absolute magic! I went on to get another hat-trick, the third goal of which was yet another right-footed looper from outside the box. The Fowler Loop might not have the same ring to it as The Cruyff Turn maybe, but I'm definitely thinking of getting the name copyrighted!

So, it was on to the final against Turkey – fittingly, for me, at Nottingham Forest, scene of my first and deepest England Schools disappointment. The ground was packed with 28,000 fans this time, though – far and away the biggest crowd I had ever played in front of. I didn't score that day. In fact, the game was something of a tight, drab affair, with Turkey sitting deep and seemingly only interested in grinding the game out to penalties. As it turned out, it was a pen that settled the game, and the tournament, though – a foul on me as I turned inside the box, ready to get a shot away. Darren Caskey was our regular penalty-taker and he made no mistake (though I don't mind saying I would have loved to have smashed it in myself).

I don't know whether making the turn that led to the foul that produced the penalty that won the Cup counts as an Assist, but let's just say we wouldn't have won without me, shall we? I went back to Liverpool as a champion, Steve Heighway's congratulations ringing in my ears. 'Next stop, the First Team,' he said with a grin – and we went out and signed Nigel Clough. Ah well, the dream was nice while it lasted, but I was off to the back of the queue, again.

Once again though, Graeme Souness took the trouble to seek me out and reassure me that he had me marked down as one for the future and that, in football, the future could always be just around the corner. He was good with me, telling me to stay positive and work hard and that, sooner or later, my chance would come. 'Just look at young McManaman,' he said. 'A regular, now. Look at Rob Jones, Jamie Redknapp, Mike Marsh, Don Hutchison ... If you can prove to me that you're good enough, age will never be a deterrent.' In fact, Souey told me that his dream team would always be a blend of youth and experience.

I don't think I was actively hoping that Nigel Clough would fail – you always want your team to win every game they play, don't you? But, by my reckoning, Cloughie was more of a Number 10 or an attacking midfielder than a bona fide goal-scorer. As the first game of the season drew nearer – a home game against Sheffield Wednesday – I was still harbouring distant hopes that I might get a place on the bench. As it turned out, I started that season leading the line for the Reserves while Cloughie hit the ground running with both goals in a 2–0 win, then bagging a goal in each of the next two games. Like I say, not a natural goal-scorer by any definition ...

Souness was right, though – the future, for me, *did* turn out to be just around the corner. The team made a pretty decent start to the season, winning three of the first four games. After the 2–0 win against Sheffield Wednesday on the first day, we won 3–1 at Loftus Road – QPR was always a tricky fixture in those days – then 5–0 away at Swindon. But then we lost away at Coventry and at home to the up-and-coming

Blackburn team that Kenny Dalglish was beginning to mould after his return to management. The turning point for me came in the next game – away at Everton. Souey had identified the left side of our defence as a weakness. He'd already brought in Razor Ruddock and the day before the Everton game, he signed Julian Dicks from West Ham to play at left-back (Bugsy Burrows went the other way as part of the deal).

Dicks was a notorious hothead; a tenacious, often reckless tackler with a fiery temperament and an even more ferocious left foot. He was supposed to be the hard man who would let the opposition know he was there and going into the derby game, a lot of our fans seemed happy enough to have that kind of no-nonsense character on board. But it just didn't happen for us, or Dicks. If anything, Everton had all the fighting qualities with Liverpool struggling for ideas and, even worse, seeming to lack guts: we lost 2–0.

For most of the squad I'd imagine it was a long, moody coach ride down to London four days later, for our League Cup fixture against Fulham. For me though, it was pure magic. The management never – or hardly ever, anyway – tell you who's playing in advance, but you know. Or, if you don't know for sure, you get a very strong feeling. It's just the way they interact with you. They're a bit more tactile, there's eye contact, smiles, the occasional slap on the shoulders or an extra word in your ear. I was starting to hear from some of the younger lads who had already broken into the team that I might be starting, but I'd had so many knock-backs that I blocked it all out – I didn't want to get my hopes up again, even though I was desperate to play.

We used to base ourselves in a hotel in Bayswater – a far cry from the spa-style hotels that most teams use today, with extensive landscaped grounds to walk around, physio facilities, or even the private jets some clubs use to get the squad in and out on the day. I was rooming with Nigel Clough – another clue that I was about to get the nod, as the club liked to put the younger players in with a more experienced head who could talk them through it all. Cloughie gave me a big grin and a thumbs-up when I got the tap on the door and Ronnie Moran called me out into the corridor. I could barely take the words in as he told me that I was going to be playing that night and it didn't even enter my head to ask him if I was starting on the bench or on the actual pitch! I was off down to the payphone in the hotel reception to tell my mum. Remember, this was before everyone had mobile phones and emails and that, and I remember my hand trembling so much, I couldn't get the money in. My dad and some of the family had come down to London anyway – it must have been on the cards that there was a real strong chance I might play – but I told Mum that if Dad phoned, to tell him to get himself right behind the goal.

The coach ride down to the ground just went by in a blur. I remember thinking, 'Come on, get us there!' I wasn't sick as in queasy, but as we crawled through the London traffic, I was beginning to feel the anticipation building inside of me. Then we headed down this narrow *Coronation Street*-type road and my heart leapt as I recognised that funny little miniature stand from *Match of the Day*! Even back then, Craven Cottage was one of the last of the old backstreet stadiums, full of history – and the place where I was about to make my debut. Souness took me to one side in the changing room and told me very calmly that I was in that team on merit. He said to relax and enjoy the occasion – I was surrounded by talented players, all I had to do was believe in myself, play my natural game and keep reminding myself that I was out there in that shirt because I had earned the right. Other than that, the only other thing I had to do was score. Simple!

It's funny the things you remember. I was out on the pitch at Craven Cottage, warming up, kicking in, all the usual pre-match routines that you do, whatever level you play at. I was buzzing just being out there in that famous red kit, with my own number on my back. I had a great big 23 (no idea why the numbers were so massive!), a number that, in the future, would become synonymous with Jamie Carragher – I made the shirt, though! Out there on the Craven Cottage turf, excited as I was and as much as I was trying to play my part in the little drills you do pre-match, my main focus was trying to locate my dad in the Liverpool end.

The backdrop to all this was that, in the wake of the Taylor Report, the world-famous Kop terrace was about to be demolished to make way for a new all-seater stand. The Taylor Report had come after the Hillsborough disaster of 1989 and decreed every single top-flight ground had to become all-seater by the start of the 1994–95 season. Most fans understood the reasons, I think. But the real hardcore who stand in the middle of The Kop and start the songs at Anfield were reluctant to see this huge part of their culture taken away from them. They started a campaign to try and have the all-seater decision reversed and it was all reaching a climax in the 1993–94 season, which was to be the last in front of a standing Kop. This is all coming back to me now, anyway, because that's how I spotted my dad! My eye was taken by this big banner behind the goal that said: 'NO KOP SEATS' and as I was reading it, there was my old fella coming down the terrace and taking up a space just behind and to his left of the goal.

I can't tell you what a buzz that gave me, not just knowing my dad was there but knowing where he was. Mum did absolutely everything for me and, straight up, without her, I would be nowhere. She was the strong, dependable, loving presence who ensured that the only thing I had to worry about was my game. Somehow or other, she always made sure I had the bus fare to get myself up to training and I will always be grateful for that. But the other big part of my football journey was all about me and Dad, on foot, buses, whatever it took to be wherever the next game was; me out there on the pitch, banging them in, him on the sidelines, cheering me on.

Any nerves I might have had just disappeared. I felt great. And I knew, 100 per cent, I was going to score. We had a good team out that night – just as Souness had said, back in the summer, a blend of youth and experience. I had Ian Rush and Nigel Clough to talk me through the game, with Jamie Redknapp, Rob Jones and Don Hutch in and around me, and now I knew where my dad was, I couldn't wait to get started and show the world what I could do. To my mind, young as I was, I'd been held back. But now I was in – and I meant to stay in!

I got in behind the last man early on and flashed a header just past the post. I wasn't daunted at all – I felt right at home, playing at this level with these teammates. I might have been trying a bit too hard, if anything, but as that first half wore on, I started to see a lot more of the ball. We were playing some nice stuff – Don Hutch, in particular, was at the heart of it all, orchestrating our counter-attacks with some lovely passes, long and short. I was involved in both our opening goals – my cross from the right was pulled back by Hutch for Rushy to tap in. At the time I remember thinking how much I'd love a chance like that, an unmissable tap-in just to get my goal-scoring account up and running. Then I played a little one-two with Rushy and put a cross in that Nigel Clough managed to scuff off his thigh, over Fulham's keeper Jim Stannard and into the net. Two scruffy goals, but they all count – and we were 2–0 up at half-time. Fulham stuck at it and pulled one back in the second half, but as the game went on, we were opening them and creating chances to kill the game off. I kept trying to work out how long was left. I assumed the boss would take me off before the end and I was desperate to mark my debut with a goal – whether it came off my thigh, my knee or my bum!

When the chance came, though, I was made up that my debut goal was anything but scruffy – it was an absolute beauty if I say so myself. I started the move with a lay-off to Hutch. He played it out to Rob Jones, who gave it back to Hutch; he looked up, saw I was making a run and whipped in the sort of lethal, bending cross that is horrible for defenders and irresistible for strikers. As the ball curved away from the keeper, I stole in and took it on the half-volley, using the weight of the cross to smash it past him with my left. What a moment! Goal number one, and I was over the moon that it was such a belter. For that split second, I could see my dad jumping up and down, pumping his fist – then all the lads were hugging me and patting my head. Rushy was grinning in my face, saying, 'First of many! First of many!' and Macca (Steve McManaman) was doing that 'We are not worthy' bowing thing. Once the lads stopped manhandling me, I ran to the Liverpool end and gave it one last clenched-fist salute, hanging on to the moment just that little bit longer. My first goal for the big team and now I'd seen the net bulge, I wanted more.

On the coach home, Ronnie Moran had a quiet word – praising my all-round game and telling me that the task now was to do it again and again and again. He said I'd done the hard bit; so many strikers are so eager to make an immediate impact that they try too hard and end up struggling to find that first goal. I'd hit the ground running and it was down to me to keep on doing it on a regular basis. I wasn't daunted in the slightest; I couldn't wait to get out there and do it again, and I didn't have long to wait.

Although the return leg at Anfield the following week might have seemed like a foregone conclusion to most people, it isn't like that at all for strikers. As a striker, what you want is goals – as many goals as possible. As soon as I knew I was back in the team I was sure I'd get a couple that evening, Fulham were there for the taking. But I'm sure Rushy was thinking exactly the same; he'd be planning on getting a hatful and I was very much the junior partner! As it turned out, the senior pros were brilliant that night. Rushy passed up chances for himself, trying to play me in, and the first goal wasn't long coming. I knocked in a rebound from one of his shots – even Razor Ruddock laid one on a plate for me from a free-kick inside Fulham's box. I was in dreamland. This was all I'd been thinking about for the past ten years – scoring big goals in big games, the crowd singing my name. We blew Fulham away 5–0 and I got all five – goals with either foot and, to cap it all, a diving header. I went off with the match ball and the sound of my name ringing in my ears. I hadn't just arrived, I'd exploded onto the scene. Surely the boss couldn't leave me out, now?

He didn't. Without any big announcement being made, I found myself part of the First Team set-up and it wasn't long before I notched my first League goal. If my debut goal at Fulham was one to savour, this one was not exactly a classic!

Not long after the Fulham game, I was involved in a shocking, scrappy tie against Joe Royle's Oldham. Once again, in spite of all our experienced internationals, we just couldn't get into any kind of a rhythm. We tried to gift Oldham goals a few times, then with about 15 minutes left, they scored. Up until that point, we hadn't looked as though we had a goal in us, but we upped our urgency and I managed to scuff an equaliser right at the end. Like I say, not a classic at all but enough to spare our blushes.

My goal seemed to knock the stuffing out of Oldham – we sensed their legs were beginning to wobble. We'd played about five minutes of time added on in an era before that was the norm and threw everyone forward for one last attack. The unlikely hero was that marauding, whippet-quick winger Razor Ruddock, who trapped a raking cross-field pass like Michel Platini, left his man for dead and fizzed in a cross so deadly, Oldham's right-back could only divert the ball into his own net.

As we came off the pitch, Joe Royle was raging at the ref about the added time, but we were elated. We knew we'd got out of jail and we simply had to do better and be better in future. It was going to be a while, though.

The very next home game I scored my first League hat-trick – at Anfield against Southampton. The Kop chanted my name to the old 'Bring on the Champions!' tune:

Roooooobie Fowler, clap-clap, clap-clap-clap!

It didn't quite scan, but did I care? Did I heck! It sounded fantastic! Some players can go their entire career without hearing their name sung and here was I, a crowd favourite after a handful of games. I loved it! I followed up the hat-trick with my first penalty, against Spurs. If anything, that was the goal that proved to the manager (and the board) that I had the temperament. I was going to make it, and that was it – the club had me in double-quick to start talking about an improved contract.

Bear in mind I was still 18 and up until then I was still on my original deal of about £200 a week. This is another part of my progression where I owe Graeme Souness a huge debt of gratitude. Technically, the club didn't *have* to offer me a new deal until my 19th birthday, but Souey made sure they had me tied down to a much better, long-term deal as soon as possible. He was always very respectful to my dad, but he told us both it was in my best interests for me to get proper representation and sound financial advice.

It was Souness who introduced me and Dad to George Scott, the straight-talking Glaswegian who has looked after me ever since. Graeme introduced George to my dad, Dad liked him, brought me in for a chat, and that was that. After George spoke to the club, I signed a five-year deal that, if I saw it through and hit my goal and won bonuses, would make me a millionaire. Jesus! I was British football's first teenage millionaire. All of a sudden, I was a real player on real money – and I felt fucking great!

6

CHANGES

Everything seemed to move at a crazy pace during the next few months. This was that insane era when Liverpool – and the UK as a whole – seemed to finally emerge from those dark days of Thatcherism and misery into a multi-coloured world of optimism. Part of that technicolor dream was fuelled by Sky TV and its magazine equivalents like *Loaded*, *Maxim*, *Zoo* and *Nuts*. TV and the mainstream media were obsessed with 'Lad' culture and they were all looking for over-the-top stories of daft excess. One of their favourite subjects was young footballers, who became almost a sub-section of the media in those days. From being quite a shy, ordinary lad, who lived with his mum and gran in a Park Road terrace, virtually overnight, I had to get used to being recognised.

The first big culture shock was just the business of getting to games. At the start of the 1993–94 season, I was light years away from becoming a regular and therefore nowhere near the list for a parking space at Anfield. I used to drive up to the ground in my Maestro and park up about half a mile from the ground on Oakfield Road, not far from where The Church bar is today. I wouldn't get any hassle whatsoever. Nobody, or almost nobody, had a clue I had anything to do with the club and I would just park up, walk to the ground and take my place on the bench.

Overnight, all of that ended. After I signed that first big contract, the club gave me a sponsored VW Golf, care of Frank Skelly of Edge Lane. Boy, was I made up! As far as I was concerned, a VW Golf was on a par with a Rolls-Royce in those days. And even though we were well past the era of players' names being emblazoned on the sides of their Ford Escorts, it was pretty common knowledge that the Skelly cars belonged to the First Team squad. I still didn't have a parking space but once I'd made that First Team debut, I literally could not get out of my car for kids banging on the side, wishing me well and asking for my autograph. 'Mind your car' went from being a mild threat ('If you don't let me look after your car for you while you're at the match, it might not be here when you get back') to a service the local scallywags would happily provide for the club's new scoring sensation. Saying that, one of my regular car-minders did call me a 'minge bag' when I only had a pound on me to pay him!

We'd moved to Hughson Street a few years previous, just around the corner from St John's youth club where me, Calvey and the gang used to play pool. Now, once people found out where I lived, there was a permanent encampment

outside the house. I've been told that I'm not convention-
ally handsome, so I doubt the letters and offers of specialist favours that dropped through our door were inspired by
lust, but let's just say it was starting to become difficult to
live a normal life.

The first thing I did was to pay my mum back for all the
love and support and sacrifice she put into helping me get
to this stage. When I say 'pay her back', there's nothing I
could humanly do that comes close to the years and years
of unconditional love and belief she showered on me. But
it was always a dream of mine to set her up in a nice big
house in a quieter part of town, so that's what we set about
doing. We found the ideal place, set back from a leafy road
in Mossley Hill – not far from the Penny Lane pitches where
I started out all those years before. Mossley Hill is only the
other side of the park from where I grew up, but it's the jewel
of the South End. Our Scott was funny when the family
moved to the posh side – he started speaking in this funny,
Blackadder-style lingo, saying things like: 'Ay em et your
service. Does one require me to nip to The Arz-darr?' (Asda,
to the uninitiated!)

He was a lot younger, our Scott, but he's always been my
mate – a great laugh and a brilliant uncle to my kids.

But, even in sleepy Mossley Hill, there were gather-
ings outside the house and little petty incidents – graffiti,
cars getting keyed – that made me think that the time was
probably right to let my family live in peace. A few of the

lads had started getting apartments in the Albert Dock, which had been a symbol of Liverpool's gradual regeneration. It started with apartments, then a number of trendy bars and restaurants began to open and, finally, Granada TV and the Tate Liverpool had set up there. Jamie Redknapp was in the Dock before he met Louise, Steve McManaman (Macca) was looking – it was the place to be. My agent George went to have a look at a discreet corner duplex, right on the other side of the dock from where the bars and restaurants were. I was in there within the month (even if I was still taking my washing home and going back for Sunday dinner!).

I say the corner apartment was discreet, but not long after I moved in, a boutique hotel opened, diagonally opposite. The Albert Dock is surrounded by restored cobbled roads and walkways but apart from the occasional taxi dropping off or picking up, it was pretty quiet in the days I lived there. You'd hear the odd slanging match, the clatter of heels and the usual soundtrack to a Saturday night, but the apartments are tucked away behind code-operated steel doors and layers of security, so the last thing you'd expect is any kind of intrusion of your privacy.

Imagine my bafflement, then, when I was padding around my newly acquired bachelor pad in my boxer shorts one evening, eating a nutritious microwave meal and scrolling through the TV channels, when I saw this brief flash of light in my peripheral vision. What the fuck was that? I went to the window and craned my neck. Was there a helicopter up in the sky? All I could see was a reflection of my unconventionally handsome dial. I was about to pull the blinds when it went again – a big, blinding, silver flash. There was no doubt about it this time, though it dazzled me so much, I couldn't be sure where it came from. I looked out again, left and right, trying to put my predator's instinct to some other use than smashing leather balls into onion bags. I'd settled on an ingenious plan – I was about to turn the lights off and stand back, away from the windows, in an 'I can see you, but you can't see me' counter-attack, when the flash went off right in front of me: it was coming from the new hotel.

I could see them now, two silhouettes up in a top-floor room, snapping away at me. That was it! I was off down the corridor in my boxers and vest, as though Macca himself had threaded a ball past the last man. In fairness to the hotel, they were brilliant about the whole thing. They sent a security guard up to the room and he came back down a few minutes later, giving it the Hollywood 'exposing the film reel' routine like a wise guy in *The Godfather*. But there was very little that any of them could do to help when I returned to my plush pad clad in just my underpants, only to discover I had locked myself out! Life had become very different for little Robert Ryder, very quickly.

It was all change at the club, too. Graeme Souness had given Phil Thompson his marching orders, supposedly after another complaint from one of the younger players. Again, you can't stress enough that these were completely different times. I can't say I actively liked being screamed at, but it didn't bother me that much, either. There was this unwritten assumption that if you wanted to make the grade at a top club like Liverpool, you had to be able to withstand a high degree of mental pressure. Ultimately, Souness and Thommo just didn't see eye-to-eye, but soon the writing was on the wall for Souness, too.

In the lead-up to Graeme Souness's swansong, I felt I had finally seized my chance and hit the ground running. I made my First Team debut in September 1993 and by the end of the year, I had scored 15 goals in my first 22 games. After the miserable start we had made to the season, Liverpool were stable and our young side – regularly featuring Macca, Steve Harkness, Rob Jones, Jamie Redknapp, Don Hutchison and me – was starting to climb the table. I was still only 18, the crowd was chanting my name and everything was going like a dream. It quickly turned into a nightmare.

We were drawn away against Bristol City in the third round of the FA Cup. For me, that was always one of the big highlights of the footy calendar, and when I was growing up I looked forward to that first weekend of the New Year. Bristol City were one of those sleeping giants who had been in the old First Division in the 70s and had the crowds, the history and all the potential to be a huge club again. We played okay in the original game down at Ashton Gate; we weren't fantastic but Rushy put us 1–0 up and we were comfortable enough as the game headed into the last 20 minutes. But an innocuous 50–50 ball was to have far-reaching consequences for me. I took a little clip on that bit of sticky-out bone where the ankle meets the bottom of the shin, felt a bit of pain, but carried on playing. The next sprint, I realised I couldn't put any weight on it at all and signalled to the physio to come and have a look. Straight away, he substituted me.

Then Bristol equalised, the floodlights failed, and the game was abandoned. It turned out that I had fractured the base of my shin – a nice clean break, but one that would take a minimum of two months to mend. In writing this, I still wince a little, because it brings it all flooding back how crushed I was. I'd only just broken into the team as a regular and now I was back on the sidelines. I was desperate to get back into the thick of things and – I wince thinking about this, too – probably rushed my rehabilitation. It's well known that, over the years, I had numerous issues with my ankle. Each time those historic issues flare up, I think back to that first ever injury at Bristol City. All I wanted was to get it mended and get back out on the pitch, but I'm sure I did myself no favours by rushing myself back as quickly as I did. Meantime, I was out of the team.

We drew the replayed game at Bristol, so they were due back at Anfield for a third game that actually took place after most of the fourth-round ties had already been played! It was obviously a massive occasion for Bristol City and their fans. From mid-afternoon, the city centre was overrun with hundreds, if not thousands, of exuberant West Country supporters. It was a thunderous day, dark by 4 o'clock, and the rumbling skies added to a growing sense of gloom and doom as I made my way to watch the game from the stands. There were Bristol fans everywhere – the entire Anfield Road End, plus little pockets of them dotted around the Main Stand, too. Their manager was the former Ipswich striker Russell Osman and he came with a plan to stifle our creativity down the flanks and hit us with extra numbers through the middle.

Watching the game from an elevated position behind the Anfield Press Box, you see the game in a completely different way. For me, it was Bolton Wanderers all over again – a disaster waiting to happen. No disrespect, but I was looking at Bristol City's defence and thinking how much I would have loved a proper go at them. But, by the same token, Junior Bent's speed was causing panic in our back line whenever he ran at them. We could consider ourselves lucky to go in 0–0 at half-time. Their goal, when it came, was a cracker – a headed clearance falling on the half-volley to Brian Tinnion, just outside the box. If you think of Stevie Gerrard's 2004 famous goal against Olympiakos, the only difference is that Tinnion hit his with his left – a beautiful, swerving strike on 66 minutes. The 8,000-odd Bristol City fans inside Anfield went berserk, running onto the pitch, enraptured, unable to believe that this was happening.

Only then did we start to apply any kind of sustained pressure – too little, too late. Right at the death, their keeper Keith Welch pulled off a miracle save to keep out a Steve

Harkness rasper – but, for the second year in succession, Liverpool were out of the FA Cup at the first time of asking. I was out of the team, sulking – and Graeme Souness was out of a job. The following morning, he asked to see the board, informed them that he felt senior elements of the squad were no longer performing for him. He suggested a new manager was needed to come in and oversee the root-and-branch surgery needed to transform a dysfunctional and unbalanced squad. I was genuinely upset – for Souness and for myself. Whatever reservations people might have had about him, Souey was the manager who believed in me and encouraged me and gave me my chance, way ahead of schedule, or certainly much earlier than another manager might have risked. I was gutted – I had waited an eternity to live my dream, then in the space of a few weeks, saw it reduced to dust again.

My big fear was that Liverpool would bring in a different sort of manager – someone from outside the fold. Everton, for example, had dispensed with the tried-and-trusted approach after they dismissed Howard Kendall and brought in Mike Walker, who had enjoyed prolific success with Norwich City, helping them punch way above their weight in the Premier League and in Europe (where Norwich had beaten Bayern Munich). I was anxious that a new manager might revert to the safety-first approach of splashing out on experienced players instead of allowing our improving young team to fulfil its potential. I needn't have worried, though. The LFC board continued with the tradition of promoting from within, by offering the job to the popular coach Roy Evans, who had been in and around the Boot Room since Bill Shankly's days. Straight away, Roy sought me out and told me to take my time and concentrate on complete recovery, even if I didn't play again until the following season.

But I had two milestones to aim at. The first was a derby game towards the middle of March – I badly, badly wanted to play in my first ever game against Everton. The second was my 19th birthday coming up on 9th April. Looking back, it makes no sense whatsoever, but at the time, you set yourself little goals. After my debut, six months earlier, I had set out to score 20 goals before I turned 19. I don't think I even told anyone – it was just a personal target to keep me focused and sharp. The broken ankle soon put paid to any idea of that, but if I could get myself back running again, the Everton milestone was still achievable.

It's all very well being wise after the event. I could tell myself I felt fine, I was match-fit (technically, I probably was), but my ankle and my ligaments could have done with an extra few weeks' strengthening. As it turned out, although he was obviously going to be given time by the board, Roy Evans hadn't had the best of starts. He knew how much kudos a win against Everton was worth, how much goodwill a derby win would buy him and how it could spark an upturn for us. He kept coming over to me in training and saying things like 'Looking good, Robbie,' and 'Looking nice and sharp today, Rob.' He was almost willing me to declare myself fit, and I was hardly going to turn down the opportunity to start against Everton at Anfield!

I trotted out in front of a packed fervent Kop, creating the kind of atmosphere I had only ever sampled before from the terraces. Everton had had a crap season, too. They needed the win as much as we did, if not more. It's a cliché to say it was electric – it was way louder and wilder than that, more of an angry, passionate bear pit. Here were two wounded beasts coming up against one another to fight for the last thing on offer that season: their pride.

The noise was off the scale as we lined up. Roy went with a lot more experience than Souey had been utilising, with Ronnie Whelan back in our midfield with John Barnes. I remember looking at Everton's defence – I always try to visualise myself ghosting past their centre-backs to prod one in – and seeing two of my old heroes, Neville Southall and Dave Watson, geeing each other up. It was a typical, hell-for-leather, no quarter taken, blood-and-thunder derby game, with wild tackles, missed chances and verbal onslaughts, on and off the pitch. Then, just before half-time, John Barnes bent a ball past Ian Snodin with the outside of his right foot. It was just a little tickle – a bit like the way a golf ball will start off well wide of the hole, then begin to come back in and come back in, almost by magic. John Barnes and Jan Molby are two players who can do that in their sleep – just clip the ball, no backlift, and it spins in an arc past the last man, leaving him for dead. A ball like that, played at the right pace, is a dream to run onto.

Snodin had played me onside and the ball wrong-footed him, completely. I was through on goal, right in front of The Kop, before he even knew I was there. Big Nev came out to narrow the angle but I didn't hesitate; I clipped it past him, exactly the same way I had practised again and again and again – aiming for the extremes of the side-netting. My shot grazed the inside of the post and hit the net, and the entire place went mental!

It was sheer pandemonium – me standing there, delighted, of course, but not really knowing what to do. I remember Rushy, then John Barnes, running towards me, laughing their heads off, and me just grinning like mad, both fists clenched in celebration, but probably a little bit embarrassed, too. I didn't even think about my Everton-supporting relatives in the crowd until we trooped off at half-time. There were some lovely, ripe comments from our brothers in blue, as you'd imagine, and only when we sat down for the half-time team talk did the enormity of what had just happened hit me. I had slotted my first-ever derby goal in my first-ever derby game, at the ripe old age of 18, in front of The Kop! After that, I started every game – in fact, I don't think Roy Evans ever left me out again for non-medical reasons over the entire time he was Liverpool's sole manager. Rushy and I got 37 between us – 19 for him, 18 for me – in an increasingly lethal partnership that only really got going properly after that Everton game.

So, it came to the last game of the season, at home against Norwich. We all desperately wanted to go out with a bang in the last-ever game in front of the old, standing Kop. Their protests had fallen on deaf ears and a new era was about to be ushered in. The crowds had been queuing outside since midday – anybody and everybody who had ever stood on the fabled old terrace wanted to be there one last time before it was all ripped out to accommodate the new, seated Kop. The entire squad, management included, could feel the emotion around Anfield as we arrived for our pre-match preparation and the welcome as we ran out onto the pitch was spectacular. Every single person on The Kop seemed to have brought a flag – the backdrop of noise and colour was like nothing I had ever seen before.

I was starting to get a real sense of the untapped potential here at Anfield. For starters, it had been far too long since we had won the League, but the club really needed to be back at the very top, along with all those other European giants like Milan, Bayern Munich, Real Madrid and Ajax, who had also fallen by the wayside as the 20th century went into its final decade. Here was a chance to set a marker down and make a statement as to what this team could achieve under its new Scouse manager – and we blew it. Somehow, the occasion got the better of us. We barely got out of first gear, barely created a chance worthy of the name. Mute, passive, we were lacking in ideas and allowed an historic occasion to fizzle out into a nonentity. We lost 1–0 and it was another somewhat downbeat procession around Anfield as we waved the crowd and the season goodbye – a far cry from the spectacular bus parades yet to come.

7

FINDING GOD

Thinking back to that close season of 1994 is one of those moments where I find myself puffing my cheeks out and shaking my head in amazement – not at any particular incident, just at how *young* I was and how enormous the responsibility was that I had taken on, almost overnight.

This was a season or two after Alan Hansen's infamous comment that 'You don't win anything with kids'. Yes, Man United and The Class of '92 had bottled it in their break-through season, but they won the League in 1993 and 1994. Frankly, I was green with envy. I had been in and around the England Youth scene with the Nevilles, Paul Scholes and Nicky Butt for years, and I rated Paul Scholes as a top, top player. But I never thought any of them – or anyone else from my age group – was as good as me. I realise, writing that, how big-headed it sounds, but it's the truth: you have to be confident in your own ability if you're going to stand any chance at all of making it as a player and that's the way I saw it. I've only ever thought of a handful of players as being as good as me, or as good a striker. I went away that summer of 1994 absolutely full of myself and what I was going to do once I got a full season under my belt.

What I was going to do there and then was go on a cheap and cheerful holiday to Magaluf. Dom Matteo and I decided we would invest some of our hard-earned fortune in a hard-earned week of frivolity with a few of our mates. In an era before budget airlines, my pal Ste Calvey discovered a thing called a Bucket Shop in Church Street, offering flights at discounted prices. The system was that the charter flight operators and package holiday companies would sell off their unused seats at huge discounts, with the prices tumbling lower and lower the nearer you got to take-off. If you were ready and able to go, there and then, you could sometimes pick up a flight to Tunisia or Crete for as little as £29. The bucket shops could sell you hotel rooms, car hire, day excursions, all sorts, but we thought we were being clever just getting the flights. Stroking our chins with the wisdom of ages, Dom and I assured the others, 'Rooms are bound to be cheaper over there,' with the two unforeseen obstacles being that we didn't get into Majorca until after midnight – and there wasn't a single hotel room or apartment to be had.

We went to a bar and straight away, this lad recognised us. He asked his ma if it'd be okay for us four to kip on their sofa and we ended up all piling back there until we could find a place of our own. Not only did she find room for us, his mum cooked us all breakfast the next morning! It was a low-key introduction to my gradual understanding of the pull that young footballers were starting to have as wall-to-wall TV coverage became the norm. We were oblivious and although we had a blast and barely saw our beds the entire time we were there, it seemed mad to us, the way our every move was being reported back home. It wasn't as though we did anything that outlandish, more a case of teenage lads letting off steam.

To any casual onlooker, it must have been obvious that us two born leaders were the lads to turn things round for Liverpool as we held sand-swimming races and competitions to see who could fart the biggest bubbles in our Swimming Pool Jacuzzi Challenge. Those same innocent bystanders must have cupped their hands over their mouths as though they were passing on tactical instructions in a World Cup final and said: 'Those two, Fowler and Matteo. The devilishly handsome sand-swimmers. Going all the way to the top, they are.' It was that obvious. But, like I say, if us younger players were expected to lead Liverpool Football Club's gradual return to international supremacy, then we had a bit of growing up to do – and fast!

Across the Med, in Ayia Napa, Don Hutchison was starting to understand the downside of all that horseplay. Don was always a merry prankster – just a fantastic, natural talent and a natural crowd-pleaser, on and off the pitch. A few of the lads – Jamie Redknapp, Michael Thomas, Don and some of their mates – had gone off for a week of R&R in one of the Med's livelier resorts. Ayia Napa was the big new party island, home to a lot of R&B clubs and already being dubbed 'The New Ibiza' by our friends in the national press. In short, it was the very last place a 24-hour party person like Don Hutch should have been let loose! There was nothing he wouldn't do for a laugh and I can imagine all too well him out there, enjoying a drink or 60, everyone egging him on.

Clearly well lubricated, the photos that resulted of Hutch have become legendary – his eyes screwed tight in laughter as he demonstrates his love of Budweiser by planting their beer label on his manhood. Is that the worst misdemeanour a professional footballer has ever committed? Far from it, but it turned out to be Don's last performance in front of the cameras as a Liverpool player. A lot of commentators have retrospectively tarred Roy Evans for a supposed lack of discipline, but he could be strict. He'd openly berate overweight players and, if anything, he was overly strict with Don over Budgate. He transfer-listed him immediately and Don started the 1994–95 season as a West Ham player (signed, ironically, by Jamie's dad, Harry!).

Not to over-egg the point, but these were the times we lived in. Those laddish magazines and the tabloid press all played their part in stirring and splashing the stories, the more lurid the better. As well as being the dawn of Britpop and all the great bands that came in its wake, this was also the time of Girl Power, The Spice Girls, S-Club 7 and all that. A voracious media wanted real-life soaps played out across their pages; footballers married pop stars, a new breed of people called 'socialites' checked into rehab clinics and us daft teenagers on our first professional contracts whipped each other's backsides with wet towels and giggled over fart jokes.

I was obviously ready to make that next big step towards Kop immortality ...

I think it was Neil 'Razor' Ruddock that first called me God, during those first few days back into pre-season training. Still a fearless, exuberant kid, I would hit a ball from anywhere, any angle and more often than not, they'd fly into the back of the net. Razor would fall to his knees and grovel at my feet and do that whole 'we are not worthy' worshipping routine. They all took the piss in the nicest way possible – Razor with this shocked expression, shouting, 'Surely he is the Son of God!' and John Barnes, doing this mad Supergran voice, saying, 'Is there nothing he cannae do?' It all made me feel ten feet tall, like I was finally a proper, valued member of the team.

We made a brilliant start to the new season, beating Crystal Palace 6–1 at Selhurst Park. It was one of the first games I can remember kicking off at midday, and I think we had a few reservations about the early start, but we found line and length straight away. I scored just before half-time to make it 3–0 and even though Chris Armstrong pulled one back for them early in the second half, Rushy got a couple and Macca finished them off right at the end. Nigel Clough was out of favour and Lee Jones never really found it in the first place. Someone always has to make way though and I'd be lying if I said I wasn't made up that I was now an automatic first choice to play up front with Rushy. Game One of the new season and me, Rushy and Macca were all on the scoresheet in an emphatic win – normal service resumed. This set the scene rather nicely for our first home game of the season against Arsenal, one that turned out to be somewhat memorable for Robert Bernard Fowler (19) of St. Patrick's Parish, Liverpool 8.

Disclaimer – I like Martin Keown as a pundit and a player. In fact, I *really* liked him as a player because I could do whatever I wanted to him! It's funny watching him as a commentator because he's exactly the same as he was as a player – eyes wide, jugular throbbing, full of passion and absolutely certain of himself. When I had my first tangle with him in that game at Anfield in August 1994, he let me know straight away what he was going to do to me, and it wasn't pretty. Fortunately for us all, I don't take these things personally and just to prove it, I stuck the ball through his legs and blew a raspberry as I ran past him.

The game was pretty much even-stevens for the first 25 minutes – and then our first real chance came along. There was a bit of a ricochet in the box as Rushy and Keown both went up for a header and grappled for the loose ball. Rushy mis-controlled it, the ball fell to me right on the penalty spot and I just hit it first time, a little left-footed chip shot across David Seaman and into the far corner: 1–0. By this time, I had a proper goal celebration – a one-handed fist clench, followed by two fists held high (alluring smile optional).

I barely had a chance to celebrate that one though, because a minute later we were 2–0 up. This time Macca spotted my run, weighted the ball beautifully (though a little too far to the left, if I'm being honest). I spared his blushes, took a touch, looked up, saw the gap and threaded a left-footed shot through Lee Dixon's legs, just inside the far post. In fact, I think it clipped the post on its way into the net. The older pros all ran over – Rushy, Jan Molby and John Barnes grinning away, shouting his Fowler Favourite: 'Is there nothing he cannae do!' I winked at Macca and said: 'Shit ball, mate!' The third goal in what would, at that time, be the fastest hat-trick in Premier League history was almost the best...

A beautiful, effortless ball from John Barnes cut their defence in half. I ran onto it, scampered away from Keown and Dixon and waited for David Seaman to commit himself. He read my first effort, getting down and spreading himself to keep my shot out, but I kept the rebound in play right on the touchline, steadied myself and clipped it in with my right foot. The crowd went berserk and I reeled away towards our dugout. I can remember thinking to myself, Christ! How quick was that? I was doing this counting thing on my fingers, but even I had no idea I was a record-breaker – four minutes and 36 seconds, to be exact. That record stayed intact until Sadio Mane shattered it with a hat-trick in less than three minutes for Southampton against Aston Villa in May 2015. A couple of days before Liverpool's Champions League win in Madrid, I was interviewing Mane for the *Daily Mirror*. I said to Sadio:

'Hey, you! Thanks for breaking my record! You better go out and score against these, or I'll be coming after you!'

He didn't quite get on the score sheet, but he certainly made a key contribution!

The season went from strength to strength. By the end of November, I'd scored 14 League goals, but the downside was that my face was everywhere. The tabloids had all these nicknames for me – The Kop Kid, The Toxteth Terror and so on – but the lads just called me Growler. I kept my head down and carried on as one of the first names on Roy Evans' team sheet as we went into 1995.

Every game was still a big game for me, but I was licking my lips as our League Cup semi-final against Crystal Palace drew near. The first leg was Anfield in mid-February. Bearing in mind that we had beaten them 6–1 on the first day of the season, Palace's sole objective seemed to be to ensure this was no St Valentine's Day Massacre, more like The Battle of the Alamo. We must have had 20 corners and at least ten shots on goal, but Palace's keeper Nigel Martyn was the equal of everything we threw at him ... until injury time. Ninety-two minutes were on the clock when Macca, for about the fiftieth time that night, skipped past the last man and pulled the ball back towards Rushy. Instinctively, he knew I was coming in behind him, stepped over the ball, leaving his Welsh teammate Chris Coleman floundering in no-man's land, and I smashed the ball in with my right. A narrow win, but it completely took the wind out of Palace's sails. Considering this was a game we'd been expected to win, and comfortably, too, our celebrations on the final whistle were pretty wild – I think it was just the relief of finally breaking Palace's resistance. The fact the goal came with just about the last kick of the game only added to the drama.

I scored in the second leg, too, but this time we all made sure our goal celebration was a little more restrained. The week before, on another rainy midweek night, Eric Cantona found himself red-carded in Man United's 1–1 draw at Selhurst Park. As he walked off, shoulders back and back typically stiffened, bristling with the injustice of it all, a Palace fan goaded him from the crowd: 'Off you go, Eric!' crowed the Palace supporter – 'It's an early bath for you!' So incensed was Cantona by this cruel and deeply personal insult that he launched himself two-footed into his tormentor's chest. For this, he received an eight-month ban, a precedent none of us was keen to emulate by riling the Palace faithful. We settled for a brusque handshake, a slight nod to one another and I might even have muttered 'Goal!' under my breath – that's how crazy I was in those days.

Still, we were into the final of a Cup competition in my first full season. I've said time and again that bringing home cups and medals is what it's all about for me, so I was nigh on delirious at the chance to actually win something with Liverpool. The fact that we'd be playing Bolton from the league below us in the final only made me more confident that we'd come home triumphant.

In a season where games were kicking off at all sorts of crazy times, the 1995 League Cup final – or the Coca-Cola Cup, as it was that year – kicked off on a Sunday ... at 5pm! The last scheduled trains back to Liverpool and Manchester were around 7pm, so even 25 years ago, the fans who turned out in their thousands to vocally support their team were being side-lined in favour of the television viewer. Not that the inconvenience deterred the hordes of Liverpool fans who descended on the capital. It was just one of those days when you wake up and you know it's going to be your day. The sun was shining late into the afternoon and we ran out at Wembley to a fantastic noise from a shirt-sleeve crowd. From my earliest days as a junior footballer I had been dreaming of occasions like this and in those dreams, Robbie Fowler would step forward to score the crucial goal with the game at a dramatic point.

It had been me who had done the business in both semi-finals, but that game against Bolton was run from start to finish by Steve McManaman. He was on fire that day and it's still hard to digest how we only won that game 2–1.

Bolton had their moments and they did come back into the game's second half, but by God we were good – and Macca was absolutely brilliant! He scored two, ran them ragged, created countless more chances and was deservedly given Man of the Match.

I got on well with everyone in those early days. There was a real nucleus of proper teammates, all young lads on their way up, fighting for the same thing. There was Dom Matteo, Rob Jones, Tony Warner, and Stevie Harkness, in particular, was a really good mate. Steve was a down-to-earth Cumbrian, one of those fellas who always had a smile on his face, yet was fiercely competitive, too – you wouldn't want to come up against him in a one-on-one!

But Macca and me were becoming especially firm friends by now: two young Scousers, living the dream. We cavorted on the pitch, big mad smiles all over our grids, congratulating ourselves as we looked for our friends and families in the crowd. I had an idea where my dad would be and what he'd be wearing, so I spotted him pretty quickly – and the icing on the cake, for me, was that Mr Lynch was sat there, right next to him. From Liverpool 8 to Wembley Way via Penny Lane had not been a painless process, but here, side by side, were two of the people whose belief and patience had helped me get where I was going. I ran over and gave my dad my winners' medal for safe keeping, then legged it to join in the celebrations. Don Hutchison was no longer with us, but Razor Ruddock was, so suffice to say, those celebrations went on long into the night. I'd say they lived long in the memory, too – but I can't remember!

A pretty good season ended with us beating Man United 2–0 to virtually hand the Premier League to King Kenny's Blackburn Rovers side with four games to go. But, from a position where they only needed five points from those final four games, Blackburn suddenly started to wobble – losing games they should have won and conceding late goals to draw when they'd been winning. This was the start of Alex Ferguson's notorious 'mind games' – he was never off the telly and the radio, talking about the pressures of leading from the front and how it was harder to stay ahead than to make a run from behind. Blackburn had a great team – Tim Flowers in goal, Alan Shearer, Colin Hendry, Tim Sherwood, Stuart Ripley supplying the crosses. They stumbled towards the finish line, but they were still top of the League going into the final weekend. All they had to do was beat us on the last day, or hope Man United failed to beat West Ham.

They started off well enough, with Shearer scoring about his hundredth goal of the season in the first half. But anyone expecting Liverpool to roll over had another thing coming, as John Barnes equalised around about the hour mark. That last 30 minutes was strange: the Liverpool fans obviously didn't want United winning a third title in a row yet they always wanted to see their own team play well and beat whichever opposition was put in front of them. They urged us on, but it wasn't exactly heartfelt. As things stood, a draw was going to be enough for Blackburn, but the tension was unbearable as we turned the screw on them, creating chances and pressing them further and further back, until everyone except Shearer was camped out in their box.

With virtually the last kick of the game, Jamie Redknapp sent a pearler of a free-kick curling past a flailing Tim Flowers. I don't think I've seen such a muted goal celebration from a squad of players – there was almost a sense of 'Shit! What have we done!' But, no more than a minute later, a big cheer went up around the ground. I could see Kenny stood up, trying to find out what was going on, and a lad with a little radio leaning over, trying to hug him. If Man United had scored one more at West Ham, they would have been Champions – but they could only draw 1–1. We had done our bit by beating Blackburn – no half measures or kid gloves at Anfield – but United couldn't quite find that elusive second goal.

I had videoed the whole last day and watched it all through later. United laid siege to that West Ham goal in the second half. Right at the death, Andy Cole was through on goal, but somehow, the ball just would not go in for him. For the neutral, it must have been fantastic viewing. Right at the end of our game, you can see the message has got through to Kenny that everything is okay – they've won the League. Everyone is smiling, The Kop is able to relax and salute our returning King – but I couldn't help skulking off to the sidelines, wishing that it was me, not Alan Shearer, holding up the big trophy.

But, I'd had a decent season. I played in every single game
– 57 of them – scoring 25 League goals and 31 in total. I won
the Young Player of the Year Award and, most important
of all, my first major medal as a League Cup winner. That
was the big thing – Liverpool had won a Cup in my first full
season and I was getting a taste for it, big time. There were
bigger prizes, home and abroad, for club and country, and I
was determined to win every single honour going. Watching
Alan Shearer cavorting on the Anfield turf with the Premier
League Champions trophy was a massive incentive to me. He
may well have been the one holding that big silver cup aloft
there and then, but I was praying it wouldn't be much longer
before I did, too.

8

THE ORIGINAL GUCCI GANG

I returned for pre-season training in July 1995 with a brand new, canary-yellow swede. Once again, I had gone on a genteel summer sojourn with Dom Matteo and my long-time best mate, Ste Calvey. Someone came up with the inspired idea of bleaching our hair with lemon juice but, by the time the Mediterranean sun set on our respective bonces, we were more Paul Calf Yellow than platinum blond. I'm saying that Matteo was the big brain behind Operation Lemonhead, he swears it was me ... so let's blame Calvey!

I also came back to a new colleague (or was he a rival?): Stan Collymore. Logic said that having paid Nottingham Forest £8.5 million for Stan, Roy Evans wasn't planning on keeping him back as an impact sub. Logic also suggested if anyone was going to be vulnerable to the new arrival, it was more likely to be Rushy, who would turn 34 later that year. From my first days training with the First Team squad, Tosh (Rushy's nickname, after the character Tosh Lynes from *The*

Bill) seemed to take to me. I learned countless invaluable tips from him – how and when to bend a run to stay onside, how to anticipate a goalkeeper's spill, how to defend from the front – and I loved playing alongside him. I thought we made a brilliant 'Dad & Lad' partnership (only messing!). But, playing devil's advocate, this was the start of Roy Evans's second full season as manager. He'd had a chance to assess where our strengths and weaknesses lay, he'd won his first cup with the squad he inherited and now came his big chance to mould his own team, back his own judgement and build for the future as well as the present. One of football's great truisms is that Goals Win Games and you can't really argue with that. For Roy, signing one of the most lethal young strikers in the country wasn't just a bold move, it was common sense.

But, just as in any workplace, in any walk of life, you're going to have colleagues and employees who don't get on. It's human nature. Anyone with their eyes open could see the ridiculous talent Stan Collymore had. He was skilful, he was a beautiful striker of the ball, his movement was graceful, his touch was good – we should have formed a brilliant partnership because, when we were good, Stan and I were very, very good. Yet, in terms of our personalities, we were like chalk and cheese: me being quite lippy and outgoing, Stan almost brooding and insular.

Looking back, we should have seen the signs that Stan had his demons. A few weeks into the new season, we signed

Jason McAteer (who had played brilliantly against us in the League Cup final against Bolton, back in April). Very recently, prompted by the suicides of two greatly loved young Liverpool fans, Mick Woodburn and Neil 'Yozza' Hughes, Jason made a thought-provoking, heart-breaking documentary with LFCTV about his own mental health called *Through The Storm*. To us, in 1995, part of your rite of passage was to be able to 'dish it out' as well as take some stick. We would forever be burning each other with jibes and practical jokes and a lot of that banter came pretty close to the knuckle. To us, everything was fair game and we would do anything or say anything for a laugh. Many of us were fortunate enough to be able to take our share of the stick, but a lot of us found it difficult, too.

To give it a bit of perspective, let me say again how young we were – a group of relatively immature working-class lads, catapulted into the limelight, playing the game we loved for a team we loved and being very handsomely paid for it. Yet we had absolutely no privacy. No normality. This is not a bleat, it's a fact – people staring at you as you sit down in a café, standing vigil outside your house, beeping you and slapping on your car window at traffic lights, continually shouting out to you – it takes a fuck of a lot of getting used to. I'm as ordinary a fella as anyone could ever meet and being absolutely honest, I would far rather be left alone to get on with my everyday life. But I very quickly realised that waving farewell to any last shred of normality is all part and parcel of the footballer's contract. There is no preparing for it; it is really, really weird.

But we develop a shell; we stick together, as players; we take the piss out of the more extreme episodes we encounter, and we take the piss out of each other. That's the culture. Unbeknown to the majority of the squad, Jason really struggled with that. It's only 20-odd years ago, but it was a different era, and no one would *ever* own up to psychological frailty then. If we'd had an inkling that Stan and Jason were troubled, the sad but honest truth is we probably would have roasted them even more. Our culture was still ingrained with the idea that Real Men don't show their feelings, so any hint of introspection would have resulted in merciless ribbing. We used to call it 'slaughtering' each other. To me, it was hilarious – I could take it and dish it out, so it never remotely occurred to me that anyone in our position wouldn't necessarily be loving every minute of it. I have the utmost admiration for Jason, standing up, speaking out and putting a name to his condition (and I'd urge anyone who hasn't yet seen *Through The Storm* to look it up on LFCTV or YouTube). In retrospect, I wish we'd all known more about Stan's issues, if only for a better understanding of why he seemed so aloof. His coping mechanism was to remove himself from the banter. To us, he seemed to think himself a cut above – and that would never be good for team spirit.

Rushy seemed destined for the chop, but when the new season kicked off with a home game against Sheffield

Wednesday, guess who was left out? Yep, it was top goal-scorer and current PFA Young Player of the Year, Robbie Fowler. I was on the bench with Michael Thomas while Rushy and Stan started up front – and I was gutted. Stan had a blinder, too. He harried, made runs, shot from all distances and all angles then just as it was looking like Wednesday would shut us out for a month of Saturdays, he cut a gorgeous left-footer from the edge of the box and curled it around their keeper for the only goal of the game.

I came on for the last ten minutes and straight away carved out a chance, but being honest about it, I was pig-sick when Stan came off with a few minutes to go and the whole ground gave him a standing ovation, like he was Liverpool's great new hero. Was it my peroxide barnet that had put Roy Evans off me? Okay, Collymore had cost us mega-millions but I felt that, as a local lad who had come through the system and seized my chance with both feet when it came, if anyone deserved the adoration of The Kop it was me. So once again, just as I was starting to think I'd earned my keep as a guaranteed starter, the gaffer reminded me that I was just another cog in the system. There never was, and there never is, any preferential treatment at Liverpool and the only solution was to get used to it and get on with it. I was finding it pretty hard to understand – I was just a young lad and I badly wanted to be the best. Realising that I still wasn't Roy's automatic first choice stung, at first. But I quickly worked out that if the manager didn't think I was his best striker, it was up to me to prove to him that I was. I was going to have to take it on the chin, get my head down and work even harder in training.

As so often happens in footy though, someone else's misfortune handed me an opportunity: Rushy twisted an ankle in the 'Tony Yeboah' game at Elland Road. All these years on, and a relatively mundane game against Leeds is remembered for that outrageous screamer of a goal, volleyed past David James by Yeboah from about 30 yards. Poor Jamo stood no chance – and poor Rushy did his ankle. So, I was in against Spurs – where I scored – and from there, I went on a run that included me bagging four against Bolton and lining up at Old Trafford in what was being billed for weeks in advance as Eric Cantona's Comeback Game.

Before that, though, was the little matter of a European hike – a 2,500-mile hike each way, in fact – as we faced Spartak Vladikavkaz (technically in Russia, but geographically closer to Azerbaijan and the Caspian Sea). In those days, especially for the longer trips, it was quite common for the press – sometimes even the fans – to travel on the same plane as the players. The local media turned up at Speke Airport (i.e. Liverpool Airport, before it became John Lennon International) and *The Echo* took a photo of me and Macca waving ourselves off. From that innocent, promising start, the Vladikavkaz game was to become one of the great European yarns. For the team and the 38 Liverpool fans who made the journey, it was a tale of bravery and suffering as they survived the ardours of Hotel Fukk Me (essentially, a grey concrete housing block) and some of the most challenging international cuisine this well-travelled bunch had ever faced. For me, though, it will always be The One Where I Came To Blows With Neil Ruddock.

Let's be in no doubt about this, Razor Ruddock is an absolute nutter. He's the original force of nature – generous, funny, loud, over-the-top, filthy, undisciplined and unfiltered. Razor drives a Porsche – at fast and furious speeds – and he's like a high-powered dynamo battery in real life. It's impossible to measure the energy and positivity he brings to a dressing room – he's just one of those non-stop comic typhoons, like Gazza, who are at it from the moment they arrive at the training ground to the moment they wheel-spin away from the car park. Me, Macca and Jason were local lads who weren't exactly naïve, but even us three would be pop-eyed at some of the things Razor got up to.

One time, close to Christmas (so he does have the excuse that it was f-f-freezing!), we were playing Arsenal at Anfield. We had a corner at the Kop end. Razor trotted up from defence but instead of his usual tactic where he would hang back and time a late run from the 'D', he went into the box and leaned against the near post. Next thing, the Arsenal defenders – we're talking Lee Dixon, Steve Bould, Tony Adams here – hardly shrinking violets themselves – are backing away from Razor, genuinely stunned as his shorts go from red to black in a matter of seconds and there's steam rising up from the pitch. The boy Ruddock was only answering nature's call and relieving himself, straight through his shorts, without a care in the world. It may sound difficult, that, but Razor made it look piss easy!

Vladikavkaz was, to be tactful about it, an absolute fucking shithole. There were insects climbing the bedroom walls that Doctor David Bellamy would struggle to identify. I swear one thing, half-cockroach, half-hornet, looked me in the eye before it leapt on me, digging its feelers into my wrist. I wasn't heartbroken to spend the game on the bench, considering no one ate or slept for 24 hours – I was knackered just watching. Miraculously though, we managed a 2–1 victory, care of a Macca tap-in and a beauty of a free-kick from Jamie Redknapp.

Everyone was in high spirits as we made our way back to the airport, though most of us had our eye on getting some much-needed kip as soon as the plane took off. I was completely flat out when I began to feel a bit of a cold breeze – so much so that it woke me up. My training shoes had been deftly removed from my feet and thoughtfully cut up into tiny pieces. Bastards! The list of suspects immediately came down to three: McAteer, who was sound asleep himself – and the giggling schoolboys a few rows ahead, Neil Ruddock and Steve Harkness. Okay, I thought to myself, revenge is a dish best served cold. I'll get them back at training tomorrow or the day after – just when they least expect it.

I chuckled to myself, knowing what Razor didn't know – which is that I had a spare set of wheels in my kit bag, stored in the overhead locker. I got up, stretched and reached into the locker to grab my bag ... which fell right through my hands, down into the aisle of the plane. Ruddock and Harkness were staring straight ahead, wetting themselves (so, nothing new for Razor, there!). They'd cut off the handles of my sports bag too and to add insult to injury, smeared ketchup, mustard and vinegar into the soles of my spare trabs. Bastards! Once again, though, I sat down and bided my time, waiting for the great ogre to nod off.

Once he eventually set the plane rattling to its axis with his Richter-scale snoring, I knew nothing could wake the snoozing Ruddock. I sneaked down the aisle, removed his soppy white slip-ons and using the snippers from the First Aid kit, cut them into strips. Satisfied with my work, I tucked the shredded remnants under his feet, patted him on the head and went back to my seat, waiting for Mount Razor to erupt. I must have fallen asleep again because, next thing, there's a big tornado cloud looming over me, whining at me in a strangely high, injured tone of voice.

'Goochy! They was Goochy!'

Being an Essex lad – or so I assumed – I took it that Razor was telling me that his daft white dress shoes had been a present from the England cricketer, Graham Gooch. I started laughing, which only made his voice go higher and more hurt.

'Listen, you mug – they cost, right? Big time! And it ain't me who's paying for a new pair!'

Before too long, the whole plane was shouting: 'Gucci, man! They fucking cost!'

But Razor wasn't taking it well. The combination of sleep-deprivation and lack of sustenance was slowly transforming him into a B-movie cockney gangster caricature. As we finally landed and everyone got up to exit the plane, he leaned into my ear and said: 'No c**t mugs me off, Growler! You're only a kid so I'll give you a chance to make this right.'

I started laughing again and carried on imitating his Ray Winstone accent as we trooped off the plane. We got onto the tarmac and were all speed-walking towards the team bus. I'd already forgotten about the whole thing, when bang! Razor chinned me. Blimey! I was, quite literally, gobsmacked. I thought we'd been having a laugh and Razor just came up and stole one on me, making me bite my tongue. As I put my hand to my mouth, there was blood trickling through my fingers. When I looked up, he was just sauntering ahead towards the team coach.

I ran after him, jumped on the bus and went for him when a pincer movement of David James, Macca and Jamie Redknapp got in between us and held me back before the whole thing escalated. Macca was hissing at me, reminding me the press were still around and this little spat could very easily end up all over the newspapers. They kept me and Razor apart for the rest of the trip back to base. By the time we were all back at training, me and him had spoken on the phone, had a laugh about it and settled our differences, though the shout of 'That was a Gucci ball, you mug!' and 'Gucci tackle!' rang out over Melwood for weeks to come.

* * *

Having cemented my place in The Kop's affections by scoring against Everton and then notching hat-tricks, fours, fives, goals in semi-finals and, already, many, many other big goals, it seemed only right that I should open my account against our great foe, Manchester United.

For years and years throughout the 70s and 80s, United had been jealous onlookers while Liverpool went out and won every prize going, but now the roles were starting to be reversed. United had won the Premier League in 1993 and 1994, and were already the runaway leaders, while Liverpool were nowhere near. The previous year, exciting as the game was, I felt we were a little too made up when we clawed back a 3–0 deficit to draw 3–3 with them in a volatile night game. Any Liverpool team should be looking to beat Man United as a benchmark, yet at 3–0, their fans in the away end were chanting, 'So fucking easy, oh, this is so fucking easy!'

We definitely owed them one.

To give them their due, Sky TV had started ramping up live football as a major event. From the days of the BBC and ITV having one camera and an almost matter-of-fact approach to commentary, Sky were bringing a rock'n'roll vibe, with multiple cameras and a huge amount of build-up ahead of the biggest games. Eric Cantona had been out since his infamous kung-fu kick back in January. If our game against

United had taken place on the Saturday, 30th September, as scheduled, then Cantona would have missed it. By pushing the game back to Sunday, 1st October, Sky ensured United's king would return in front of his adoring supporters, against their biggest rivals, in a live television spectacular.

All week, they whipped up the anticipation, visiting Manchester to speak to the fans. 'God is back,' said one. 'So I am!' said me. We walked out that Sunday afternoon to a sea of French tricolours. Old Trafford was being redeveloped, which meant our following had been cut to a hardy few hundred – but they were in for a treat. The 1995–96 season was a good one for kits and lining up in that bottle-green and white 'harlequin'-style jersey, I had a real strong feeling that we were going to make a statement in front of those cameras.

A feeling that lasted exactly two minutes as Man United came storming out of the blocks and Nicky Butt put them into a 1–0 lead before we'd even worked out which way we were kicking. Needless to say, Cantona was heavily involved, pulling the ball back for Butt to run onto. His first touch was a mis-control, but the ball ran kindly for him and his second touch lifted the ball over Jamo, into the net. Cantona just stood there, nodding his head as though this was exactly what he'd envisaged. It used to do my head in the way someone else would score, but Eric would stand there with his collars up, hands on hips, waiting for everyone to run over and congratulate *him* – which the entire Man United team duly did.

Maybe we should have taken a leaf out of their book and treated our own maverick loners to the praise and affection they craved – it certainly worked for Cantona. But we gradually started to grow into the game, Macca drifting past Phil Neville at will and getting crosses into the box – we were looking good. There's always a part of you, when you're creating chances against a strong team at their place, that thinks, we need to slot one of these, they're not going to give us many more opportunities. We were into the last part of the first half and, apart from their high-tempo start, United's intensity had slowed and with half-time beckoning, they'd gone into their shell a little. Macca picked me out over on the left flank with a nicely weighted ball. I took a touch, saw that Peter Schmeichel had taken a step forward and a step to his left, anticipating a cross – and smashed it right past him on his near post. Schmeichel just stood there, barely able to believe what had just happened. His face just seemed to say, where did *that* come from? It was far and away the best goal of my young career so far, and what a place – and what a time – to score it! We went off at half-time buzzing, knowing we had United rattled.

We came back out and I did it again. This time it was a gorgeous, 40-yard through-ball from Michael Thomas that dissected their defence. Gary Neville was half a yard ahead of me, but I burst past him, easing him out of the way with my comely builder's hips. (Big thanks to my dietary consultants, Mick's of Windsor Street, for calorific assistance – I knew those chippy dinners would serve me well in the long run!) As Neville Senior floundered to catch up with me, Schmeichel came out, spreading out in a 'star' shape, trying to close me down. I didn't even think twice: he'd left three-quarters of the goal wide open to me. As nonchalantly as you like, I just sand-wedged it over his outstretched leg with my right foot. It was one of those that you just knew was in from the moment you hit it and I stood there with one arm raised, ready to take the acclaim. Our tiny band of followers was going mad in the corner, while the Old Trafford faithful stood there in silence.

'God is back,' indeed!

Needless to say, the ref gave them a highly questionable penalty when Jamie Redknapp made an immaculately timed challenge on Ryan Giggs as he burst into the box. If there was VAR back then, it would be an immediate No Penalty, but the script had already been written and Cantona stepped up to claim his goal. Still, we knew we were the better team on the day. The confidence flowed through the squad and we went on a little run that included an away win at Southampton – never an easy place to go, with Matt Le Tissier in his pomp – and a thumping 6–0 win at home to Man City (Fowler: 2). Ian Rush was back and the gaffer was rotating the squad, picking horses for courses. Rushy would generally start the away games, where we'd naturally have more defensive duties and Stan Collymore would start in those games you'd expect to be more open. I was back to being a first pick, home and away, and before you knew it, we were up against

United again – only two months after we beat (sorry, drew with) them at Old Trafford.

Even though the scoreline shows that we only beat them 2–0, we absolutely stuffed Man United that day. I got both our goals and the win signalled the start of a tremendous run right through Christmas and into the New Year. We beat Arsenal 3–1 (Fowler: hat-trick), drew at Stamford Bridge and then, on New Year's Day, we were up against Stan's former club, Nottingham Forest. I gave us an early lead, but Forest went 2–1 up after about 20 minutes. Their fans made the elementary mistake of booing Stan every time he touched the ball and singing, 'What a waste of money.' Oh dear! I equalised just on the stroke of half-time and Stan shoved the Forest fans' words back down their throats with a second-half brace. Having won 4–2, we found ourselves at the dizzying heights of second place in the League. We went on to beat Leeds 5–0 (Fowler: 2), Villa 2–0 at their place (me and Stan: 1 each), away wins against QPR (Fowler) and Blackburn, and Aston Villa again at home, where I bagged another two and we went 3–0 up after eight minutes. Villa would be sick of the sight of us – and me – by the end of that season!

Stan was getting his share of goals, too – things were generally starting to work – and we were right back in the mix for the title. United were top, Newcastle were second, and now we were only four points behind them. This, then, was the backdrop to one of the greatest games it has ever been my privilege to take part in – the visit of title-challenging Newcastle United on 3rd April 1996. Anyone in that rare minority who hasn't witnessed this remarkable game, do yourselves a favour right now and go look it up – it was astonishing!

The bare beats of the game are that we were on the front foot from the first whistle and I put us 1–0 up after a minute. It was a delicious cross from the left by Stan just begging to be buried, which I duly did – nodding it down and into the net. We seemed a little dazzled by this, stood back to take stock, in which time Newcastle were devastating on the counter. Les Ferdinand equalised and David Ginola put them 2–1 up, all in the first quarter of an hour.

Second half – I scored again. Macca seemed to bamboozle half their team just by shaking his hips; he feinted right, he feinted left, he steered the ball into my path as I ran in and I punched it, hard and low, right under Pavel Srnicek in the Newcastle goal: 2–2, with half an hour to go. Newcastle had only signed Tino Asprilla right at the end of January to help see Kevin Keegan's team over the line as they battled Man United tooth and nail for the title. Rob Lee slid a pass between Steve Harkness and Neil Ruddock, and Asprilla just hit it past Jamo first time with the outside of his right foot: 3–2 to Newcastle and difficult to see any way back for us at this stage. Cue Stan Collymore – and possibly his finest moments in a Liverpool shirt …

His first – our equaliser to make it 3–3 – came from an unplayable bending cross by Jason. What a ball! You just can't defend against those. He curved it inside the nearest defender but away from the keeper, who just didn't know whether to come for it or stay on his line. In the end, he did neither and Stan ghosted in at the far post to prod past him: 3–3, and the scene set for a grand finale.

This is where fortune favours the brave, arguably. Roy Evans brought Ian Rush on for Rob Jones in a bold, aggressive statement of attacking intent. Kevin Keegan's answer was to bring on Steve Howey to shore up their defence.

With the Newcastle fans content seemingly to settle for a draw by now, and the game entering its second minute of time added on, we launched one last attack. God knows (well, I don't, to be fair!) how our senior statesmen, John Barnes and Rushy, stayed calm as they patiently picked out passes to feet on the edge of the Newcastle box. Every single player was crowding the area when, somehow, Digger had the composure to look up and see Stan Collymore, once again all alone to the left of the box. Wiggling a bit of room for himself, he clipped a nice left-foot pass for Stan to run onto. He took one steadying touch and blasted it inside the near post with his next. I don't think Stan ever felt so much love in a football match! We all ran after him, delirious, while the fans went wild. It was an unbelievable end to a phenomenal, end-to-end game of football, which is often voted by TV viewers as the greatest game the Premiership has ever seen.

We could, and should, have kicked on from there but in true Liverpool style, we managed to come unstuck at

Coventry, a few days later. So that was that – any lingering hopes we might have had about making a late charge for the title hit the buffers once and for all. Still, we had an FA Cup semi-final to look forward to. The draw had kept us away from our old adversaries, Manchester United, though we'd be playing – you guessed it – Aston Villa at United's ground.

Brian Little had made some shrewd buys and turned Villa into a very slick outfit. Mark Bosnich was an under-rated keeper, the late great Ugo Ehiogu was terrific, with Paul McGrath at the back, and Savo Milosevic and Dwight Yorke made a pretty deadly partnership up front. We seemed to have twice as many fans as Villa inside Old Trafford. Today, there's a lot of resistance to the idea of both semi-finals being held at Wembley and I'd go along with that. Wembley should be special – the FA should keep it sacred, for finals and inter-nationals. A big part of the argument against playing a semi at Wembley is that it's so expensive for fans, more often than not involving a lengthy trek and an overnight stay. Yet, here was a semi-final between two highly attractive, very attack-minded football teams played at a reasonable hour in a stadium no more than 90 minutes away from Villa Park, an hour from Anfield – and it didn't sell out.

Not that that bothered us – our fans had three sides of the ground and there was no way we weren't winning that game! As the game started, it was actually Jason who had our first decent shot on goal, before I got on the scoresheet with a diving header. Somehow, I managed to get in front of

Ehiogu and steer a low cross away from Bozzy and into the net. We didn't really look back from that point. Digger hit the post, I went on a run past three or four Villa players, that very nearly ended in a goal – then netted one of my all-time favourites. Jamie Redknapp sent a deep cross in and Agent Staunton provided a lovely assist, nodding the ball out to the edge of the box. It dropped at a nice height for me to chest it down, lean back and curl it on the volley, just inside the post. That was 2–0 to us, Jason added a third and Jamo kept out a piledriver from Alan Wright towards the end, to keep it 3–0.

We were off to Wembley for a mouth-watering FA Cup final against Manchester United!

9

THE CALL-UP

In what was turning out to be a brilliant season for me, personally, I got my first call-up to the senior England squad. Terry Venables had been to watch me a few times and the last time he'd been up at Anfield, he came to find me and told me to keep on doing what I was doing and I'd get the call-up. How many times had I heard that one before? This time, though, I was double-keen to believe him as Euro 96 was around the corner. Skinner, Baddiel and The Lightning Seeds were in the charts, football was coming home and every single one of us wanted to be a part of it. The major obstacle for me, though, was the players I was up against for a place in that squad – let alone a starting place, or a role from the bench. Absolutely nailed-on to start, and probably the first name on Venables', or any manager's, team sheet, was Alan Shearer – simply the best striker in the Premier League.

With England hosting the tournament, there were no competitive games for almost two years, but in the succession of friendlies leading into 1996, Shearer had struck up a great, intuitive partnership with Teddy Sheringham. They seemed more or less guaranteed to start. After that, there was a glut of hopefuls – Les Ferdinand, Peter Beardsley, Andy Cole, Stan Collymore, Ian Wright, Nicky Barmby, Robert B. Fowler ... Everybody wanted to make it into that 22-man squad, but someone, somewhere along the way, was going to be left disappointed. Meanwhile I clung to El Tel's words of encouragement. I was doing my bit, scoring screamers virtually every week and keeping Shearer in my sights, but as we left the New Year behind and headed towards Easter, I was beginning to lose hope.

As so often happens, just as I was starting to let go of my dreams of making the cut, I got my chance. I'd made it onto the bench for the friendly against Bulgaria at Wembley and spent most of the second half warming up. On 75 minutes, I got the nod to strip and get ready, and with just over ten minutes left to play, I was on.

This was it, I was about to become a full England International!

Playing for your country means different things to different people but, honestly, I was on cloud nine. I think the rejection all those years before at the England Youth trials still rankled with me on some level. It was always important to me that I achieved due recognition as being a top, top striker at every stage of my career. In public, I might have said I wasn't that bothered about not being picked, but privately, I wanted it and thought I deserved it.

As I was waiting on the sidelines, about to come on and make my full debut, it felt like another part of the journey was complete: it was huge for me. I basically moon-walked onto the Wembley turf and if I'm honest about it, did very little other than run around and try my best. Still, we won 1–0, and Venables came and put his arm around me afterwards to reassure me, again, that he wanted to get me into the starting line-up, somehow.

True to his word, I started the very next friendly a month later, against Croatia. And I got the Professional Footballers' Association's Young Player of the Year for the second season in a row. With an FA Cup final on the horizon and another fine haul of goals already, the last few weeks of the 1995–96 season were starting to look tasty. An FA Cup win to go with my League Cup winners' medal was the overriding priority – then, if I could just nab one of those last few places up for grabs in the Euro 96 squad, it would be a season to look back on with real satisfaction!

But there was a problem. No matter how well Liverpool played as a team, no matter who we beat, no matter how emphatically we beat them, we found we were dogged by name and reputation. To our utter bemusement, we had become The Spice Boys. We laughed it off, at first – in that era of *Loaded* magazine, it was almost a back-handed compliment. By calling us Spice Boys, the press were saying the Liverpool lads were living their lives in 3-D. At that time, in that era, you were almost expected to 'have it large'. There was a fabricated rivalry between Blur and Oasis, the two biggest bands in the country, that was more focused on their excesses than their music. There was a whole type of telly called 'zoo' TV – shows like *TFI Friday*, where people would essentially sign up to humiliate themselves in public. The new Leader of the Labour Party, Tony Blair, sold himself as a future Prime Minister not by virtue of his policies, but the fact that he used to be in a band himself, and might possibly, once upon a time, have indulged in a bit of (nudge-nudge) horseplay. New Labour were keen to tap into pop culture and football's huge nationwide profile, with Blair adapting The Lightning Seeds' Euro 96 anthem at the 1996 Labour Party Conference, when he said the immortal line: 'Seventeen years of hurt never stopped us dreaming. Labour's coming home!'

Even Radio 1 – part of the BBC, remember, moral guardians to the nation – had a popular daytime strand called *Bird or Bloke*, where listeners had to guess the gender of some former celebrity (or nonentity) they'd plucked out of a hat. The UK was a little lairy, in truth, and this was the backdrop to the so-called Spice Boys – stars on the pitch and stars off it, too, allegedly.

And that's the part you find hard to live down: your life away from football, blown-up in full, all over the tabloids. Full disclosure – we didn't deserve the Spice Boys tag. If we'd won the Cup that year, things might have been very,

very different. Further disclosure – we probably didn't help ourselves, either. Not one single thing pointed to a collective breakdown in standards, but it's fair to say Bill Shankly might have struggled with some of the choices we made. David James modelled Y-fronts for Armani. Jamie Redknapp went out with (and subsequently married) pop star Louise Nurding from Eternal. Lads like John Scales and Phil Babb would go to parties and clubs in London – but mainly after Saturday games against London teams. Jason McAteer did a shampoo commercial. Steve McManaman's manager (say that with your mouth full!) was Simon Fulwell, who looked after – you guessed it – The Spice Girls. And, because of that connection, and because Jamie was seeing Louise and because Jamo's fashion-world connections led to Armani supplying our Cup final suits, we became collectively dubbed The Spice Boys.

Macca and I used to go to Wade Smith, a designer clothing shop that had opened in Liverpool on the back of the craze for wearing hard-to-get training shoes and sportswear. We loved our clothes, but the Armani suits were another level up. I mean, come on, who wouldn't want Giorgio Armani designing their suits? Did being a footballer mean that you had to wear some dowdy off-the-peg number to show how 'grounded' you were? I don't mind saying it, I was made up when Armani came on board. I thought the suits were smart and, in that age of Cool Britannia, yeah, they were cool!

Of course, our light, stylish Armani outfits passed into folklore as an enduring symbol of the way footballers were turning into feckless playboys and losing sight of the game itself. Hand on heart, nothing could have been further from the truth. I'll say it again – if we'd have won that final against United, the 'ice cream' suits would have become part of the folklore, the day the Liverpool cool cats outfoxed and outdressed the Manchester Steady Eddies. But we didn't beat them, did we? Somehow, this lip-smacking final just never got going, and one of the dullest games in FA Cup history was petering out towards the prolonged agony of extra time, when the cruellest of blows was struck by ... yep, Eric Cantona!

What made it worse was that the 'assist' bounced off Ian Rush in what turned out to be his last touch as a Liverpool player. We were gutted. For a team that had supposedly lost sight of who we were and where we came from, we were inconsolable.

I didn't want to go up for my medal, I just wanted to get away from there – confine a very bad day at the office to history and start, as quickly as possible, to put it all behind me. But, it hurt ... It hurt badly.

10

FOOTBALL'S COMING HOME
(ONE DAY...)

We were all still guessing about Euro 96, too. In the back of my mind, I knew I wasn't going to displace Alan Shearer or Teddy Sheringham, even though Shearer was on a prolonged barren spell that, by his standards, was starting to border on a crisis. He'd gone 12 games without scoring for England but El Tel held his nerve, carried on showing the faith and kept on picking Alan and Teddy as his first-choice strike partnership. It was more of a question of who would be joining them in the squad. In the end, it came down to a straight choice for Terry Venables – the experience and guile of Peter Beardsley or the raw talent and goal-scoring prowess of Yours Truly. I got the nod, and I was ecstatic.

Macca and Jamie Redknapp had already had the word that they'd be in the squad and now I would be joining my pals for the biggest competition in years. Having been in and around the England set-up for a while now, I was beginning to feel part of the family and, truth be told, I would have been gutted to have missed out. I liked the coaching staff – Bryan Robson and, in particular, Ted Buxton, were top-notch with me. And I really liked Venables' approach to man management. Like all great managers, he had his steely side. The previous summer, there'd been a kind of rehearsal for Euro 96, a low-key mini tournament called The Umbro Cup featuring England, Brazil, Japan and Sweden, played out across a few venues, including Goodison Park and Elland Road. With the best will in the world, the tournament failed to capture the fans' imagination, with most of the games played out in half-empty stadiums. Nevertheless, I don't think Venables ever forgave Paul Ince for his refusal to make himself available for the tournament – he certainly never featured for England again under Terry's watch.

Yet, for all his uncompromising, tough side, Venables was brilliant tactically, great at focusing on the small details that might make a difference and knew how to get the best out of each and every player. Terry would quickly suss out who perhaps needed an arm around their shoulder and a word of encouragement in their ear. He was also great with the motivational side of management – he could make you feel like you were the best in the world, even if you were only on the subs' bench. But, above all, he put his trust in you. Most managers today – and I'd count myself among them – will want to know what you're eating, whether you're looking after yourself and so on. But Terry treated you like a grown-up and left it up to you – how much sleep you required or what you did between training sessions. That turned out to be particularly relevant in the case of one Paul Gascoigne, an absolute jack-in-the-box who looked like he needed almost 24-hour round-the-clock nannying! Honestly, Gazza was a one-off – a unique talent with the attention-span of a gnat. I loved him, but I was glad we didn't have to deal with him all year round.

Meanwhile, Euro 96 hysteria was reaching fever pitch. Every newspaper, every petrol station, every supermarket was giving away Three Lions and 'Goaliath The Lion' merchandise. Every car had St George flags fluttering from its wing mirrors; houses were re-painted or decked out in England paraphernalia. The nation was going football barmy and Football was Coming Home. Venables and the FA decided to remove the squad from this pressure-cooker environment by taking us off to a pre-tournament training camp in China and Hong Kong. It worked a treat. Gazza was as hyperactive as ever, doing our heads in, but at the same time, endearing himself with his non-stop jokes and chatter. We played a couple of exhibition matches, I got another start and another cap against China and we all felt good, relaxed and raring to go. Terry told us we could all go out on our last night – assistant coach Bryan Robson would follow along later to make sure things didn't get too out of hand. But the message was 'kick back, enjoy yourselves – there's a nation's hopes and dreams waiting to be delivered when we get back home'.

From this…

A Toxteth lad obsessed with footie.

To this...

How did this happen?!

Above left: UEFA Under-18 Championship final against Turkey in July 1993, at Nottingham. *Above right:* 1993, in action for Liverpool.

Below: Celebrating with Ian Rush and Rob Jones after scoring the second goal in an FA Premier League match between Liverpool and Aston Villa at Anfield.

Three goals, four minutes... What a game.
Against Arsenal in August 1994, where we won 3–0.

Above: Signing autographs for the young Liverpool fans.
Liverpool vs West Ham United, September 1994.

Below: Receiving the PFA Young Player of the Year
award from legend Ian Rush in March 1996.

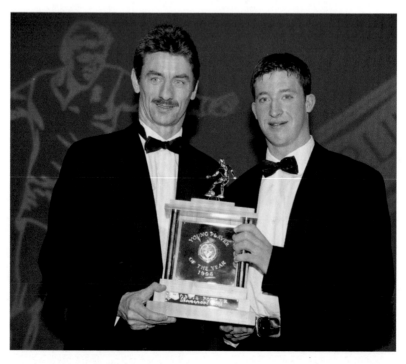

Below: Peak Fowler-mania.

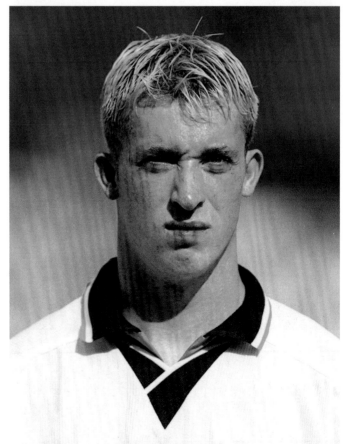

'You looking at me?'

YT auditions for
Miami Spice, 1995.

A Scotsman walks into a bar...

Above: Terry Venables always had the right blend of intensity versus relaxation ahead of Euro 96.

Left: Riding high with Macca, during a Premier League match against Man City, 1995. These are the moments that are so easy to forget, but make for the best memories.

Above: I said to Ian Walker, 'I'll do a one-arm press-up and still score a hat-trick past you...'

Below: January 2001, versus Middlesbrough. Duck, Incey!

Celebrating then lifting the UEFA Cup in Germany in 2001 – as triple cup winners.

We went to a Hong Kong bar that was well known – notorious, in fact – for its signature attraction, The Dentist's Chair. Customers, usually high-ranking bankers or professionals celebrating their retirement or promotion, would be strapped in the chair and have shots poured down their gullets until they could take no more. Gazza was in his element, goading us all to take the Dentist's Chair Challenge. The weird truth about that night, considering the way it has passed into notoriety, is how tame it was. Well, okay, that's not strictly true – there'd been a group of students in earlier, graduates out celebrating the end of their academic careers by ripping their student gowns. We copied them, doing our own footballer's version – ripping each other's shirts to strips – for a laugh. It sounds a bit silly in retrospect but, in the moment, when you're all starting to gel as a team and that great camaraderie you get among players is really coming to the fore, this is exactly the sort of thing that just happens. It's a laugh, everyone joins in.

Next thing, Gazza was in The Dentist's Chair, that huge, gummy grin lighting up his face as me and Macca poured drinks down his wide-open gob. I don't even remember a photographer being there, we were all laughing so much. Then Gazza took things a step too far by ripping Bryan Robson's shirt off and before we knew it, the night was called to a halt, the bill was being paid and we all trooped off back to bed, neither particularly drunk nor entirely sober.

Next morning, all hell broke loose. There had been press in the bar and the infamous photo of me, Macca and Gazza in The Dentist's Chair was all over the news back home. It did not look good, admittedly – England's great footballing heroes in tattered shirts, taking their task to heart by getting outrageously blotto, or so it seemed, from the photos. The thing I felt particularly bad about was the way Terry Venables felt we'd betrayed the trust he'd put in us. I can blame my youth, I can protest that it wasn't anything like as bad as it looked until the stars come out, but the truth is, going out on the lash in Hong Kong probably wasn't the cleverest way to prepare for a major tournament, full stop.

We were left in no doubt that we'd have to deliver on the pitch – which, initially, we failed to do. The opening game against Switzerland on 8th June turned out to be much trickier than it looked on paper. Thankfully, Alan Shearer broke his scoring hoodoo with an absolute rasper in the first half, but Switzerland surprised us with their technical ability, playing the odd killer pass and getting past our full-backs a bit too easily. One player in particular, Kubi Turkyilmaz, posed a constant threat and it was he who popped up right at the end to draw a handball from Stuart Pearce when he was through on goal. Turkyilmaz himself drilled the penalty past David Seaman, leaving us feeling like we'd lost the game. Fortunately, the other two teams in our group, Scotland and Holland, played out a drab 0–0 draw at Villa Park so all four teams were all square after Match One.

Holland then beat Switzerland 2–0, meaning we had zero room for manoeuvre. We absolutely had to win our next game – against The Auld Enemy, Scotland. Once again, it was slim pickings, with Scotland rising to the occasion and giving as good as they got in a blood-and-thunder first half. Macca switched wings with Darren Anderton in the second half and started to give the Scotland back line a torrid time, but the game was turned on its head by a crazy period that seemed to flash by in the blink of an eye.

Firstly, Macca sent a ball out wide to Gary Neville, whose cross was met with a thumping header from Alan Shearer: 1–0 to England in the Wembley sunshine. Then, a cross from the left found Teddy Sheringham all alone in the box. He did everything right, headed the ball down hard, but somehow Andy Goram got to it and kept it out. At 2–0, it would have been game over. Instead, Scotland went down the other end and now it was David Seaman's turn to produce the heroics, parrying a thunderous Gordon Durie header out when their whole team – and their supporters – had already started celebrating the equaliser. A moment later, Durie turned in the box and Tony Adams clipped his ankle as he went past him. Penalty. Up stepped Gary MacAllister (passable head of hair, suggestion of a combover in the middle section), who never missed. He struck the pen well enough – so hard, in fact, that David Seaman's save sent the ball high over the bar and way out into touch.

Still 1–0 to England.

The stage was set for Gazza to redeem himself, which he did in typically outrageous style. In the very next attack,

David Platt helped an awkward ball into Gascoigne's path. In one balletic movement – honestly, it was Gazza, but it was pure Geordie ballet – he flicked the ball up and around the last man, side-stepped past him and volleyed it in. In less than a minute, we went from another likely draw to winning the game in style and Paul Gascoigne was loving it! He veered off behind the goal with arms out wide like an aeroplane then lay down flat on his back, his mouth wide open as his teammates re-enacted The Dentist's Chair. How I would have loved to have been out there with them, taking part in our redemption. As it was, I was there on the bench.

As the celebrations started, Gazza's fellow Geordie Bryan Robson nudged Terry Venables and said: 'Daft sod!' They were both laughing their heads off.

England's Euro 96 campaign was up and running. I actually got on in the next game, a reunion with many of the Holland team we'd drubbed at schoolboy level, three summers ago. Obviously, the Fowler magic rubbed off again and we finished the Group Stage as comfortable winners, beating Holland 4–1. This left us with a quarter-final against Spain the following Saturday. Although Spain have always had a very handy team, they were nowhere near the level of recent years, where they have been consistently among the best in the world for at least the last decade. With the momentum building and the force of the nation behind us, driving us on, we went into that game as clear favourites. If anything, though, we were lucky to make it to extra time as Spain had a very good shout for a penalty waved away by the ref. At this point, my own personal moment of pride arrived as I was invited into the Euro 96 party as a substitute for Teddy Sheringham, who had given everything and was – not to put too fine a point on it – knackered.

Both teams were tiring and with penalties looming, I probably tried a little bit too hard to make an immediate impact. Neither side was giving much away, so the game went to pens. From all our preparation and training, we knew who the first five penalty-takers would be and what order they'd go in – with one notable exception. Teddy Sheringham was always down to take the fifth spot kick and he'd gone off. Terry Venables ambled over to me, put his arm around me and said: 'Say no if you don't fancy it, no one will think any the less of you, this is all about...'

'Yes,' I said.

'You're only a kid still, so if you have even a shred of doubt in your mind...'

'YES!'

'Oh. You sure, Robbie?'

'I WANT it! Try and stop me...'

And off I went, into that little cluster of Chosen Ones who were slightly removed from the rest of the squad – the ones on whose shoulders the hopes of the nation now rested. Although I wasn't to know it at the time, I was about to embark upon a lengthy quirk of fate in which I was destined to become the Nearly The Hero. In the shootout with Spain, I was down to take the final penalty.

Fernando Hierro missed Spain's first spot kick, Alan Shearer nearly blew the net off with his, Spain scored their second... If things went down to the wire, I would be taking the crucial, potentially match-winning kick. We scored, they scored, we scored, they scored. At 3–3, Gazza stepped up to take our fourth – and scored. This left Miguel Nadal to take Spain's fifth penalty. If he scored, it would all be on me to deliver the victory.

I couldn't decide if I was excited or terrified. I never, ever suffered from nerves; my technique was, and always had been, to visualise the outcome. Picture the goalkeeper diving one way and the ball flying into the net on the other side. Yet, somehow, out there, in the Wembley centre circle, my mind was conjuring up another image – me with my head in my hands, the Spaniards all rushing to hug their goalkeeper. Even there, though, in that scenario, it wouldn't be the absolute end – just, simply, that I would have blown my chance to be the country's hero, and I really, really wanted to be the hero. Who doesn't? As Nadal placed the ball, I came out of my trough of negativity and was back to imagining where I was going to place the ball, how it was going to fly past their keeper like a comet, how I would just stand there with my arms aloft, waiting for my teammates to pile over and dive on top of me, how I'd lead a charge across to Dave Seaman... Who, as I looked up, dropped down like a hawk on a mouse and saved Nadal's well-struck penalty. So that was that, then. Seaman was our hero, I would have to wait.

And wait, as it turned out. Nearly The Hero syndrome kept on striking. In the 2001 League Cup final against Birmingham, my all-time classic of an opener looked like being the decisive and winning goal, right up to the last minute when Andy Johnson popped up with an equaliser and stole my moment of folklore. It happened again in the UEFA Cup final against Deportivo Alavés – right up to the final moments of the game, my little beauty was the difference between the teams. The headlines were being written – Robbie's Rhineland Rocket Kops The Cup for Rampant Reds – when Jordi Cruyff managed to get up above our defence and nod home yet another equaliser, sending the game into extra time. We all know what happened next. Don't get me wrong, it's the result and the cups that matter and I'm half-joking about wanting to be written into the history books as the main man – except most footballers under hypnosis would have to admit that we all dream about being the hero of the hour. I was a few seconds away from Dortmund being The Robbie Fowler Final, which is now of course The Gary Mac Final. Time and again, it happened to me, with the shootout against Spain being only the first.

England went out against Germany in the semi-final – on penalties, naturally. Terry Venables stood down almost immediately after the tournament, to be replaced by Glenn Hoddle. I went on a belated holiday and reflected on another good season with another 35 goals – a more than decent haul. I'd won Young Player of the Year again and established myself in the England squad, but I just wasn't satisfied. Deep inside, I was burning for more silverware to go with the League Cup medal I won in my first full season.

That promising young squad we had at Liverpool was starting to come of age, now. Rushy had reached the stage we have all been at, where he felt he had more to offer than being a bit-part player warming the bench. He was leaving the club for a new challenge at Leeds. Ronnie Whelan had gone, too, and it was now down to our youthful core to step up to the challenge. We'd shown that we had the beating of Man United – in fact, we had the beating of anybody, on our day.

Now we had to make it Our Day much, much more often and find the consistency to perform on a regular basis. Everybody from the chairman, David Moores, down to the apprentices and kit men knew that winning the League again was our big priority. It had been six years now since we'd won it and to make matters worse, Manchester United had won three out of the last four titles. Even though we were way, way ahead of them, on 18 League titles, United were now into double figures – it was time to pull away from them again.

11

PAYING THE PENALTY

I was gutted that Ian Rush had gone. It wasn't just the advice and encouragement that he gave me as a young player trying to break into the first team, there was also something reassuring about having players like him and John Barnes around. They were the sort of players that gave you confidence. You'd look to your left and see Digger (Barnes), look to your right and see Tosh (Rush), and even if you were a goal down you'd think, 'We can win this.'

But the baton had now been well and truly handed to the next generation and I was more than ready for the responsibility, as well as the challenge. As a gesture of his belief in me (and, I'm sure, there was an element of the boss throwing down the gauntlet), Roy Evans gave me Rushy's prized Number 9 shirt. Finally, it had happened! The shirt that Phil Thompson told me I would never be fit to wear was, for the time being at least, mine. It was a big, big moment for me. That jersey had been worn by legends like Ian St John and Steve Heighway, before Rushy became synonymous with both the shirt and the countless goals he scored in it. No player ever owns Liverpool's Number 9 jersey of course, we're all just part of a dynasty – but boy, was I proud!

Almost as soon as I was given Number 9, The Kop had a new song for me, too – that simple chant based on a 60s hit called 'Let's Go' by The Routers. It would only work if you have a two-syllable surname, and the chant was only ever bestowed upon true Kop idols. It started with 'St John', then when Kenny was at his height, it was his turn – you know, the simple clap, clap, clap intro, kind of '1, 2 ... 1,2,3 ... 1,2,3,4 – DALGLISH!' Well, now it was my turn to inherit the shirt and the song. Kenny, Rushy and Steve Heighway had all played a part in getting me to this point and I promised myself I would do the shirt justice and score bucketloads of goals.

Like every other club in the wake of Euro 96, we splashed out on overseas talent. Up until this point, Liverpool had only occasionally looked abroad for signings – players like Jan Molby and Ronny Rosenthal being the exception rather than the norm. But we were now looking towards Europe for the value and quality that certain markets offered. In Patrik Berger, I felt we'd landed a proper, international-class midfielder. I would have loved his compatriot Pavel Nedved alongside him, too, but Paddy was class. He fitted in straight away and we started the season well enough: a goal for me in a 3–3 draw at Middlesbrough, followed by the usual home win against Arsenal. We were consistently inconsistent, yet, by December, we found ourselves top of the League.

On the Saturday before Christmas we faced Middlesbrough again, this time in a reverse of the opening day fixtures. We leathered them 5–1 – satisfying enough in itself, and also solidifying our position at the top. But, for me, that win was extra special for another reason: I scored with virtually the first kick of the game and managed to rile their players by consulting an imaginary watch as if to say: 'How quick was that one?' (It was 23 seconds, by the way.) They treated me to a few extra-special tackles, digs and elbows, after that, though nothing that would deter me from bagging my all-important second goal of the game on the half-hour mark. Not that the goal itself was particularly outstanding, it was what it symbolised – my 100th goal for Liverpool in just 165 games.

This was extra satisfying as I brought up my century in one less game than Rushy. I wish he'd have been there on the pitch to celebrate it with me because even though every one of us desperately wants to be the best – and strikers are worse than anyone, in that respect – Ian Rush was always the ultimate team player. He would have been over to me like a shot to ruffle my hair and remind me that, however many goals I went on to score, he would always have a much bigger nose than me! I went on to score four in that 5–1 win and celebrated the 100-goal landmark by taking off my shirt at the end of the game to reveal a cheeky T-shirt saying; '100 Up. Job's a Good 'Un' – a popular phrase at the time, coined by Bez from my namesake Shaun Ryder's band, Happy Mondays. Unofficial T-shirts were to loom large over the next few months.

In the New Year we were back in European action and, once again, I found myself in the news for reasons other than kicking footballs into goal nets. I might have mentioned once or twice that both myself and Steve McManaman are proud Liverpool lads. Neither of us considers ourselves flash – far from it – and we have always tried to stay connected to the communities we come from. One of Macca's uncles was a docker and by the winter of 1996–97, the dispute between the dockers and the Mersey Docks & Harbour Board was entrenched. It all started in September 1995, when the dockers came out in support of colleagues who had been dismissed without warning. The Liverpool dock workers found themselves, too, being sacked and, by March 1997, the detente was showing no signs of any kind of settlement being reached.

From our point of view, the dockers and their fellow workers had been denied basic civil liberties under new anti-union legislation. Their families had suffered two successive, very harsh Christmases, but worst of all, their plight was starting to be taken for granted. The support would always be there in a city like Liverpool, but it was becoming all too easy for people, no matter how well intentioned, to forget about the strike altogether. But Macca came up with a very effective plan to make sure the dockers stayed in the public eye.

Someone had designed a T-shirt, initially to raise awareness as well as much-needed funds. It was red with a message of support and the word DOCKERS prominently highlighted in the middle, using the Calvin Klein CK logo at the centre of the word. We had the second leg of our Cup Winners Cup tie against SK Brann coming up, which was guaranteed to be shown on TV. The idea was that Macca and I would wear the doCKers T-shirts under our LFC shirts so they would be seen by a TV audience as well as those inside Anfield on the night. Even though we both wore the shirts, I was first to score so, naturally, I lifted up my Liverpool top to show the Dockers message to the TV cameras that were honing in on me. We won the game 3–0 and all seemed to be well.

Next day, Roy Evans called me in – not to discipline me, but to tell me he'd had a call from Glenn Hoddle to say I'd be leading the England attack against Mexico in the forthcoming friendly. Happy days!

Before that though, we had a night match against Arsenal and controversy followed me to this game, too. It seems funny, looking back on this incident now, when Liverpool are known to many as 'Penalty Pool'. The inference is that Liverpool go down too easily in an attempt to win penalties. Biased as I am, I just don't see that at all. I can clearly remember incidents where Mo Salah, who is seen as the chief offender, has stayed on his feet when he's being clipped and impeded and could very easily have given the referee a decision to make. I don't think Liverpool have one single player who is consciously looking for a foul. I certainly never went to ground deliberately myself and this Monday night game against Arsenal towards the end of March 1997 was the living proof of that.

Both ourselves and Arsenal were still just about involved in the title race – we were third, they were fourth. The game at Highbury (remember Highbury?) was billed as a clash of the purists as the country's two most attacking teams came up against each other. The first half was anything but – two unadventurous teams, each of them scared of losing, cancelling one another out. Then David Seaman had a ten-minute spell he'd rather forget. Firstly, Macca squared a ball to Patrik (Paddy) Berger, who sent in a hard, low shot that Seaman could only parry. Stan Collymore followed up and slotted the rebound to give us a 1–0 lead. Then Mark Wright sent a speculative ball for me to chase after and I found myself leaving Tony Adams in my wake, with only Seaman to beat.

I slightly overran the ball, giving Seaman a sniff of a chance, and he rushed out to try to smother it. But I got there first, nicked the ball past him and, in so doing, my momentum (and the change of direction) unbalanced me and I went sprawling in the box. Seaman hadn't touched me and had no intention of doing so. Gerald Ashby, the referee, was chasing the play from behind and from his point of view, it probably looked a stone-cold foul by the keeper. I've watched the incident countless times since and I can understand the ref's perspective. The speed Seaman came out, he would have clattered me if I hadn't jumped out of the way and we would have both ended up hurt.

On the night, though, Ashby caught up with play and immediately pointed to the spot. Straight away, I jumped up and went over to the ref, waving my hands to say, 'No contact, no contact.' I assured him that David Seaman hadn't touched me, but he'd already made his decision. A couple of our players arrived, telling me to shut it, the ref had already given the pen. I made one last, slightly more muted attempt to tell him Seaman hadn't touched me. The ref muttered something like, 'Maybe not, but the intent was there.' This turned out to be a little-known but technically accurate reading of the penalty laws that came back to us again, much later in my Liverpool career, when the referee gave us a penalty at Sheffield United after their goalkeeper 'intended' to scythe down Stevie Gerrard! Anyway, the penalty was given, the Highbury crowd was baying for blood and while I didn't, and would never deliberately miss the spot kick, I didn't exactly put my bootlaces through it, either. Seaman got down to it and pushed the ball out, but Jason McAteer followed up to smash the ball underneath him into the net. It was Jason's 60th game for Liverpool and his first ever goal. Understandably, he went potty with his goal celebration!

So potty, in fact, that clearly still on a high from his debut Liverpool goal, he made the gloriously ill-advised decision to accept an offer to film a shampoo commercial in Dublin. Jason was by now a well-established Republic of Ireland international, care of the Irish heritage that just about every single person born in and around Merseyside can trace. He was also the recipient of a new nickname – Dave – let's just say it was a tribute to his often slow responses to everyday situations. It just sounded right for him, especially when you said it in a certain way: 'Oh Day-ave!' Anyway, Jason – Dave – was offered a well-paid gig to shoot an advert for Wash & Go shampoo, to be screened exclusively on TV, exclusively in Ireland. Not that he discussed the matter with us lot, but anyone could have told him that things like that tend not to stay secret. Understandably, however, Dave kept the deal along with his gorgeous, flowing locks – under his hat. He would have been better advised consigning that deal to the bin, though. However much Wash & Go paid Jason, nothing could compensate for the absolute mullering he got when the advert inevitably made its way across the Irish Sea. It featured a pouting McAteer, walking in slow motion towards the camera, shirt off, tossing his hair like a horse shaking its mane. As he gets nearer the camera, a voiceover goes:

'One thing Jason will NOT tolerate is dandruff!'

A-HA-HA-HA-HA-HA-HA-HA! Brilliant. Priceless. As one would imagine, indeed, as one would *demand*, Dave was massacred for this indiscretion. It went on for weeks. The poor lad would turn up for training and the likes of Neil Ruddock would come jogging towards him in slow motion, arms out like he was greeting a long-lost friend and the rest of us would shout: 'One thing Jason will NOT tolerate is dandruff!'

Over a period of a few weeks, dandruff was replaced by whatever we found amusing. Cheese. Pointed shoes. Farting. 'One thing Jason will NOT tolerate is yellow! He simply will not have it!' It all added up to a great camaraderie, though. We were a happy camp and that translated to our performances.

The Arsenal non-penalty game was on the Monday night, 24th March 1997. On the Wednesday, the club received a fax, addressed to me, from Sepp Blatter – the President of FIFA. He was basically telling me how refreshing it was that I'd tried to get the penalty decision overturned. The very next day, I received a letter from UEFA, telling me they were fining me £1,000 for displaying a political slogan on my T-shirt at the SK Brann game. All these years on, and I still wasn't sure whether I was a Scally or a Saint!

But a season which had promised so much fizzled out into disappointment. In one of the most wretched displays of my time at Liverpool, we were beaten 3–0 by Paris Saint-Germain in the semi-final of the European Cup Winners Cup. The final was in Rotterdam that year and we felt we'd got the easiest draw, avoiding Fiorentina and Barcelona. This was an era before Paris Saint-Germain were a force in European football. It was a game we were expected to win and so we collectively approached it as though we expected to turn up and roll them over, just because we were Liverpool. We were awful that night in Paris, and we had more than just our pride to play for in the second leg at Anfield – we owed the supporters a proper Liverpool performance.

As always happens in these games, the crowd was right behind us – the noise was incredible and it really did feel as though we could turn the three-goal deficit around. We started well enough, too. Stan Collymore won a loose ball in the box, turned it back to me and I hit it first time, right across their keeper and in at the far post: 1–0 after ten minutes, game on! The Kop had this song based on 'Rotterdam (Or Anywhere)' by The Beautiful South and they were belting it out as we surged forward, attack after attack, chance after chance. Mark Wright got up above their defence to smash a header in from a corner: 2–0, with ten minutes left. We laid siege to PSG's goal, but there were to be no fairy-tale heroics this time and, in spite of the song, no final in Rotterdam.

At the end of the 1996–97 season, Roy Evans came to the decision that his Collymore gamble hadn't worked. Stan was a gifted, instinctive, often brilliant footballer but a very complex man. The fact that he never committed to a full-time home base in Merseyside should have set the alarm bells ringing, but if anything, Roy veered too much towards the Terry Venables school of nurture. He worked around Stan's needs to a degree that, I think, pissed off the rest of the squad in the end. Stan was a home-loving lad and, ultimately, it suited all parties when Liverpool got £7 million for him from Aston Villa.

Since Roy Evans had come in as manager, he had gradually eased out the older players – John Barnes being the latest to leave in that summer of 1997. Roy brought in the promising young midfielder Danny Murphy from Crewe, a local lad and a die-hard Liverpool supporter from childhood. We also had a couple of highly rated kids coming up from the Academy, Jamie Carragher and David Thompson, plus a promising little striker called Michael Owen. Roy had already brought in Patrik Berger the previous summer and he now added Paul Ince and Oyvind Leonhardsen to inject a bit of energy and drive into the midfield, as well as the experienced German striker Karl-Heinz Riedle to replace Collymore. There was never any big announcement from the directors, but it was widely understood that we had to finally deliver on our promise this next season, or Evans would be out, too.

Looking back on all the ups and downs of my career, there were things that didn't seem too significant at the time that, on reflection, turned out to have a huge impact. One horrible example of this syndrome happened right at the end of pre-season, in August 1997. It was a tradition, up until then, for Liverpool to step up the pre-season conditioning programme with a trip to Norway, the rugged terrain being good for endurance work. The range of opposition we could play against varied from rank amateur to a good standard of highly competitive European-level teams too. And there were Liverpool fans literally everywhere you went, so the welcome was always abundant.

As players, we weren't exactly thrilled at the prospect of the Norway tour. There was a feeling that a few too many of the players we came up against went in that little bit too enthusiastically against us – either because they supported Man United (the other huge team in Norway) or maybe they wanted to leave a lasting impression. Either way, we thought they were a bit keen and we made our feelings clear to the management – tell them not to kick us this year! But, that year, my demise had nothing to do with being kicked. I'd lined up against Oslo FC alongside that little striker from the Academy, Michael Owen, and we clicked straight away. Both of us played well and each of us bagged a brace. Michael went off first, then Roy Evans signalled across to me that I'd be the next to be subbed and I should get myself ready to come off. No matter that this was a low-key workout against a part-time team, there is always a part of any striker that wants to get a hat-trick.

Knowing I'd be coming off any second, I made a run into the box, attempted to get on the end of a cross, jumped, landed awkwardly and tried to carry on. But there was this huge stab of pain right through my knee up to my thigh, and straight away I knew it wasn't a 'shrugger-offer'. I managed to hobble off and get the knee wrapped in ice, but by God, it hurt! When they got me back to Liverpool, our worst fears were confirmed: I'd jarred my knee ligaments and only rest and physio would get me back to full fitness. In all, I missed the first seven games of the new season, by which time Owen had seized his opportunity to be the main man, scoring against Wimbledon in the first game of the season.

Over the next few weeks, both Michael and Karl-Heinz scored important goals and, even though I immediately got right into the scoring groove as soon as I returned, I always felt as though as I had some catching up to do. It was as though I still felt the need to prove to myself and the manager that the Liverpool strike force should always be a case of Robbie Fowler +1. I reckon I conned the medical team, rushed my comeback by at least a fortnight and put myself under unnecessary pressure. In my first three games back, I scored then stupidly got myself sent off at Bolton – a game I'd scored in during the first bloody minute! That meant I was out in the cold again, waiting to get back and, belatedly, get this 'new' season on track. Meanwhile, we were the same old Liverpool we had been since I broke into the side as a kid – beating teams like Leeds and Arsenal at their own grounds (Steve McManaman's goal at Arsenal that November is one of my all-time favourites!), then coming unstuck at Anfield against a team like Barnsley. It was so frustrating, but I had only myself to blame.

We had a better run of form over Christmas, winning six out of seven and drawing the other – then it was Everton next up. Thinking back to that original break against Bristol City – the way I'd rushed back to face Everton and the way I had always rushed myself back from injuries ever since – it's no great surprise that I did myself in that night. It was a bitterly cold night and with the score at 1–1, with Liverpool throwing everything at them, I was as desperate as ever to get that derby-winning goal. A ball came over from the right and I remember thinking to myself, this is it! It's on! As I focused on the ball and where I was going to guide my header, I felt two sharp pains – one in my head as Everton's keeper, Thomas Myhre, tried to punch the ball clear. The other, sharper pain ripped through my thigh, just above the left knee.

I'll never know for sure whether Myhre did me with his knee as we both went up for the ball, or whether Gavin McCann came across me as he tried to block my run. Two things I *am* certain of, though: firstly, if I'd come off in that pre-season game in Norway a minute earlier, if I hadn't jarred those knee ligaments and rushed myself back from injury, I doubt the impact that night would have been anything like as serious.

But it *was* serious – as I landed from the challenge, I knew it was a bad one. And that's the second thing I know for sure – that I have never, ever known any pain like it. It was horrific, like a nuclear bomb going off in my brain, thousands of stabbing pains rippling right through me as my knee gave way as I landed. I went down on the pitch, tried to sit up, barely able to take in what was happening. It's funny, the protocol of getting injured: you're conscious of the cameras and the opposition fans and you don't want to make yourself look stupid, crying and writhing on the grass, but that's exactly what I felt like doing. What's worse is that you lie to yourself. By sitting up and trying to come across as though it was just another knock, I was already plea-bargaining with myself, trying to tell myself it wouldn't be too bad. Maybe a bit of rest and a bit of physio and I'd be back in action for the climax of the season.

Then another panicky thought – what about the World Cup? It was still four months away. I'd be fine for that, wouldn't I? I had just about worked my way into Glenn Hoddle's trust and I reckoned I stood a great chance, not just of making it to France 98 as a squad player but actually being in his starting 11. Maybe I'd be out for a month or two with this, but I'd be okay for the World Cup, wouldn't I? Our physio Mark Leather's face told another story: he could barely look at me. All I wanted to know were those two basic, but definitive things – how bad? And how long?

But my season was over and, deep down, I knew it.

12

HOU KNEW?

Everyone knows what happened over the summer of 1998. While I was ploughing that lonely furrow, taking those first excruciating steps back to fitness, Michael Owen seized his chance and made himself one of the big stories of the World Cup. Even though England were eliminated by Argentina, Owen announced himself on the world stage. 'Babygol', as the international press dubbed him, became a folk hero back home – and he deserved every bit of it. Brave, skilful, single-minded and deadly, he was a true striker dressed up as an innocent kid. Glenn Hoddle might have had his hand forced when it came to picking him, but boy, did Michael seize his chance!

His arrival as Liverpool's new goal-scoring superstar was not the only big news to come out of France that summer. Liverpool announced that the French team's technical director, Gérard Houllier, would be joining the management set-up. I was in the latter stages of rehabilitation at Melwood the entire summer, so I was hearing whispers on the grapevine before the story broke big. At first, we were told that Houllier would come in as director of football – all very modern and progressive. But, as the 1998–99 season approached, it became clear that he saw himself as joint manager with Roy Evans. It's easy to say now, in hindsight, but come on, that idea was doomed from the moment it was first floated.

There were the expected teething problems, but we didn't start the season too badly. Owen picked up where he'd left off, scoring a first-half hat-trick away at Newcastle (the 'hand-rubbing' celebration with Paul Ince), then bagging four at home against Forest. But there were problems, the biggest of which was the basic question of who was in charge. There was one memorable night away at Valencia in the UEFA Cup, when we were 1–0 down at half-time and Gérard started giving the team talk. He wasn't really getting the message across, so Roy stepped in and basically, hot-wired the team with this impassioned *Braveheart* kind of speech. The lads went back out there and turned the entire game on its head, drawing 2–2 and going through to the next round on away goals. That particular game was memorable at the time for a flare-up at the end that led to Macca and Paul Ince both being sent off. It was like the Battle of the Alamo, as we clung on through about ten minutes of injury time.

But, in many ways, that Valencia game was more significant for what it symbolised – the basic and obvious disconnect of having two managers. As skilled and respected as they both were, Roy and Gérard could not both be boss at the same time. I got myself back to full fitness ahead of schedule and hit the ground running in my first game back mid-September – a strange 3–3 draw at home to Charlton. They scored early on, but I equalised for us with a penalty. They went ahead again and we equalised, then I thought I'd won it for us with a screamer in the 82nd minute, but they went down the other end and equalised again. Disappointing after you think you've won the game but, on a personal note, I was overjoyed – if knackered! – just to be back.

I was in and out, played then rested, as I began to build up proper match fitness – which is a whole different beast to simply being able to run without restriction. Your match fitness requires you to be able to sprint, turn, run, track back with ease – no resting your hands on your thighs as you try to catch your breath. But on the fateful night of 12th November 1998, I was in the starting line-up for what turned out to be Roy Evans' last game as joint manager, a bad defeat at home to Tottenham in the League Cup. With typical dignity, Roy took responsibility and fell on his sword. Up until that point, my agent George had been talking to the club about extending my contract. Now, I wasn't sure where I stood.

Looking back now, with the perspective that time gives you, I still don't know whether Gérard Houllier and I could have ever made a real go of it. I've played under many different managers over the years, each with their own distinct style, their own ideas as to how the game should be played, their own strengths and weaknesses. Houllier, as a former teacher, was a staunch disciplinarian and a stickler for physical prowess. One of the first things he did was to bring back Phil Thompson to organise the First Team training and instil some structure into what was being caricatured as a talented but unruly bunch.

Having come back from an injury so serious it could have ended my career, I can see how a more regimented physical routine might have benefited me. Yet, in my eyes, the standard by which I judged myself and had always been judged, right from schoolboy days, was the goals I scored – and I had never stopped scoring goals. In one of my first games back I scored a hat-trick in a 7–1 win against Southampton – normal service resumed, as far as I was concerned.

My slant on things was that I was there to win and I wanted to push myself to be the very best I could possibly achieve – but that didn't mean it had to be all dour, nose-to-the-grindstone drills and circuits. The best teams I was involved with had, at their core, terrific team spirit. For me, the idea of enjoying your work, having a bit of a laugh as well as doing the hard yards was conducive to fostering a brilliant team ethic. On this key issue, sadly, myself and the management differed. Training was tough, physical and highly focused. Gérard had quite a scientific approach to the game which was founded on solid defensive principles which, in turn, tended to elim-inate risk. If that sounds safety-first, then that's pretty much how it was – his philosophy was, primarily, to make the team hard to beat then, layer by layer, add the flourishes and finesse once the basics had been embedded. You can't argue with the results. Liverpool entered a period of comparative success and you have to attribute that to the root-and-branch change of regime under Houllier. For me, it was difficult, though. I quickly formed the view that, whatever I did, it might never be enough for him.

Saying that, I didn't exactly ingratiate myself. For me, there was no point in trying to be something that I wasn't. I'd always been a player who liked a laugh and I'd always been one to embrace the piss-taking that is part and parcel of football, for better and – occasionally – for worse. Not long after I made my comeback from injury, we played Chelsea at their place. The past couple of games against them we'd had proper aggro, particularly between Paul Ince and Graeme Le Saux. Now Le Saux was one of those very clever fellas who was very easy to wind up. If you look at someone like Dele Alli today, they have all the ability in the world, but there's a hair-trigger temper simmering under the surface and you just know that certain players will play on that and see if they can get him going. In all honesty, that's how we were with Le Saux.

Of course, this was a long time before Chelsea's renaissance under Roman Abramovich. Back then, they were a so-so squad who would make a go of it in the FA Cup every few years but hadn't made a serious challenge for any of the major trophies in decades. They were still a handy team though and Graeme Le Saux was one of their key players.

So much of their attacking play started with him marauding down the left flank that we felt it would be remiss of us not to wind him up a bit and try to put him off his game.

An opportunity came when he tried to take a quick free-kick in an advanced position. I stood in front of him, bent down and displayed my pert derrière – and Le Saux literally saw his arse! He went mad, yelling at the ref to send me off for unsporting behaviour. I went over and ruffled his hair and he lashed out at me, but – for me, at least – the whole situation was comical: I was just a kid on the wind-up, and it worked. The more I laughed, the madder he became, so in that respect, it was job done. It was only afterwards that I realised how ridiculous and embarrassing the whole thing came across. Quite some years later, I got the chance to apologise directly and, to his great credit, Graeme accepted that I hadn't meant anything malicious. But, at the time, Gérard Houllier found the whole episode entirely unacceptable. He had his ideas as to how Liverpool players should conduct themselves and left me in no doubt that I'd fallen short. Among ourselves, most of the lads were scratching their heads, trying to work out what was so bad about taking the mickey out of an opponent so effectively that he had zero impact on the game. But, by that stage, I probably should have read the signs and started to rein it in and curb my enthusiasm.

Fat chance of that – our very next home game was against Everton. The background to this was that, as a general observation, the derby games had started to become increasingly toxic. University dons have done entire thesis papers on the causes and contributory factors of the decline in friendship at the friendly derby. But the basic elements were that Everton, having won the League in 1985 and 1987, had been on a slow decline since, consistently flirting with relegation for the last few seasons. A lot of their fans laid the blame for this squarely at Liverpool's door. As a result of the Heysel Stadium disaster of 1985, English clubs were banned from Europe from 1985–90 (Liverpool a year longer).

Having won the League in 1985, Everton felt they'd been cut down in their prime and had their chance of a prolonged period of domination taken away from them. You could argue that they in fact strengthened, if anything, over the summer of 1985 – signing Gary Lineker, finishing second in 1986, then winning the League again in 1987. But nothing is ever logical in football. It's a game of passion and instinct and the Everton fans felt badly let down by their neighbours in Red.

On a personal level, I had by the late-90s become a figure of hate for the Blues. Almost since my debut I'd had to endure abuse in the street, graffiti outside my house, petty vandalism at my mum's even after I moved out. I don't think the fact that I was a boyhood fan had anything to do with it. Macca and Jamie Carragher both seemed to escape the vitriol I faced – it was more to do with the goals I scored against them and the direct damage I caused, right from my very first derby.

But the physical attacks from our Evertonian friends were nothing compared to the onslaught against my reputation. By the time we played the Blues in April 1999, things had reached pandemic proportions in the city generally and for me personally. There had been a consistent rumour campaign about me supposedly being a drug addict – in spite of me taking and passing numerous random drug checks both for Liverpool and for England, and in spite of me being a happy, engaged-to-be-married man. I had met the love of my life, Kerrie, on a night out in Liverpool with her family and, in scenes reminiscent of Michael Corleone courting Apollonia Vitelli in *The Godfather*, we'd been chaperoned by her numerous sisters as we got to know each other over the passing months. If I was a drug addict then I was also a fool, as only a certified nutter would risk the wrath of the Hannon sisters! Added to the personal spice was the fact that Everton, under Walter Smith, were floundering at the bottom of the League and the stage was set nicely for me to twist their melons a little.

Things did not immediately go to plan, with Olivier Dacourt scoring with an unstoppable scorcher from outside the box. The Blues packed into the Anfield Road end went delirious, bouncing up and down while still finding the time to remind me, whenever I touched the ball, that I was a Judas, a bastard, unorthodoxly handsome and, of course, a smackhead. So, when Marco Materazzi was penalised for a foul on Patrik Berger inside the box, there wasn't a wall high enough or a rope strong enough to hold me back from taking that pen. The fact that I laced it past Thomas Myhre, whose uncompromising challenge had put me out of action for the best part of a year in my last derby game, made the moment all the sweeter. I'd love to say that I reeled away with one clenched fist in the air, ready to greet my admiring teammates – nah, would I heck! I'm sorry, but even now, I don't regret for a second the crazy celebration that followed – I knew exactly what I was doing.

Since childhood, I'd had sinus problems on and off. It wasn't that serious, but I'd been told by a boxer mate that if you stuck an 'airstrip' over the bridge of your nose, it opened up your nasal cavities, helped you breathe deeper and, in turn, perform better. I'd been wearing one for a while – it became such a part of my persona that my little Twitter avatar fella has a cheeky air strip across his nose right now! Anyway, I got down on my hands and knees and 'snorted' the touchline, my big, air-strip hooter buried in the white paint. Macca ran over and tried to get me up. He was laughing and shaking his head, shouting, 'Get up, you mad get [git]!' but I just carried on.

Eventually, I got up and ran over to the Everton fans to show them a bit of love, too – but their fume levels burst the thermometer glass, so I got back down on my knees and did it again, just in case they hadn't got the joke first time round. Finally, play restarted and, just before half-time, I added another one, this time getting my bonce on a flick-on to put us 2–1 up. It's strange to look back on this and even stranger to say it now, but for what was left of that first half I revelled in the abuse of the Everton fans – I loved it.

It seemed like the more they insulted me, the more I could torture them in return.

Second half, we began to turn the screw and after we spurned at least four good chances to put the game to bed, Patrik Berger slotted one in the 85th minute to spark mass delirium in the crowd (apart from the Angry Corner in the Anfield Road). But, as the cliché goes, we started singing too soon. Right at the end, Francis 'Franny' Jeffers nipped and stole a proper poacher's goal: 3–2, with four minutes added on. It was a nervy last few minutes and the Blues would have snatched an undeserved equaliser right at the death if it wasn't for the intervention of a little-known young hero in the making. Everton had brought on Danny Cadamarteri, a speedy striker who had caused something of a hoodoo over Liverpool. Sure enough, he ran onto a through ball, went around Jamo and rolled the ball into an empty net ... or so he thought.

The young Number 28, who had come on just 15 minutes earlier to replace our injured right-back, Vedge Heggem, came racing in like a whippet and threw himself after the ball, just getting there in time to keep it out, clear it and keep the scoreline 3–2 to The Mighty Reds. The kid celebrated like he'd just scored the winning goal, punching the air and taking the congratulations of his teammates: his name was Steven Gerrard. When you consider that I have played along-side midfielders of the calibre of John Barnes, Jan Molby, Ronnie Whelan, Steve McManaman, Xabi Alonso, Gary Mac (McAllister), Danny Murphy, Dietmar 'Didi' Hamann,

Paul Ince and Jamie Redknapp, it's no exaggeration that Steven is the finest of them all and, along with Macca, I'd say the greatest I've played with in any position.

Any short-term euphoria from that 3–2 derby win was quickly extinguished as the British media went into meltdown over my snort-the-touchline goal celebration. As with many of my actions – like scoring incredible goals out of impossible situations! – the celebration was mainly impulsive and instinctive.

Gérard Houllier's attempts to defend me only made matters worse. The boss came out with the baffling explanation that getting down on my hands and knees and 'eating the grass' was a typical Cameroonian goal celebration that Rigobert Song had brought to Melwood with him. By crawling along the line with one hand over my nose, my face buried in the lush Anfield turf and a big stupid grin on my dial, I was merely imitating a sheep or a goat doing what came naturally and having a good old chomp on the L4 grass. Gérard meant well, but the press went to town on that story and he ended up making us all look a bit daft. The club didn't wait for the FA to act: I was fined an eye-watering £60,000 for breaching the terms of my contract and bringing the club's name and reputation into disrepute. I was already due before an FA disciplinary hearing over the Graeme Le Saux affair and before the day was out, I discovered I was going to be charged over Grassgate, too. To say I felt a little hard done by would be an understatement.

★ ★ ★

In the midst of all this controversy, the tenth anniversary of the Hillsborough disaster arrived. When the terrible event happened on 15th April 1989, I had just turned 14 the week before and was about to sign my Associated Schoolboy forms with the club. Even at that age, I was hugely touched by the tragedy. You couldn't fail to be – the feeling of numb disbelief that this could happen at a modern-day football match was everywhere. But it was only as a Liverpool player, ten years on, that I started to truly feel the profound and lasting effect that Hillsborough had on the families, survivors and their loved ones. The club always held its own memorial service, which the entire staff would attend, but with this being the tenth anniversary and the families no nearer to getting the justice they sought and deserved, the Anfield service was due to be bigger and more poignant than ever.

Sitting there, listening to the names and ages of all those fans brought home the sheer scale of loss. If it was difficult for me to comprehend, what must it be like for those closest to the people who had lost their lives? They were fans of all sorts of ages and backgrounds, who had gone along to watch their beloved team play in an FA Cup semi-final and didn't come home from the game.

13

BEATING THE ODDS
(PART ONE)

I have a 13-year-old son of my own now – Jacob – and he's currently showing a huge amount of natural ability. There isn't, and there never will be, any pressure on him from me. If he decides he wants to be a doctor or a builder or an aeroplane pilot, that's more than good enough for me, so long as he's happy and secure in what he's doing. But if Jacob does go down the path of becoming a professional footballer, the support he'll get from his mum, from me and his three sisters will ensure that all he has to think about is his game. God knows, I made enough mistakes early on in my career to be all too aware of the pitfalls. I'm often asked what the grown-up me would say to the cheeky young lad who took Liverpool by storm in the mid-90s. I think the big message would have to be: Just Don't Go There.

What I mean is that, for all we can justify to ourselves that we were never *that* bad, we just did what every other player did in those days, which was tame compared to the generation that preceded us, the reality is that you're better off eliminating the risk altogether. And I'm not just talking about our social lives either, although late nights are part of a cycle that includes daft injuries, bad diet and, in my case, unwanted headlines. It took a while for the penny to drop that once you sign that big contract to become football's first teenage millionaire, *everything* changes – including the way people behave towards you. If you think, by carrying on the way you've always been, you're 'keeping your feet on the ground', there's a rude awakening coming your way. People want a piece of you. Sometimes that's just an autograph, a chat or a photo – but, all too often, they want to exploit you in some way and as sad and as wrong as it may seem, you have to break with your old habits and your old routines if you want to prevent that from happening. I'm not talking about your lifelong mates – by God, you're going to need them more than ever – but if you plan to carry on going to your usual bars and pubs, then you have to expect some paparazzi to snap your picture with a drink in your hand. Expect someone you barely know to sell a story about you to the press. Expect some opportunist to set you up, snap your picture and splash it all over social media.

Welcome to my world.

Part of the problem, undoubtedly, was the perception the general public had of modern-day footballers as overpaid playboys, disconnected from the harsh realities of everyday life. Obviously, we would all dispute that. The majority of us came from pretty tough backgrounds and our attitude was that we would have played for nothing, for the love of the game. But it wasn't us who invented the Premier League, it wasn't us who negotiated those eye-watering television deals. As the millennium headed to its climax, the Premier League was awash with money and the very best players tended to be the very best paid. Although the 'bling' lifestyle hadn't quite come home to roost by the late-90s, it got to a point where most of my teammates had money to burn or, in my case, to invest.

Remember, the rise of big money in football coincided with the boost to the economy that New Labour brought. Suddenly, everybody wanted to be a property developer and that's how I became Robbie Fowler, beloved landlord to the many. The idea was to invest in rundown properties with a bit of development potential, make the repairs and improvements and either re-sell the houses or let them out to tenants. I'm not saying I was down there doing the plastering and re-wiring, but I could see the commercial sense in it to the point where there's now a Robbie Fowler Property Academy offering investment advice and expertise to prospective developers – not bad for a Toxteth tearaway, eh?

Another Toxteth lad, my pal Ste Calvey, also carved a living from masonry – literally, in his case. Calvey was always a massively skilful craftsman and after serving a long apprenticeship, he began to specialise in stone restoration.

After he left school, our Anthony joined Calvey Restoration too, so it's fair to say we've all made a few quid out of bricks and stone.

David Moores, the Liverpool chairman, was not short of a bob or two, either. He had an expression for those irrational passion purchases and investments that you occasionally make, like racing cars, paintings – or, come to think of it, football clubs. They're going to cost a lot of money. More than likely, you will not see a return on your investment but you're going to dive in and do it anyway, because you love the world and the thing you're buying into, and above all, because you want to!

Mooresy used to call those investments 'Buying A Racehorse'. Well, the other thing we dabbled in, just for a bit of fun was, er ... horse racing! Not as in gambling, though that obviously played a small part in a day at the races, but more as something that just fascinated us and that we grew to love – especially me and Macca. Growing up in working-class communities, you see enough of the bookmaker's end of the business. But me and Macca discovered we had a real interest in the breeding, training and ownership side of the racing game. A few us had met the jockey Tony McCoy the year Aintree was abandoned after a bomb scare. We'd subsequently bump into Tony at sports dinners and awards ceremonies and so on, and we got on brilliantly with him. Tony was one of the people who planted the seed of our racehorse interest by opening up that world to us. He offered an open invitation to race meetings, introduced us to other jockeys and trainers and breeders and, over time, racing grew into a real passion of ours – a welcome escape from the world of football.

Although that general curiosity and interest was there, the ownership thing really all started by accident. Dom Matteo is a Southport lad and going back to the 60s and 70s, there has always been a tradition of Liverpool and Everton players living up by the seaside in Formby, Ainsdale and Birkdale, just outside of Southport. That area between the coast and Ormskirk is honestly like the Netherlands – it's completely flat for as far as the eye can see, regularly gets flooded and is mainly just fields, farms and yet more fields.

Anyway, it turns out those never-ending flat fields and, by contrast, those good long stretches of sand are an ideal environment for horse breeding. It's pretty well documented that Ginger McCain used to train Red Rum on Ainsdale Beach (less well-known trainspotter fact: Red Rum got his name from the last three letters of his mum and dad's names – Quorum and Mared!). So, it turned out the flatlands around Ormskirk were a breeder's dream and Dom knew a trainer from the area called Mick Meagher. Mick agreed to look out for an entry-level buy into the horse trade and a few of us – Dom, Razor Ruddock, me, Macca, Jamie Redknapp, John Scales, Rob Jones and Phil Babb – formed a gung-ho, swashbuckling buyer's club, ready to transform the racing landscape with our audacious, instinctive, *Wolf of Wall Street*-style investments. Well, we put a grand each in, anyway, which was just about enough to buy a pit pony.

Our pit pony turned out to have something about him though, winning his first race at decent odds. That was a lot of fun, just the simple fact of having some skin in a race – though nowhere near as much of a laugh as our naming session. I swear we could have gone on for days, coming up with daft names like Cunning Stunt and Easy Balls (he was a gelding – think Lord Varys in *Game of Thrones*!). I take exceptional pride in the fact that it was me who came up with the ingenious and unforgettable name we stuck with … Some Horse! It's ridiculous how much amusement that gave us, the idea of a random punter in the bookmakers going, 'Who's winning?' or 'Who won the 3:15 at Haydock?' and the bookie saying, 'Some Horse!' That was just our sense of humour, but I'm convinced it all added to the great team spirit we had among that squad.

The consortium bought another horse – surprisingly enough, named Another Horse, in the hope that they'd compete in the same race and the commentator would have to go 'and Some Horse eases past Another Horse on the final straight' – but that was as far as the enterprise went for most of our LFC Buyer's Club. I think the likes of John Scales – or James Bond, as we called the handsome Yorkshire brute – just wanted to go to their showbiz parties and gallery openings and impress some debutante by saying: 'Yah, I have a minor interest in bloodstock, own a couple of nags, actually. You should come to my stud sometime …'

There was an unforeseen side effect for me, though. When Some Horse won in its first outing, I went into the winners' enclosure as an owner. It was the first time I'd seen our nag close-up and in fact, the first time I'd ever been that close to any kind of gee-gee. I found out pretty quickly that I had an acute allergy – several, as it turned out! My eyes puffed up and I came out in these attractive red blotches, and I think I broke the world record for consecutive sneezes. Channel 4 had the racing in those days and they were waiting for a cheeky interview, but I just went legging it to the First Aid tent.

Ah-ah-ah-achoo!

In spite of my allergies, me and Macca had caught the bug, big time, and went into a proper partnership, which, after a great deal of spit balling and head banging, we decided to call The Macca & Growler Company. Beats me how we came up with these winners, time and time again! Through Tony McCoy, we met a top bloodstock agent, Graham Bradley, and with his input, took the whole thing up a level or two. Whereas, up until then, we'd been concentrating our modest interest in flat racing, Graham and co introduced us to a whole new turf game – the National Hunt hurdle circuit. A bit like the way certain football clubs and scouts will look for quality and value in untapped territories – Arsène Wenger, for example, bringing in so many players from France and the African nations – Graham Bradley was one of the first buyers to move into the German market. He found us a whole string of top horses, like Auetaler, Bernardon, Samon and our best-known nag, Seebald, all trained by Martin Pipe.

With me and Macca so busy with our football, the horses became a lovely pastime for our dads. Dave McManaman and my old fella, Bobby, had become firm friends since I broke into the Liverpool team and the nags were something they grew to absolutely love. They would travel to all the race meetings and phone us from the racecourse with all this jargon they'd picked up – we didn't have a clue what they'd be on about. Dave had actually worked in one of those unlicensed backstreet bookies that every major city used to have, mainly because it was illegal for women to lay bets! Can you imagine that, women having to go and see so-and-so in such-and-such a pub or grocer's or whatever, just to lay a little bet? Anyway, Dave McManaman was a shrewd tipster and The Macca & Growler Partnership started to flourish. With horses of this calibre and Martin as trainer, we had quite a few winners, which, in turn, raised our profile. You get the picture? High-profile, earning megabucks, prancing around, swigging champagne at Cheltenham and Aintree, giving it the big one? I didn't – and I never would (for the record, I can't stand champagne!) – but it's easy to see how a certain type of person could start to get the wrong impression, maybe even bear a grudge.

I still don't know for sure whether the incident at the Holiday Inn was a set-up. What I do know is that, if I hadn't been there at 2am, it couldn't have happened at all. It was after our home game against Aston Villa, towards the end of April 1999. I was banned for four games for the line-snorting incident and a further two games for taunting Graeme Le Saux. There was a fine of £32,000 to go with the £60,000 Liverpool had already fined me – if the club had been hoping by getting in first and going in hard on me, they'd soften the FA's stance, then it backfired – badly. My ban was due to start after the Villa game, which was effectively, therefore, my last game of the season. With pre-season training three months away, I felt fairly safe in having a drink in town after the match and putting an up-and-down season behind me.

Coming back to my message from Present Day Me to Young Robbie (or Jacob), we footballers might feel entitled to wind down like ordinary people do – but are we ordinary people? In pursuing our dream, do we have to accept that 'ordinary' has gone for as long as we're in the limelight? Apart from my long-standing, close circle of friends I had always kept myself to myself. I never actively courted publicity, always, always tried to stay private – but can you ever stay private when your day job places you slap bang in the public eye? There's always going to be an element that decides they don't like you, even though they've never even met you. So, are you, in a way, asking for trouble, exposing yourself to the haters just by being out in the first place?

The fact that, to this day, I only drink bottled beer when I'm out, my thumb permanently clamped over the neck so no chancer can slip anything into my drink, tells its own story.

Even in a coffee shop, I always have the plastic lid and drink through the little slot. Is that too high a price to pay for the celebrity – some might say infamy – that comes hand-in-hand with being good at a popular sport? For the almost inevitable flak that comes with the territory, especially in today's world of smartphones, Instagram, Snapchat and immediate (often fake) news, is it worth it? On a different day, I might give a different answer, but I think I'd steer Jacob in the direction of a discreet meal in a restaurant that he knows and trusts rather than a city-centre bar.

Saying that, we'd always wind up at the Holiday Inn in Paradise Street *because* it was discreet – or at least it was supposed to be. This was the hotel that LFC had used since Bob Paisley's time as manager. It was a tried-and-trusted (and lucky!) routine. On match days, he'd bring the team down – especially before a night game – to give them a team talk and let them get their heads down for a bit of a kip before heading up to Anfield on the team bus. Whether I was out with old pals like Gordon and Ste Calvey, or on a night out with my teammates, we'd generally head back to the Holiday Inn for a nightcap while we waited for a taxi. There was a little private lounge where we knew we wouldn't get hassled and that's where I found myself after that game against Villa, feeling pretty sorry for myself.

We'd lost the match to an Ian Taylor goal, I was out for the season and I was suddenly, in my mid-20s, no longer a kid with the world at his feet, but an experienced pro who was expected to deliver. There's no doubt about it, I was at a low ebb, starting to think for the first time that I wasn't tasting the kind of success I'd always imagined I would do – the cups, the medals, the international caps. To my mind, one League Cup medal wasn't sufficient reward enough for a lad who'd been expected to go all the way to the top.

My cab was due, so I went through to the toilets for a wee. The bogs are in the main hotel, meaning that guests staying there or people using the public bar will stumble into those same facilities, too. As I was washing my hands, two lads came in. Looking back, I think they'd seen me go in there and had followed me in – only they know for sure. What is on record (it came out in the court case and was never disputed by the fella's legal team) is that one of them offered me a line of coke. I'll admit I wasn't in the best of moods; I'll admit that, if it happened again, I'd be a little more diplomatic. But, at that time, on that night, I brushed him away, told him to fuck off and made my way out of the toilets, back towards the private lounge.

I'm told by eye witnesses who gave evidence that one of the lads appeared behind me and whacked me in the back of my head. I reeled from the sucker punch and his mate then joined in. The two of them started filling me in before guests and security broke it up and gripped my attackers. When it went to court in the summer of 2000, the lad admitted every-thing, apologised and didn't dispute my account of what had happened. The judge agreed – he was sent down for 18 months. But, the way it was reported, it was yet another of those 'no smoke without fire' stories that seemed to dog me. I'm sure it played a part in the way that Gérard Houllier came to look upon me and I have to say, I gave him reasonable cause to think that way – not in so far as I did anything so bad, but I put myself in that situation in the first place. Like I say, the moral of the story is: Just Don't Go There.

It was horrible, being fit yet being out of action. As I sat there after our final game of the season, watching the Lap of Disgrace, I began to feel emotions up until then alien to me. I was despondent, dejected – not just in the way that footballers feel down about losing a game, this was more of a personal low. When I had been in this situation previously, looking on in despair at a situation I was powerless to affect, it was through injury – an occupational hazard. I would try to take it on the chin and use my disappointment as motivation to get back into the thick of it ahead of schedule. This time, I was out on a limb and it was mainly of my own making. I could moan and gripe about things being taken the wrong way, but I was starting to realise that, all too often, there was a common denominator in all these incidents: me.

For the first time in my adult life I experienced genuine self-doubt and as a result, plummeted into a kind of despair I had never known before. As a kid and now, as a professional, playing football was all I had wanted and all I'd ever known. I was always one of these naturally happy, optimistic characters who instinctively expect things to work out for the best. Now here I was, just turned 24 years of age and for the first time, beginning to doubt myself. At least this time it was within my gift to sharpen up and do something to bring about change. Yet, in my heart of hearts, I knew I had already blotted my copybook with Houllier – he had me down as a disruptive influence, someone who didn't respect his own talent, let alone his teammates and peers. To me, nothing could be further from the truth and I determined to knuckle down and prove myself once and for all to the new regime.

14

A NEW DAWN FADES

Major surgery to the squad was afoot ahead of the last season of the millennium. Gérard Houllier said farewell to Paul Ince, Jamo and Bjorn Kvarme. Somehow Liverpool's Chief Executive Rick Parry managed to get £1.5m from Sochaux-Montbéliard for Jean-Michel Ferri, too – a player who managed a grand total of 37 minutes of football in the red shirt over the two seasons. I think Mr Parry deserves the football administrator's equivalent of a gold medal for that one! And it was farewell to my old mate Macca, who left for Real Madrid on a free transfer. Fans will always have their own perspective on these things and it usually goes along the lines of players' greed coming ahead of loyalty to the clubs who made their name for them and the fans who adore them. As with all things, there are usually at least two sides to any story and Macca would have felt aggrieved at the way he was made available to Barcelona the season before, only for him to be left sitting in a hotel room for 24 hours before being flown back home again without him ever speaking to anyone from Barca.

The point is not that any particular person is right and another party is wrong, but more than ever before, football is a business – and a huge, cynical, voracious business at that – and players are increasingly seen as commodities. Everything, including loyalty, has its price. If Macca came back from that Barcelona farce feeling as though he was last consideration in the trade, then you couldn't blame him for looking out for himself when the next opportunity came along. He was off to lift domestic titles and Champions Leagues with Real Madrid, while Gérard Houllier set about rebuilding Liverpool from the ground up. Literally.

Gérard brought about some basic changes that had both immediate and longer-term impact. He oversaw the remodelling of the club's Melwood training base, bringing in dieticians, fitness coaches, performance analysts and specialist scouts for different territories. He also brought in a new central spine – Sander Westerveld as goalkeeper, Sami Hyypia and Stéphane Henchoz in defence, Dietmar Hamann and Vladi Smicer in midfield and Titi Camara to provide a more physical foil to Michael Owen and myself up front. Later in the season, Houllier would also bring in Emile Heskey – a net spend, after sales, of around £25,000,000 and serious money in those days. Over the summer of 1999, Liverpool had sold 9.8 per cent of the club to Granada, which paid for the bigger part of this transfer splurge; suddenly, things were looking up. From my utter dejection at the end of the previous season, I felt as though this newly assembled squad was suddenly starting to look like a nicely balanced mix of experience, youth and local brio.

August 1999 felt like a real significant milestone for me, on and off the pitch. Kerrie gave birth to our first child, Madison. Talk about love at first sight! I was besotted and couldn't wait to get back from training every day to see the baby. And, although there was no thunder-flash from the heavens, it felt like the right time to knuckle down and really prove my worth to Gérard, the club and myself. I worked harder than ever before throughout pre-season and with a new, five-year contract agreed to put all those doubts and thoughts of under-achievement to bed, headed into the season with a renewed zest and self-belief.

And it all started so well. I scored in our opening day win at Sheffield Wednesday then got an absolute belter against – who else? – Arsenal, a half-volley from the edge of the box that went in off the bar. If you could design your own goals, Minecraft-style, then I reckon I'd have a fair few of mine flying in off the bar – there's just something dramatic and immensely satisfying about it. But, as seemed to be the pattern with me over these last few seasons, my excellent early form was just the tail wagging the dog. It goes without saying, with the Everton game coming up at the end of September, I was eager to play. Yet, deep down, I knew I was struggling with that first burst of pace, that initial head start you need in your duels against the best defenders. When I planted my foot to make a sprint, there'd be a brief, sharp pain that went away as quickly as it came. I should have gone straight to physio Mark Leather, but with all this added competition for places, I kept it to myself.

The derby game arrived and, as ever, I was busting a gut to make that crucial difference in the game that meant more to me than any other. By the time the first half ended, I knew I'd made my ankle twinge worse. Still, I said nothing. The second half started, but I only lasted another quarter of an hour before I had to limp off. In the back of my mind I was thinking, okay, it's out in the open, now. At least Gérard and Phil Thompson can see how much it means to me to play for Liverpool. I've been playing through the pain barrier these last few weeks; a bit of ice, elevation and rest and the swelling will come down. I'll come back in a couple of weeks stronger, faster and fitter ...

No chance. The prognosis was a ruptured peroneal tendon, meaning I would need a small operation that, in turn, would require at least 10 to 12 weeks' rest.

It'll sound crackers in the context of my having just signed a new, long-term contract that would keep me at Liverpool for the best years of my career, but I just never got the sense that Gérard was 100 per cent sold on me. I'd have games when I was hitting the net and, I don't know, his praise always seemed a little muted somehow, or qualified. It would be words to the effect of, 'Yes, Robbie has done well in this game, now he has to show he can do it in every game.' That sort of thing. And, partly as a result of that sort of thing, I was desperate to get back in action.

There had already been rumours that Liverpool were seriously interested in Leicester's big young striker Emile Heskey. The last thing I wanted was to give the club an easy decision to make so I defied medical logic (and, no doubt, advice!) and got back in the team before the year was out. In the last game of the millennium, I scored the third in a 3–1 win against Wimbledon – my 150th goal in six years for Liverpool F.C. Of those, 95 had come with my left foot, 30 with my right, and 25 with my head – I think that pretty much qualifies me as being a natural, all-round striker! Disastrously, though, I felt that old familiar ankle twinge once again during that game and this time, I was out for the rest of the season. What a washout! All that hope, all that promise, and I was invalided out of the action all over again. Now, there was no question that Gérard would bring Heskey in. Michael Owen had played alongside Emile quite a few times at England Schoolboy and Under-21 level and he rated him as the ideal complement to his own, more predatory skills.

For me, it was back to a now all-too-familiar world of rehab, physio and psychological motivation. That process is a long and lonely road, and it was here that I started to think in earnest about one day moving into coaching. I'd always had an intuitive interest in the academic and technical side of the game. Anything I could pick up that might, however marginally, improve my game, I was open to it. And I'd often say to my dad that I reckoned I'd be just as good a manager as I was a striker when the time came, but in rehab, you really do focus on the big What If … and What Next … questions. So, I started on that daily slog on the journey back to recovery once again and gradually found my rhythm. It's not that it got any easier, the grinding, remorseless routine of that first step, then the next, and the next, but it held less fear for me. The only other option was not to play again – so no option at all, in reality. I accepted the situation for what it was, gritted my teeth and got down to it – literally one step at a time.

Kevin Keegan was, by now, England manager and he was good enough to call me and offer words of encouragement. Even though his long-term plan was to blood younger players in the expectation of building a core that would stay together over the next ten years or so, there would always be a place for an instinctive, out-and-out goal-getter. He said some really nice things and I felt a whole lot better about the road ahead.

The gradual overhaul of the Liverpool squad continued over the summer of 2000, too. Some of the players Gérard shipped out had featured so little over the previous season or two that you'd half-forgotten they still played for us. Brad Friedel, Phil Babb, Stig, Rigobert Song, Stan Staunton, Titi Camara and my old mate, Dom Matteo, all left. So, too, did two of our more recent Academy products – David

Thompson, a fiery and skilful winger from Birkenhead, went to Coventry and Jon Newby, who had been at the club as long as I had, left for Bury.

Among the new recruits were Christian Ziege and Markus Babbel, two highly experienced German full-backs who would surely add even more steel and maturity to our defence. Houllier also brought in Nicky Barmby and Jari Litmanen – graft, craft and creativity to support the front men. Jari's arrival was a real coup, not least because he was rumoured to have been a childhood Liverpool fan. He had plied his trade with two of the purest footballing institutions in the world in Ajax and Barcelona. Already I was licking my lips at the idea of getting back into action and being on the receiving end of some of those defence-splitting passes Litmanen had become renowned for – and Barmby's energy and skill were to provide even more chances, too.

Perhaps Gérard's canniest signing of all, though, was his decision to bring Gary McAllister in from Coventry on a free. Although Gary might have missed that crucial penalty at a critical time in the England v Scotland Euro 96 tie, he was one of the coolest customers in the game and had personally ruffled our feathers quite a few times over the years with his goals and assists. Part of the management's thinking was that, along with the creativity and emotional maturity Gary Mac would bring to the mix, people like him, Didi Hamann and Jari Litmanen would all help in developing the precocious talent that was Steven Gerrard.

Stevie reminded me very much of myself at that age. He had already shown that he had the ability to punch his weight against the very best; all that was standing in his way was his tendency, on occasion, to try that little bit *too* hard, resulting in some reckless tackles and the inevitable sending-off in the derby game. Everyone was excited about his potential to go all the way to the very top of the game. Now we had Gary Mac and Didi to help him decide when to make a tackle and when to hold back, when to spray a long ball and when to give it short. Between them, these two older heads were to be the perfect foil to the greatest young midfielder in years to break through at Liverpool.

I was naturally excited to get back to the coalface and play my part in this dawning of a new Liverpool – I worked like mad all summer, got myself into the best shape I'd been in years – and promptly got myself whacked in pre-season. We'd gradually been stepping up the intensity in our warm-up games and things were going well, both on a team and a personal level, when we headed into Belfast first week in August for a game against Glentoran – what could possibly go wrong? We were strolling it, 4–0 up without really having to break sweat, when their goalkeeper decided he'd come charging out and slide tackle me on the edge of the box. To this day I don't know what he was thinking or whether he meant to do me, though plenty enough Belfast Reds told me subsequently that he was a big Manchester United supporter. What I do know is that my ankle was knackered again and I was going to miss the start of the season.

It's hard to explain just how weird it feels to be in that situation. You're a long-term, fully committed member of a team and a club, and you badly, badly want that team to do well. But – especially when you're a striker – you want to be at the centre of the stage, the heart of the story. In football, you're very quickly forgotten – especially when your teammates do well in your absence. And that's the hardest, oddest part of the long-term injury phenomenon. Week in, week out, Michael Owen was scoring goals – odd ones, doubles, hat-tricks. When he wasn't scoring, Emile Heskey was chipping in with his fair share, too. I was pleased for them, delighted for the team – and I was pig sick not to play any part in it.

*　*　*

I got back into the team towards the end of 2000, and the Cups – particularly the League Cup – turned out to be my salvation. In the back of your mind, you know that the League Cup is the lowest priority for any team that has serious designs on the big prizes. But, as I've been saying, to me cups are cups. Medals are what it's all about. Plus, by then, I just wanted to play! As it turned out, one of my first games back was an encounter with Chelsea at the start of November. We were locked at 1–1 after 90 minutes but, just on half-time in extra time, I scored the winner. 2–1 to the Reds and we were in the hat for the next round draw. It felt brilliant just to be playing again and making a contribution – the only way I knew how to. The next round was even better: we won 8–0 (eight!) away at Stoke City and I bagged a hat-trick. It's not as though we fielded a weakened side, either. This was a proper Liverpool team, staking a proper claim on the first silverware on offer that year. We beat Fulham next, to set up a semi-final with our trusty old foes, Crystal Palace. They were fantastic in the first leg at their place, winning 2–1 – but we blew them away at Anfield, with me getting our final goal in a 5–0 romp.

This led us to the first-ever League Cup final – in fact, the first final of any sort – to be played at Cardiff's Millennium Stadium, the temporary venue for football's biggest games while Wembley was being rebuilt. It also led me to the strange and quite moving occasion of being on the same football pitch as Dele Adebola for the first time since we were both lining up for Liverpool Schoolboys together. Dele was leading the line for Birmingham City, who were very much the underdogs against us. In the run-up to the game, myself, Michael Owen and Emile Heskey were vying for the two starting positions up front. Even though I'd led the line throughout this League Cup campaign, managers want to win cups as much as players do. It's not unusual for the players who have done the dirty work in getting a team to a final to find themselves dropped for the big game itself – especially goalkeepers and strikers. To compound all the usual considerations, we were firing on four fronts – the FA Cup, UEFA Cup and still very much in the hunt for Champions League places.

The games were coming thick and fast and as much as everyone wants to play every game, rotation was to be a key part of managing such a congested schedule. Nevertheless, as the weekend approached, I had a pretty strong inkling I was going to get the nod. You just develop a feel for these things from the way the coaching staff interact with you. It's not scientific, but you can generally tell whether you're going to figure by the day before any major match. This time it was Michael Owen who missed out and, like any top player, he wasn't happy.

There was a sobering backdrop to this incredible run of Cup success the team went on, in that our mate and club captain, Jamie Redknapp, suffered a devastating knee injury that led to him having to go to the US for total knee reconstruction. I, of all people, could sympathise with what Jamie was going through, looking on from afar as his teammates went on a spectacular, triple-headed journey at home and abroad. Jamie would be proud as punch, but with his own route back to football being a long and incredibly lonely one, he was going to have dark days and mixed feelings, too. With Jamie out for the season, I was captain and it was one of my proudest moments ever in the red shirt, leading the team out at Cardiff on 25th February 2001 for the League Cup Final against Birmingham.

As can happen when a racing certainty faces a team from the lower leagues, the opening exchanges were cagey. I had a half-chance with a header from a Vladimir Smicer cross, before the game exploded into life on the half-hour mark. Sander Westerveld cleared long, and Emile Heskey got above Darren Purse to flick the ball on. I let the ball drop past me, took one stride and thrashed it on the volley with my left foot, high into the net past Ian Bennett. It was one of those where you know it's in the second you hit it, and I was wheeling away, both hands pumping the air, as I ran to the Liverpool bench. The first person I jumped on was Mark Leather, sort of a thank-you for all his faith and hard work in helping me get back to full fitness.

It was a glorious moment, banishing all those dark thoughts and endless hours on the road to recovery as I reeled around, taking the acclaim and savouring the moment. With Birmingham reeling, now, we thought we'd doubled our lead when Vladi got on the end of my flick on and lifted over their keeper. The net rippled – but, sadly, it was only the side netting.

The remainder of the game didn't live up to that one fantastic moment, but while we never truly threatened to add another goal and put the game out of Birmingham's reach, it never really felt as though we were going to let them back into it, either. Yet, somehow, as we edged closer to the final whistle, Liverpool started to retreat deeper into our own half, trying to contain and stifle Birmingham and see the last few minutes out. This played right into their hands. They could sense how much we wanted this first trophy since 1995 and they could sense, too, how our desire was affecting our play, making us stiff and tense so that even the simplest passes were going astray. Birmingham were launching ball after ball into our box, and we were clearing them straight back out to them. With seconds remaining, I was starting to believe we'd weathered the worst of it. I was going to lift the Cup and my goal was going to be the decider – then Nearly The Hero Syndrome struck again.

Urged on by their manager, Trevor Francis, Birmingham advanced one last time. Their midfielder Brian Hughes – a Scouser, who had copied my avant-garde nose strip with a homemade effort of his own – sent an evil ball skidding through no-man's land into our box. Their midfielder Martin O'Connor turned Stéphane Henchoz in the 18-yard area – but Steph just carried right on, right through him, giving David Elleray no choice but to point to the spot. There were literally only seconds left on the clock when Darren Purse stepped up and made no mistake with his side-footed pen. I just stood there, not quite able to take it in.

In extra time, Birmingham were dead on their feet, yet they gave as good as they got. Andy Johnson could easily have earned them another penalty when – get used to this – Steph Henchoz went tonto in the box again. Somehow Elleray didn't give it. Then, straight after that, Sander Westerveld made a miraculous, cat-like save, spooling backwards to keep out an audacious chip from Stan Lazaridis. Right at the end, Christian Ziege lobbed a beautiful cross right into my path. I did everything right with my header, getting a great connection on the ball and tensing my neck muscles to send it up and past Ian Bennett – who, somehow, managed to spring to his right and claw the ball out from under the crossbar. This one was going to penalties, and I was down to take our fifth and last kick – maybe I would turn out to be the hero, after all! Everything was on course for that to happen after Birmingham missed their first pen, and Gary Mac, Nicky Barmby and Christian Ziege calmly slotted our first three. If Dietmar Hamann scored our fourth and Brian Hughes nailed his, it would all be down to my trusty left foot to deliver the silverware.

Once more, I make no apologies for thinking like this. Footballers rarely move beyond their childhood self in this respect – it's all about dreams of glory, and mine was to score the winning goal in a big, big final. It was all down to Dietmar – cometh the hour, cometh Hamann. There was no way Didi was letting the side down. He was German, for starters, and Germans never, ever miss penalties. He was also completely unflappable, too. Calm as you like, he stepped up, took a moment to confirm in his mind where that ball was going ... and missed! *Dietmar! How could this happen?* Brian Hughes extinguished any last lingering hopes of Growler Glory by slotting his penalty away, leaving it to my Scouse comrade and fellow Number 23 Jamie Carragher to do the business. He side-footed his high into the net, Sander Westerveld saved Andy Johnson's crucial kick and that was that – we won the Cup. I was proud and happy though, holding that trophy up above my head and cavorting around the Cardiff pitch in front of our fans. Things had not been great since my clash with Thomas Myhre three years previously, but maybe we had all turned a corner, now.

We were certainly going great guns in the other cup competitions and even though I've always found it a leap of faith to consider second, third or fourth place a 'prize', we were on course for Champions League qualification, too. We'd made steady progress in the UEFA Cup, beating Rapid Bucure ti, Slovan Liberec and Olympiacos, but in the New Year, some of the biggest teams in Europe who had finished third in the group stages of the Champions League dropped down into the UEFA Cup, and we were drawn against Roma. Things were getting serious. Yet, far from being daunted by a trip to the Stadio Olimpico, we gave one of our finest European performances ever. Michael Owen played particularly well, notching both goals in a convincing 2–0 win, which could have been even better if Nicky Barmby had converted a good chance right at the end.

And there was no letting up back home. Two days after getting back from Rome, we had a really tricky FA Cup quarter-final away at Tranmere Rovers, who had been on a tremendous run. They had a skilful midfield schemer, Jason Koumas – a boyhood Red whose style of play and range of passing was similar to Gary Mac's. There was no way we would be underestimating them, especially not with another potential final now only two games away.

But having been captain for these huge games and having made a real, serious contribution to our results and our progress on four fronts, I was gutted when I found myself hooked against Man United after Danny Murphy was sent off. The game had been going brilliantly – I scored a cracker, we were 2–0 at half-time then, with about 20 minutes left, Murphy picked up a dubious second yellow for a supposed foul on Denis Irwin. As captain in what would now be a backs-to-the-wall finale, you'd have expected me to be the last one to be substituted, but my number was up. Me and Patrik Berger came off, Gary Mac and Nicky Barmby came on, and you could argue that Gérard and Phil got that one right. We held on and won the game 2–0, but I felt I needed to air my grievances.

I still don't know whether it was a mistake that I made an appointment to speak to the manager the following morning. I wasn't rude or confrontational, but equally I'm not so good at simply taking it on the chin if I think there's been an injustice. I wanted to sit down with Gérard, like men, and have an open conversation with him about what it meant to me to play for this club and to have the honour of wearing the captain's armband. I put it to the boss that the captain is the physical and symbolic leader of the team. He should *never* be subbed while he was still fit and able to lead his troops – and Gérard seemed to agree with me. I thought the meeting had been mature and sensible, and I felt the manager respected me for airing my views face-to-face. Maybe he did – but he dropped me for the next few games!

15

THE IMPOSSIBLE DREAM

All of this momentum drove us on towards one incredible week, which remains one of the topsy-turvy roller coasters of my entire career. First up was to be the FA Cup final. Growing up and during my time as a player, I absolutely loved the FA Cup. I'd grown up at a time when Liverpool or Everton seemed to be in the final every year – quite often against each other. There would be flags and bunting all over the city, special editions of the *Liverpool Echo* – it was like Christmas, the day itself could not come around quickly enough. I loved the all-day coverage on *Grandstand* – interviewing the players in the team hotel, following them onto the team bus, mingling with the fans on Wembley Way ... even *It's A Knockout* was a hoot. It was a huge dream of mine to win an FA Cup, maybe even score the winning goal, and as captain, I would be the one to raise the trophy up high as my devastatingly handsome smile lit up the Cardiff sky.

But form is everything going into these big games, and even though I scored our second and clinching goal in the semi, I'd only been getting a few minutes coming on as sub in the weeks leading up to the final against Arsenal. Since the start of May, Michael Owen had scored away at Bradford, then a hat-trick at home to Newcastle and another couple against Chelsea. With six goals in a fortnight, he was on fire and there was no question he would be starting. The big question now was, who would be partnering him up front? I was beginning to get the vibe from some of the coaches that it wasn't going to be my day.

Saturday 12th May was a glorious, sweltering hot day – almost too hot, as we made the short drive from our hotel to the Millennium Stadium. As has always been the way with these huge games, our fans clearly outnumbered Arsenal fans on the streets and outside the pubs, even though both clubs get the same allocation of approximately 25,000 tickets each. Somehow, our fans always seem to hoover up the spares and the neutrals' tickets and we always have huge support inside the stadium. I think only for Manchester United in 1996 do I remember the support being anything like equal. That was my first and only FA Cup final and I badly wanted to extinguish the memory of it.

But it wasn't to be – not from a starting position, at least. The boss went with Emile Heskey up front and taking the traditional walk around the pitch, waving to the sparse collection of fans who had come into the ground early, I had mixed emotions rattling around my head. As captain, I knew I still had a role to play, yet I wanted that role to be so much bigger. There were warring, conflicting thoughts, one after another: had I done enough to warrant a starting place? Did Gérard really trust me? Was this simply a case of him picking the 11 players he thought best equipped to beat a very good Arsenal side, or had I somehow contributed to Houllier's lack of belief in me, when it came to the biggest games? In the end, I just tried to shut out any negativity, get behind the lads who would now be representing the club and all our fans and hope that, before the end, I'd get on and play some part in bringing the Cup home to Liverpool.

We started abysmally. I don't know whether it was the heat, the weight of expectation, or whether Arsenal were just very good on the day, but we couldn't get near them. It was only some great goalkeeping by Sander Westerveld and some myopic refereeing (Stéphane Henchoz reprising his Edward Scissorhands role in our box, every time he went in for a challenge) that kept things level at half-time. Second half, though, we just couldn't hold back the tide. With 20 minutes to go, Freddie Ljungberg burst onto a Robert Pires ball right through the heart of our defence, nipped around Sander and clipped the ball into the empty net. All I can remember is seeing his mad crimson-dyed head disappear under the celebrations and congratulations of Patrick Vieira, Thierry Henry and Co. – and feeling completely, abjectly shite. I checked the scoreboard: 18 minutes. There was no way we were coming back from this. But then, hello, Thommo was telling me and Patrik Berger to warm up! We all know how this particular fairy tale ends …

As a direct result of Gérard Houllier's inspired decision to bring me on, the game began to swing in our favour. Okay, I'm half-joking, but me and Paddy suddenly opened up space and carved out chances that hadn't been there up until we came on. Michael Owen turned the game on its head and literally stole the Cup from out of Arsenal's pocket. The 2001 FA Cup final became known as The Michael Owen Final and deservedly so, but again, I'm convinced mine and Paddy's introduction was a huge factor. My shot on goal was blocked, leading to the corner which created our equaliser. Then Patrik had the presence of mind and the mental composure to look up, pick and play a beautiful through-ball for Michael to run onto, outpacing both Lee Dixon and Tony Adams to somehow produce a left-foot shot that had both the power and accuracy to beat David Seaman.

We all went potty, diving on top of Michael, certain it was too late for Arsenal to get back into the game. We were right – they were dead on their feet and dead, emotionally, too. They'd done more than enough to win the game but now, somehow, Liverpool had pipped them. If anyone was going to score another, it was us. I found myself through one-on-one, with Michael running in to my left, screaming for a tap-in. It wasn't greed, honestly – it wasn't the selfish desire to score the clinching goal. I spotted David Seaman take half a step towards Michael, ready to cut out the pull-back. In so doing, he left me a little gap to aim at and I genuinely thought the better option and likelier chance of a goal was for me to take the shot. Seaman smothered it, but it didn't matter – the referee's whistle went literally the second he hoofed the ball upfield, and Liverpool were the winners.

As the dignitaries were getting ready for the prize-giving ceremony, myself and Sami went to find Jamie Redknapp. He'd have been feeling those same mixed emotions that any player in that situation faces – delight for your teammates mixed with a bit of despair at your own predicament. But, above all, seeing your comrades lift a cup stirs your own determination to get right back in the thick of things as soon as you humanly can.

We hauled Jamie up to his feet and all three of us went up to receive the Cup from Prince Andrew, with me and Jamie holding the big silver trophy aloft. His face was a picture – as made up as any one of us! That was Game Number One of the three safely navigated, and trophy Number Two of the season tucked away. From Cardiff, it was on to Dortmund for the UEFA final against Deportivo Alavés on the Wednesday, then home again for that crucial last game of the season on Sunday 19th May, which we would have to win in order to qualify for the Champions League.

I've got to be honest, not many of us knew where Alavés was when we ended up in a final against them. We quickly established its population was the size of Birkenhead and the club wasn't much bigger than Tranmere Rovers. Yet here they were in a major European final. Something I've gleaned over all my years in the game is never to underestimate anybody. Having just about managed to see Cardiff off, we of all teams should have known that any team that makes it this far has got something about them. But we couldn't help feeling confident.

Dortmund was awash with red and white – Liverpool fans were literally everywhere. But the blue and yellow of Alavés was prominent, too, with their boisterous, beret-wearing fans making a hell of a racket with their cow horns as they ambled around, gloriously drunk a good ten hours before kick-off, slugging red wine from these calfskin flagons they all seemed to carry. There was a proper atmosphere in the city centre, Basque people mixing with Scousers mixing with the German locals – everyone seemed to be up for the party! I was back to worrying whether I'd be starting, though, and as God's Law had it, I started … on the bench again.

What a start we made, though! Perhaps Alavés were overawed by the occasion, but nobody tracked Markus Babbel, who got us into the lead at three minutes and another from Didi Hamann made it 2–0 soon after. Alavés got one back but then, just before half-time, the Alavés keeper Martin Herrera decided he was bored being a common goal-stopper and came haring out of his area to play sweeper. Unfortunately, he found himself in a straight race for the ball with Michael Owen, who beat him by about five minutes, took the ball around him and, just as he was about to fire us 3–1 ahead, had his legs taken from under him. There was utterly no doubt that it was a penalty, the only remaining debate was whether Herrera had been the last man back – in which case he'd be given his marching orders. As things panned out, the keeper stayed on the pitch and Gary Mac drilled the penalty under his despairing dive to make it 3–1 to us at half-time.

Somehow, though, we let them back into it. It has to be said that Alavés were a very handy side. They were mainly comprised of pros who had been around the block, clocking up the miles. Players like Javi Moreno (he of the studs-up tackle on Gary Neville all those years ago) and Ivan Tomic could always hurt you (ask Gary Neville!). And in Cosmin Contra, they had a lively wing-back, who was more than capable of supplying the ammo. That's the way it turned out, with them making it 3–2.

I've got to hand it to Houllier, he got creative at this point and the changes did the trick. With 25 minutes remaining, he put me and Vladimir Smicer and on. Stevie G was moved to right-back in place of Stéphane Henchoz and we went with much more variety, pushing back and getting behind them. On 75 minutes, Gary Mac knocked a lovely through ball for me to run onto. I dropped my shoulder and took it inside my man and as the ball ran on, the goal just opened ahead of me. For a split second I stumbled as I tried to get myself set, then the ball just spun out and sat up beautifully for a right-footed strike. It was one of those chances where the ball does all the work – it was rolling at the ideal pace, just to my right, and all I had to do was use the ball's momentum to guide it past the keeper.

Goal! Fowler!

Oh, dear me, was I happy! I ran over to the corner flag, where our remaining subs were warming up, and we all went into this berserk hug, bouncing round and round, delirious. Finally, I had scored the winning goal for my team in a big, big final – or had I?

You just couldn't make it up. With seconds remaining, Nearly The Hero hour struck zero: Alavés were awarded a corner. The ref checked his watch and fingered his whistle. I knew exactly what he was thinking: let them take the corner. The moment it's cleared or goes out of play, that's it. Game over. God knows I've been involved in enough games before and since where it's us who has benefited from that last throw of the dice. I know how it feels to be on both sides of the divide, the ecstasy and horror. For Alavés it was a quadruple boost of euphoria right into their veins as Jordi Cruyff, formerly of Man United, somehow got up above everyone to glance a header: 4–4.

Unbelievable.

I just stood there, half-laughing at the way these things seemed doomed.

That year, UEFA had implemented a Golden Goal system. What this meant was that, throughout the 30 minutes of extra time, the first goal would be the winning goal. Effectively, it was sudden death. Only in the event of extra time remaining goalless would the game be settled by penalties. Extra time kicked off, and so did Alavés. Their barrel-chested midfield general Magno slid in late on Markus Babbel and saw red for his trouble. With the Basques down to ten men and only minutes of the first period remaining, I thought I'd won it for us, sliding in to prod the ball home – only to see the linesman's flag go up.

Bastard! It had happened again!

Then, at the start of the second period, Antonio Karmona got a second yellow and Alavés were down to nine men. Surely, now, we could slow the game down, use every inch of the pitch to wear them out, grind them down and find that one, definitive goal? Gary Mac lined up the resulting free-kick, just in from the left touchline. From his nasty, curving free-kick, the ball skidded off the top of the centre-back's head into the net. It took us a moment to realise that that was it – we had won the UEFA Cup! Gary stood there with both arms raised aloft, more in hope than belief and then, one by one, we started running over to him, realising that the ref was signalling game over and we had, for sure, won our third trophy of the season!

I was elated, overjoyed, so proud that I thought my head would fall off as I stepped up with Sami to lift the Cup. For this one, I felt I had earned the moment, the medal and my piece of the folklore as it began to dawn on me just how insane the game had been – one of those that would live long in the memory and the re-telling of it.

We were knackered, but we had to get back, regroup and start preparing for what was, certainly in financial terms, the biggest game yet: away at Charlton in the last game of the season. We couldn't catch Arsenal in second place anymore, but we were a point ahead of Leeds in third. A win would guarantee that things stayed that way. I was pleased as punch when the gaffer told me I would be starting and captaining the side – the perfect end to the season. Somehow, our fans made it back from Germany to pack out the away end on another sizzling hot May day. They did everything they could to lift us up and generate the energy to help see us over this final hurdle, but this was now our 63rd game of a highly competitive season and our legs just could not respond at first. The only upside was, although Charlton were huffing and puffing and seeing a lot of the ball, they weren't really causing too many problems, either. It was 0–0 at half-time and you just felt that one goal might relax us enough to get the job done.

Ten minutes into the second half, from the corner, a moment of magic! Gary Mac floated one of his hanging, bending corners in and Dean Kiely didn't get a proper connection. The ball dropped over my head and behind me, but I managed to swivel, drop down and execute a falling overhead kick with my left. It was more of a lob than a volley but, with Kiely still off his line, it looped into the net. I could see Houllier on the touchline, beaming more brightly than I'd ever seen him.

These days, the manager is under huge pressure from his club's directors and owners to steer the team into the top echelons of the Champions League, where the prestige, the glory – and the money – lies. The prize pot for last season's Champions League was a head-melting £1.75 BILLION, so it's no surprise that clubs now prioritise qualifying over actual domestic silverware.

I think, in the moment where the ball arched into the net, Houllier knew that he had at long last delivered on his brief. He'd brought the glory days back to Liverpool and returned the club to the very top table in the best restaurant in Europe – and I'd scored the crucial goal! We went on to win the game 4–0, with me notching another and both Stevie Gerrard and Michael Owen scoring, too. With my wedding to Kerrie later that summer and an open-top bus parade around Liverpool to come, the good times were finally back.

16

HOU LET THE GOD OUT?

So, the good times were back? Were they fuck!

Well, our wedding was bliss, at least. Me and Kerrie tied the knot at Duns Castle in Scotland – a proper fairy-tale wedding for two normal, working-class kids like us. For a so-called 'celebrity wedding' it was a low-key affair, attended mainly by our two huge families, our friends and a few of my closest teammates (including, for conspiracy theorists who are hell-bent on insisting me and him never saw eye-to-eye, my pal Michael Owen). I've never seen my wife look so beautiful as she did on 9th June 2001. The sun shone down, our guests danced the night away, our daughters Madison and Jaya stole the show as the cutest little bridesmaids ever and us newlyweds had the time of our lives.

And the open-top bus tour around Liverpool was spectacular. I knew that Liverpool was an absolute beast of a club just waiting to be reignited, but the scale of the parade was staggering. The city is supposed to be equally divided between Everton and Liverpool supporters, but if that's the case, Liverpool must have a population of about 2 million! It was quite literally a sea of red, from start to finish, as far as the eye could see.

Jürgen Klopp has just been through the exact same thing and I know exactly what he means when he says that it's being so up close to the fans that makes you realise how enormous football is in this city, to this club. You can see the adoration in their eyes, you can really see what all this means to them – it's their life. After Liverpool won the double in 1976, the club brought out its famous pinstripe scarf, one of the first examples of a football club dipping its toe into the world of official merchandise.

Klopp said he was always aware of Liverpool as one of the great, historic teams in Europe but he'd never quite realised that we were the biggest club in the world. That's no exaggeration – a million people lining the streets of Liverpool, with mirror celebrations taking place in Egypt, Indonesia, Australia, Nigeria – quite literally all over the world. I felt like a king as I sat at the front of that bus as it made its way through the city, past elated, euphoric faces, just as I'd been when I was a kid, dreaming that one day it would be me up there on that bus, waving to the crowd, the hero of the hour. I'd been God for a while, but that day I was a king, too.

And then pre-season started.

Often, when something inexplicably goes wrong, you retrace your steps to the point when things were still trundling along as normal. You look at what happened between then and now and try to work out what changed. For example, if you have a pint with Bill and you part as the best of mates, then Bill is weird with you next time you see him, you'd want to know what had happened in between, wouldn't you? You'd want to find out who Bill had seen since your friendly pint and what that person might have said or done to make him change gear with you. This was the position I found myself in, scratching my head in the stands as the Charity Shield kicked off between Liverpool and Manchester United on 12th August 2001.

Our pre-season had gone well, culminating in us easily beating FC Haka of Finland in the qualifying round of the Champions League. Gérard Houllier didn't usually announce the team prior to the day of the game, but on the Wednesday before the Charity Shield, he took the unusual step of telling me that I would be captaining the side. I was a newly married father with another child on the way, working hard at the challenge of earning (and keeping) my place in a team full of exciting attacking talent and now, I would be walking out once again as captain of the club I adored. After numerous false dawns and setbacks, I was finally beginning to find some quality and consistency, on and off the pitch.

I threw myself into training sessions, doing extra routines and practice on free-kicks and long-range shots into an empty net. One practice session, Phil Thompson came and stood behind the goal to watch. Wanting to impress him with my accuracy, I leathered a beauty, high into the net – no way any keeper, anywhere, would have got a hand to that one! But Phil Thompson jumped back like he'd been shot and started screaming at me that, with the ball travelling at that pace, I could have seriously injured him. My mistake, in retrospect, was to challenge him on this. Instead of apologising and defusing the incident there and then, I laughed at how upset he was and reminded him that there was a net between him and a potential trip to casualty. That was that. Thommo trooped off, I carried on with my shooting practice and the whole thing was forgotten.

Or so I thought. Even though Thompson was a little more remote than usual, neither he nor the manager gave me any indication that anything was amiss. We travelled down to Cardiff in good spirits, speculated about how weird it would be, playing in the first-ever 'indoor' game (the Millennium had a retractable roof, which was to be closed against the rainstorm forecast for Sunday's game). But the real storm happened inside our changing room: Gérard announced the team, and I wasn't in it. To add insult to injury, I wasn't even on the bench – I'd been bombed out completely. I was stunned. Horrified. Heartbroken. Embarrassed. All of these emotions shot through me, one after another, as the message sank in and the implications hit me.

Why? That was the question I found myself asking as the game kicked off and Liverpool raced into an early lead. Why am I not out there, captaining that side? The truth was staring me in the face, of course, but I couldn't see it. Maybe I was in denial, but it simply didn't enter my head that a juvenile incident on the training ground had escalated into a disciplinary matter. Houllier hadn't even been there, so how would he know about it? How would he be able to judge the rights and wrongs of it? I sat there trying to trace things back, trying to recall any conversation or interaction between myself and the manager that might have been taken the wrong way, but I was coming up with nothing. I had no idea whatsoever why I'd been dropped.

I found out the next day, when Gérard called me into his office. As I went in, he was doing that routine of shuffling through papers, his glasses halfway down his nose, acting like he was a bit distracted – then he suddenly looked up and came out with it: he dropped me because I'd been disrespect-ful to Phil Thompson. Phil had told him that I had deliberately tried to humiliate him in front of the squad, by kicking the ball at him in training. Thommo was adamant that I'd been trying to hit him and that Houllier had to make an example of me. I remember standing there, thinking, who's the boss, here – you or him? Gérard told me that, until I apologised in person, I would not be considered for selection. I told him that this was all my arse – there was nothing to apologise for. If I'd wanted to hit Thompson, believe me, I was pretty sure I could have done so.

There was a horrible stand-off for the first few weeks of the 2001–02 season, during which I missed the curtain-raiser

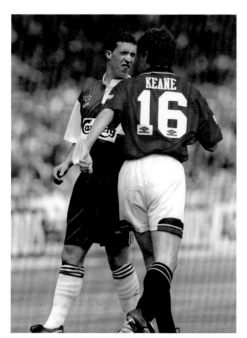

Recognise them?

Above left: Exchanging pleasantries with noted peacemaker Roy Keane.
Above right: Hair we go! Myself and Lord Beckingham celebrating my
last-minute clincher against Albania in the World Cup qualifiers, 2001.
Bottom left: Auditioning for *Strictly* with Crouchy after his goal against
Reading in 2006. *Below right:* Steven Gerrard and me in 1999,
celebrating my goal against Derby County in the League.

*You've been waiting,
and I always promise
to deliver…*

Right: Godrophenia?
Bootlemania? All
these years on,
The Armani Affair is
still tricky viewing.

May 2001, and the goal
against Charlton that finally
delivered Champions League
football for Liverpool.

Above: One of my favourite pictures. Celebrating a goal with the fans in 2006 at Portsmouth.

Right: My absolute favourite. Waving goodbye with my kids after the Barclays Premiership match against Charlton in 2007.

Sing a bit louder at
the back!

Liverpool fans
were and still are
unparalleled.

Walk On.

Above: March 1997, showing my support for the dockers strikes during the European Cup Winners Cup quarter-final match against SK Brann at Anfield. I was fined £1,000 but won the match 3–0.

Below: I couldn't not include it…! 'Snorting' the goal line to celebrate my goal against Everton at Anfield.

A footballer's life after the big games end...

Above: Reporting during the Premier League match between Liverpool and Tottenham Hotspur, March 2019 in Liverpool.

Below: Myself, Aldo and Tosh engage in a Mismatched Shoe-Off ahead of a Legends match versus Borussia Dortmund, 2018.

Above: My beautiful family.

Right: The Son of God keeps the trophy count ticking over.

My life as a footballer has literally come full circle – Granty and me, still living the dream.

against West Ham, the Super Cup win in Monaco (our fifth trophy in six months!) and the Goodison derby. It was an awful period, professionally, knowing I had done nothing to justify this prolonged punishment yet slowly realising, if I was to come through it, I had no option but to grit my teeth and apologise. Like I've said, I like Thommo a lot and given my time again, I would have just apologised for the near-miss straight away. We're both stubborn Scousers and there's no doubt, even after it was all over and dealt with, the spat created an awkwardness that was hard to shift.

Around this time, I started hearing and reading stories about other clubs coming in for me. At different times, Arsenal and Man United were supposed to have made enquiries, but my agent George told me the only serious offer had come from Chelsea. Clubs were getting wind of the fact that I was not starting games and having kept up my scoring ratio whenever I played, it was a back-handed compliment that I was in demand – just not at my own club.

But then the day came that put everything into perspective: another of the clubs supposedly in for me, Leeds United, were our visitors for a midday kick-off. It was an odd one – even though I wasn't remotely sure whether I was coming or going, I was in the starting 11, possibly because Emile Heskey was injured.

We started badly and Leeds went in 1–0 up at half-time. It seems mad to say this now, but Leeds were the Man City of the era, spending big money on all the best players as chairman Peter Ridsdale gambled on returning this sleeping giant to the big time. They had brought in Rio Ferdinand for a world record fee for a defender and added Robbie Keane, Mark Viduka, Lee Bowyer, Seth Johnson, Dominic Matteo, Jonathan Woodgate, Olivier Dacourt and Danny Mills, all for top money.

At half-time, Houllier started to go through the motions of a rousing team talk, but his voice seemed to be getting weaker and weaker as he grew more and more short of breath. He just stopped talking, nodded for Phil Thompson to continue and left the changing room. We went back out, played a much better second half and – putting all modesty aside, as per – I was 95 per cent responsible for our equaliser, with Danny Murphy running in for a simple header into the empty net. I reeled away and sprinted down the touchline, still feeling I had a point to prove, wanting to remind the manager I still had plenty to give – but he wasn't there. Even then, that struck me as highly unusual. Gérard was one of those managers who was always pitch side, analysing the game and looking for the little details that might turn a draw into a win.

As soon as we got back into the dressing room at the end of the game, Thompson explained to us why Houllier was absent: he had suffered some kind of seizure at half-time and been rushed to hospital for emergency surgery. The next 24 hours were going to be critical and we should all prepare ourselves for the worst. No matter how revered Bill Shankly may be in Liverpool, he was wrong about one thing: football is not, and never should be, a matter of life and death.

* * *

This was the start of a surreal period for me at Liverpool and it ended with me leaving the club.

Gérard had suffered a ruptured aorta – which is the main arterial valve to the heart – but an incredible medical response (starting with the first responder, our own club doctor, Mark Waller) led to the surgeon and his team placing him in an induced coma to stitch the aorta and save his life. There were differing reports coming out of the hospital saying he had been moments from death, but what was for certain was that he'd been through a serious trauma.

We flew off to Kiev for a Champions League game determined to win for the boss and, although I didn't play, we dug in for a solid 2-1 victory. Next was an away game at Leicester – always a tough place to go – where we won 4–1. Having scored a hat-trick, I started looking forward to the next run of fixtures, but Thommo left me out for both of our next matches. Beyond gutted, all I could think was that it was my goals that had got us into the Champions League in the first place. I hated being left out in any circumstance, but seemingly being dropped at whim, with no explanation offered, was more than I could bear.

A ray of hope and perspective came with the arrival of our third daughter, Mackenzie, born on 27th September 2001. As I held her in my arms, I thought to myself, okay, football is important, but it'll never be as important as this. I wanted to get a handle on things now and had various thoughts and plans whirling around my head – I was going to speak to George about a move. I was going to speak to the chairman or the club's chief executive to see if either of them could get to the bottom of what was starting to feel like a prolonged Cold War. I was even going to speak to Phil Thompson – fully installed as caretaker manager, now – try to clear the air with him, see what it might take to put the past behind us and work together to ensure a better future. In the end, though, I decided just to bite my lip, keep my head down, work as hard as I humanly could and see where that might take me.

Where it took me was into the loving arms of David O'Leary and his emerging young Leeds United side – though not without one final slap in the face. Towards the end of November we'd been soundly beaten by Barcelona and with the team obviously needing a bit of freshening up, I was back in the starting line-up for our next game. Furthermore, with Jamie Redknapp still not back to full fitness, I was captain for this mouth-watering clash with Sunderland at our Anfield bastion. Sunderland were struggling, and I had high hopes of announcing my return with a few goals – but 25th November 2001 was to be significant for other reasons.

The first half was dull but – more or less – we stuck to the regular script and Emile Heskey scored, putting us at 1–0. Then came the 'less' part of the scenario. Didi Hamann was sent off for a high challenge; at the break, Phil Thompson went through the motions of an apology – with only ten men, we'd have to shore up the defence and midfield and try to grind out the win. This was all by way of telling me that I, the captain, would be the one coming off, which turned out to be my final act (hold your horses!) as a Liverpool player. The bare statistics for the day read Liverpool 1 (Heskey) Sunderland 0.

For me, though, it was a whole different story.

17

LEEDS, LEEDS, LEEDS!

I got home and just sat there, listless. Kerrie and I spoke and concluded it just wasn't good for any of us if I was constantly feeling bitter and suspicious and unappreciated. The next day, I spoke to George and told him, though it broke my heart to be saying this, I felt it was in everyone's best interests if I looked for a new club. It turned out there were two serious offers – Chelsea had been interested for ages and now Leeds United had started to make overtures, too. As often seemed to be the case where I'm concerned, there was a glorious irony in what came next.

George did his due diligence on Chelsea and a lot of people who knew the ins and outs of the club told him they were on their last cigar. They were heavily in debt, struggling to sustain themselves and gambling on qualifying for the Champions League to attract the level of sponsorship and kit deals that could help save the club. But there was a rumour that their debts were secured against the prime real estate of

Stamford Bridge itself and predators were circling, waiting to starve the club out so they could foreclose on its assets and make a fortune from developing that prosperous little corner of Chelsea. It sounded unthinkable, but Chelsea was supposedly in real danger of being the first Premier League football club ever to go bust.

But, while Chelsea seemed to be hovering on the precipice, Leeds United was going from strength to strength. The club had won the Premiership in 1992 and got to the Champions League semi-final twice (in fact, if they'd have beaten Valencia in the second semi, they would have played Macca's Real Madrid in the final!). Now, under David O'Leary, Leeds had a policy of recruiting and developing the very best young British talent available. They played the kind of fast, creative, attacking football that is a striker's dream. I felt that, while Liverpool were once again winning trophies and making a realistic challenge for the top prizes, their football under Gérard Houllier veered towards the defensive and pragmatic. Michael Owen was top scorer that season with 12 Premier League goals. I'd never be so blinkered as to dispute the outcome of Houllier's revolution – a club moving forward – but, for a goal-scorer, it was slim pickings at Anfield.

If I needed any confirmation that it was time to go, the feedback we were getting from Leeds and Chelsea was that Houllier had already sanctioned the sale. He flatly denied that he had put me up for a sale and maybe that's the case, but he certainly wasn't going to stand in the way of my departure. It came to a point where I just thought, if we were able to do a deal with Peter Ridsdale, the chairman at Leeds, that's where I would go. I would fit in nicely there and score plenty of goals – win-win.

I'd met David O'Leary a few times and really liked him as a fella. He had that nice combination of humour, enthusiasm and a real love for the game, but you could see he was not one to be messed with, either. He spoke to me about how he'd see me playing alongside Harry Kewell and Mark Viduka, with other creative attacking players like Mickey Bridges, Jason Wilcox and Robbie Keane coming into the picture, too. I didn't take too much persuading. So, the important things discussed, we headed on to talk terms with Ridsdale himself, then the other Leeds directors. We met up in a nice hotel by a canal, in a neglected, formerly industrial part of Leeds city centre that was all being redeveloped. The directors were warm and confident, talking up their plans to transform Elland Road into a 70,000-capacity super stadium. They had Man United in their sights and held huge ambitions for the club. It seemed to me as though the city as well as the club was on the up and I was keen to play my part. On 27th November 2001, two days after the Sunderland game, the transfer was done for £12,000,000 and I'd like to think everyone got a good deal!

I was 26, newly married and now father to three young girls. I'd seen how it could backfire for players like Stan

Collymore when they make a big-money move to a new club, but don't then commit to living in the city. When Stan arrived at Liverpool, he stayed with David James and his family for a bit, but in the main, would drive up to training every day from Cannock in Staffordshire, where his mum lived. The monotony of that can't have been good for him or the club. Somehow, it always felt as though he had one foot in Liverpool, the other elsewhere. Looking back on my own experiences now, particularly some of the dark times I went through at Manchester City, I can sympathise with Collymore to a degree. I can see how that long drive symbolised his state of mind – he must never have really felt at home after he moved to Liverpool.

I'd signed a long-term contract and I was determined that, as a family, we should commit ourselves to Leeds wholeheartedly. We found ourselves a nice house with a big garden for the kids in a quiet suburb near the club's Thorp Arch training facility. A few weeks after we moved in, I came down one morning to find the place had been burgled while we were asleep upstairs. It took ages for it to sink in, because they'd removed an entire glass panel in the kitchen door and gone through the house while we'd been sleeping. For anyone who has been through that, you'll know what a destabilising shock to the system it can be – you feel violated, vulnerable and unsafe.

For Kerrie, spending a fair bit of time on her own while I was at training, or away from home playing for the team, it was a difficult, unsettling introduction to our new life. Her sisters, her family, her friends and everything she knew was back on Merseyside. With Christmas on the horizon, we agreed that she and the girls would move back for the holiday and we'd take things from there. But, over that period, we saw and fell in love with the house on the Wirral that is still the Fowler residence today. Kerrie and our three girls moved in and, secure in the knowledge that they were happy and settled once again, I got my head down and got on with trying to make a proper impact at Leeds United.

* * *

I had to smile when I found out my debut would be at Craven Cottage, where it had all begun almost eight years before. This time, however, there would be no debut goal – no goals for either side at all, in fact – and the 0–0 bore draw was one to forget. But I didn't take too much longer to open my account, scoring the second and third goals in a 3–2 win just before Christmas – against Everton. Happy days! I then got a hat-trick in a 3–0 win against Bolton on Boxing Day and then, on New Year's Day, scored an absolute beauty against my old sparring partner David James in a 3–0 home win against West Ham. We were top of the League, playing some beautiful football, and I was scoring goals again – the Ridsdale plan was working!

Looking back, the start of 2002 was the time when more and more rumours began to circulate that perhaps it was Leeds United, not Chelsea, who were staring the Grim Reaper in the face. There will always be whispering campaigns in football. It's almost a sport in its own right in the British press that, when a team starts doing well, stories will emerge about some murky skeleton lurking in their wardrobe. You only have to look at Raheem Sterling at Manchester City – as fine a role model as there is in modern-day football. Yet the press spent more time obsessing about his gun tattoo than all the work he does with City's schools and community programme, let alone the kids from the estate where he grew up. Raheem bought tickets for last year's FA Cup Final for 500 kids from his old school – but he's got a tattoo to show that he's a top marksman, so clearly, he must be advocating gun crime! That's just the way it is with football and certain elements of the press in this country – so-and-so has a gambling habit, such-and-such had a scrap with the manager in training, Club X has been holding secret talks with Player A's agent.

Almost as soon as I got to Leeds there were rumours that Rio Ferdinand and Lee Bowyer would be leaving – to Man United in Rio's case and, ironically, Liverpool in the case of Lee. And so we ignored all the fluff and carried on winning games – except that the winning run stuttered, then petered out altogether. We got a bit of bad luck with injuries, suspensions and the occasional dip in form, but nothing that really explains a winless run that stretched from New Year's Day 2002 all the way into March.

A low point for me was a crushing 4–0 defeat at home to Liverpool in the February. They were brilliant – Michael

Owen and Emile Heskey both scored. I didn't get a sniff – but the thing that really got to me was the way the Liverpool support sang my name all the way through the game. You could write it off as them just being in high spirits because they were playing us off the park and about to go top of the League, but that loyalty and love from them made me think – for the first time since the move, really – that I might have made a terrible mistake.

Our form picked up again, we started creating chances and I was finding the back of the net. We beat Ipswich, Blackburn and Leicester in successive games, with goals from R.B. Fowler in each match (two against Blackburn!). But that Leicester game, in farcical fashion, summed up the way trouble had a knack of finding me and smacking me on the arse. The whole thing was reminiscent, in a way, of the non-event when I supposedly tried to take an inch off the fabled Thompson that time on the training ground. As we were warming up and kicking in before the match at Filbert Street, the Leicester mascot – a grown man, by the way, dressed as a fox – ran into the box, waving to the crowd and making funny gestures at the Leeds players to get a laugh. All good, harmless fun. As he turned to take his applause, I chipped the ball at the fox's head. Bang, goal! The crowd laughed, one or two of them jeered and I ran over and kind of ruffled the fox's head and mock-wrestled with him/it. It was all a bit of fun and that was that. We all trooped off for our pre-match team talk, then out we came, won the match 2–0 (Mark Viduka and I both scored), business as usual.

Try then, dear reader, to imagine my dismay when two stout officers of the Leicestershire Constabulary attended Leeds United's Thorp Arch training facility the following Monday to file a complaint of assault against one Robert Fowler, employee of said football club. I was stunned.

'Approximately 14:30 hours last Saturday, sir ...' they began, unable to make eye contact.

'14:30 hours? That's half two! I was getting ready for a football match!'

Leicester Copper Number One looked at Leicester Copper Number Two. Each of them did a general excuse-me, inviting the other to break the bad news.

'What exactly am I supposed to have done at approximately 14:30 hours in the Filbert Street area of Leicester?' I enquired. Copper Two rolled his eyes, looked down and tried to spit it out.

'It's been alleged ... well, suggested ...'

He was having difficulty in finding the words. Copper Number One came to his rescue.

'Look, Robbie, we're genuinely sorry about this. I mean, it's embarrassing, but we *are* obliged to investigate ...'

'Investigate *what*, though?'

It was back to Copper Two for the *pièce de resistance*.

'Filbert the Fox says you assaulted him.'

Five full minutes later, we were all still rolling around, laughing.

It was genuinely hilarious, yet it summed up the more cartoonish, hapless side of my career. I'd made this big move to a new club – a brave move, in many respects, one I didn't really have to make. It had all started well – the team was winning, we were top of the League ... Then players started to be linked with other clubs. Suddenly, the momentum slowed. There was a sense of impending doom beginning to hover around the place. The things we were doing instinctively became laboured, confidence seemed to drain away – and to top it all, I found myself being cautioned for GBH against a comedy fox.

By the end of the season I was equal top scorer with Mark Viduka on 12 goals from only 18 games. Having played alongside some very special strike partners over the years, I'm often asked who was the best of them? Unquestionably, that is always going to be Rushy – simply the greatest striker I have ever known. But, in terms of pure finesse and technique, Mark Viduka is the most talented partner I've ever had. If Ridsdale could have steadied the ship and given David O'Leary the means and the security to push this fabulously talented squad of players on to the next level, who knows whether his new gold dream could have been delivered?

As it turned out, the 70,000-capacity stadium stayed resolutely and forever more at the planning stage – then the first departures began, in what ultimately escalated into an exit stampede. Rio went to Man United. Robbie Keane went to Spurs. Lee Bowyer went to Liverpool ... Then he didn't. I still to this day don't know for sure what happened there. It was all around the training ground that Lee had packed up and gone, and we were reading about his £9 million switch across the Pennines when he came ambling into the canteen with his shaving bag. Didn't say a word about it – it was one of those that quite simply didn't work out.

We still had an outside chance of making the Champions League, which would have been a (drum roll!) godsend for Peter Ridsdale. In the penultimate game of that 2001–02 season, I picked up an injury to my hip away at Derby County. It was just a twinge, a little pull – or so I thought. I had actually torn the labrum, which is the soft tissue around your hip that allows smooth, easy movement. To me, it was just a tweak – nothing so bad that I couldn't finish the game, though my mobility was a bit stiff, especially those little turbo-bursts you need to steal a yard on your marker and get on the end of a pull-back or a through ball.

I played on in that one, then we beat Boro in our final game of the season. Again, I felt a little restricted, but by then we were down to the bare bones of a squad. Besides that, though, after all the upheaval, rumour and counter rumour, we were once again picking up a bit of form and I was determined to see the season out. We won our last five games without conceding a goal and I think we all felt that, with a bit more consistency, we should be back with the big boys next season. We just missed out on the Champions League places, but we qualified for the UEFA Cup – still a very prestigious tournament in 2002.

I went to the World Cup finals in South Korea and Japan that summer – you might remember this as David Beckham's broken metatarsal tournament – but, apart from the odd warm-up game, I didn't play. By the time I got back, players were being sold and David O'Leary had been dismissed. Downer. But the good news – for me, at least – was that Terry Venables would be coming in. I had huge respect for him as a tactician, a manager and as a man.

We went on a pre-season training trip to Australia, but in our first semi-competitive game, the hip that had been giving me gyp went, big time. I knew it, straight away; I could feel it shoot through me. This was the worst possible start for me under a manager I was so eager to impress, but Venables was calm about it – he just told me not to put myself or the injury under any more pressure. The key thing, for him, was that I should take my time, get myself properly 100 per cent fit, then gradually reintegrate myself into the team. It didn't help that more and more players were leaving what was now beginning to feel like a sinking ship, but at least I had a viable personal goal: full fitness.

When I got back home, my sister Lisa reminded me that, when I was very little, I used to have a 'clicky' hip. At the time it was such a common thing that the received wisdom was just to let the body compensate and adjust – in other words, give it time and it'll sort itself out. That's exactly what happened with me. My 'clicky' hip seemed to disappear as I grew and through adolescence and into my early career, I never had a problem. Now, though, Lisa had got me thinking: was there an underlying issue that was, after ten years of professional level intensity, coming back to the fore? When the specialist examined me, it transpired I was going to need a hip operation – the last thing I wanted to contemplate with everything still to prove at my new club.

Leeds started the 2002–03 season well enough under Venables, but, by the November, they started to slip down the table again. I had only just started the gentle jogging stage of my rehab. Theoretically, I wasn't even due to make any comeback until Christmas at the earliest. Terry was brilliant. He would keep coming over to me in the gym and telling me to take my time – he wanted a fit, hungry Robbie Fowler, raring to go whenever I finally came back into the team. Whether that was weeks or months away, he was counting on me to transform our fortunes.

But then things changed, again. With a slightly resigned, hang-dog expression, Venables asked me to come into his office one afternoon towards the middle of December. This was the first season that the transfer window had come into play, so the clubs interested in tweaking their squad mid-season would be getting their chance to do business in the coming weeks. Terry told me that Peter Ridsdale had asked him to raise more, much-needed funds by selling a couple more players. He told the boss there was really only me and Mark Viduka left that he could sell for any kind of decent money, so Leeds were going to have to think about letting me go. As I let all this rattle around my head, he also mentioned that Kevin Keegan – by now the manager at Manchester City – had made a tentative enquiry about me. Venables had knocked City back, of course, but he was now saying, if I wanted to speak to them, he wouldn't stand in my way.

Manchester City was another sleeping giant. Although the big takeover and the move to the City of Manchester Stadium was still at an embryonic stage, City was a club with almost unlimited potential, and that's what Kevin Keegan sold to me. Keegan is one of life's great enthusiasts, a born optimist who seems permanently immersed in the moment. There's no doubt that everything he said and everything he promised was what he fundamentally believed. He painted a picture of a club about to rise up like a phoenix – in that, at least, he was right (just not with him, or me, at the wheel!).

With my four girls all living on the Wirral, Manchester City was geographically much more accessible than West Yorkshire, so the proposition became more and more tempting. My Liverpool team had broken Keegan's heart when his Newcastle team were battling Man United for the League in 1997, beating them with the last kick of that incredible 4–3 game, but he'd always been great with me when he was the England manager and now he'd given me food for thought.

I went back to Leeds to mull it over, at which point one of the directors effectively made the decision for me. As I was heading into Thorp Arch, he was heading back out to his car. Barely breaking his stride, he leaned into me and whispered, 'Take the money and run! This place is going to the dogs!' So that was me – a homeboy for all those years at Liverpool, now ready to up sticks and move on again after barely a year at Leeds.

18

WE ALL LIVE IN A
ROBBIE FOWLER HOUSE

If I could edit my football career in the same way that my kids seem able to edit an Instagram clip on their phones, I would take out most of the near three-year nightmare that started with my initial, undiagnosed hip injury around the time of Filbert The Fox, right through to the January of my last season at Man City. Like every player, I've had highs and lows. I've made good decisions and, just as we all have, I've made some dodgy ones, too. There are things I'm proud of, and things that were maybe not so clever. But I don't regret joining Leeds. I don't rue signing for Man City. What I'm a bit sad about is that the fans of those great clubs didn't see more of me at my very best. The reason they didn't is almost entirely down to injuries – and my subsequent rush to get myself back fit and playing. I fully believe that, if I'd heeded the warning signs when I first tweaked my hip around March 2002, I could have nipped it in the bud, there and then.

Instead, the underlying issue went untreated and every time I played, I was putting more pressure on a fragile area of my upper thigh that, ultimately, just raised the white flag, threw in the towel and packed in. That's the start of a spiral that saw me, repeatedly, con myself into thinking I was fit enough to play again, at a time when the game was getting faster and faster. Consequently, my last months at Leeds and my first two seasons at City were way below the standards I expect of myself.

Correction – I was shite.

There were some funny moments, though. When I was finally fit enough to take to field as a City player, I found myself thrust into the merciless glare of a derby game against United in front of 67,000 at Old Trafford. Talk about a baptism of fire – this was early February 2003 and it was freezing out there, but the fury of the atmosphere was enough to singe your ears. It was the same on the pitch, too. I trotted into the box for a corner, only to hear the mellow tones of Gary Neville in my ear:

'Robbie! Fancy seeing you here! And so much more of you, too!'

I wasn't going to stand there taking stick from The Bury Adonis.

'My gut may have grown, Gary, shame your dick never did ...'

'Robbie, you should get sponsored by Tampax. You're in for a week and out for a month, you are ...'

'You should concentrate on the game, your nose is playing me onside, here …'

That was about as polite as it got. From there, our spat descended into vicious, personal name-calling – quite a good laugh, but extremely puerile stuff. The footnote to my first ever Manchester derby is that, with us losing 1–0, I was subbed. Shaun Goater came on, scored with his second touch (his first was to control it) and, to this day, has the freedom of Eastlands.

It's fair to say the fans were not exactly enamoured of their new Scouse spearhead – with some justification. It wasn't for the want of effort, but I just didn't click, at first. Nothing I tried would come off. Perhaps, for the first time, I was playing with a bit of trepidation and over-thinking that had always come naturally to me. It's easy to blame your teammates for not playing you in or not seeing your run, or just not being good enough, but it's no exaggeration that this was by far the worst team I had ever lined up with. Fact. The big-spending superstar era at City was still a few years away yet.

In the meantime, I was, to the Man City faithful, a major, major signing. I arrived there with a great deal expected of me – and I just couldn't find a way of adapting to what the team was and how Kevin Keegan expected me to fit into his system of play. It was a dark, forlorn period in my life where I simply couldn't make the pieces fit together. When Jason McAteer made his film about mental health in 2018, there was so much that I recognised and identified with. Going back as far as games in my boyhood, I had always been able to visualise a goal in a split second and more often than not, make it happen in reality the way I pictured it in my mind. Yet, those first two seasons at City, while my mind could still conjure the magic, my feet couldn't deliver it. I was leaden – and I started to dread coming into training.

Light-hearted moments were few and far between, but one funny thing did happen at the end of my first season with City. In all the time that Macca had been at Real Madrid, I hadn't been out there to see him once. I was always playing, or recuperating – something or other always got in the way of a visit. He had already won the Champions League and Real Madrid were about to win La Liga yet again. City didn't have a game that weekend, so I went out to watch my mate, at long last, live and dangerous in the Bernabéu.

Macca had gone all-in with his new life in Spain, integrating immediately by learning fluent Spanish, getting married in Majorca and mixing well with teammates and neighbours alike. He always was a clever, talented lad and I was genuinely made up that his move had worked out so well for him. Real won the League, needless to say, and there was going to be an open-top bus parade around the city. I said I'd see him later once the bus tour was over, but Macca was having none of it. He chucked me one of the *Campiones* T-shirts the club had had made in anticipation of them winning. I stuck it on over my shirt, and security waved me through onto the bus.

It's worth saying, considering Real Madrid are often referred to as 'The Biggest Club In The World', the turnout to greet them, though boisterous, was nothing compared to our Homecoming in 2001 – which, in turn, was dwarfed by the multitudes that lined the streets to welcome the six-times Champions League winners home after their own Madrid triumph. But the crowds were out in force and a sea of jubilant supporters cheered the bus along its route. I was goofing around with Macca, waving to the crowds and acting like I was one of them. I have to say, it was nice to experience the joy of winning the League, at long last!

We pulled up by a fountain and suddenly I thought I could hear my name being chanted. No way! I said to myself and carried on waving and having a laugh with Macca. Then it got louder – the familiar old clap-clap-clap FOWLER! chant that The Kop used to sing. I looked down to see about six or eight lads jumping up and down, grinning their heads off – obviously Liverpool fans in Madrid for a stag night or something. I gave them a cheesy thumbs-up and the bus trundled away, but Macca was laughing all night after that, about how I'd gatecrashed their party and ended up getting as much applause as Raul!

★ ★ ★

Back at City, the 2004–05 began – a brand new season, but the same old story for yours truly. I'd train, I'd play, I'd get substituted – usually around the 65-minute mark. One of the big disconnects was my partnership with Nicolas Anelka –

not that 'partnership' in any way describes our dysfunctional, wholly unproductive pairing. It quickly became obvious that myself and Nico didn't, and probably never could, gel as a duo. He did just fine on his own – his scoring ratio wasn't bad at all, even though the less initiated liked to caricature him as Le Sulk.

Both Macca and I played with Anelka at different times and, like most rational people, we eventually concluded that he was just stupendously shy. He had talent to burn and it's not like we didn't try everything we could to hit it off on the pitch. It was simply the case that, if he was through, or if he thought there was even the glimmer of a shot on, he would always, always shoot. Hand on heart, I have no problem with that. Strikers have to be single-minded. Greedy. Opportunistic. Call it what you will, but Nico carried on scoring and I carried on getting hooked. Things came to a head a few games into the season when we played Everton – of all teams – and I was taken off around the hour mark.

I couldn't get my head around it: we were the home team. Although Everton had just gone 1–0 up, they were down to ten men. Surely, if we wanted to turn things round, we'd need strikers on the pitch? And what sort of signal did it send to the fans, seemingly giving up the ghost in a game that was there to be won? As I trudged off, something much, much worse occurred to me: in taking me off, the manage- ment could only be saying one thing – that, even though they badly needed goals to transform this game, they couldn't rely on me. By this stage, whatever patience the City fans had with me was well and truly gone. There were groans and boos, where once I had had acclaim and adoration (just not in Manchester). I went straight down the tunnel, into the changing room and sat there, catatonic, unable to comprehend what was going wrong. How had it come to this? Was I finished? Was this what so many pros meant when they trotted out that immortal line of 'Nobody has to tell you, you'll know before anyone else when it's time to quit.'

Throughout this time, it was only my family that kept me going. My dad had been suffering more and more with his health. Earlier that year, he'd had a stroke – something I never mentioned outside of the immediate family circle. Seeing such an active, positive guy so diminished put my own woes into perspective. I kept trying to see the positives and reminding myself that I had it all – I had my health and I had my girls back at home. More and more, I was beginning to understand the bigger picture – that, as much as I loved and lived for football, my family were the people who mattered more than anything to me and knowing I had them to come home to was a huge leveller. So, this time, after the substitution, I decided I'd just get out of there, get home and see the girls. At least *that* part of my reasoning in electing to move to City – the proximity to home – had worked out very well. I left and within an hour, was back at home playing with my kids, feeling a lot better about the things that were truly important in life.

On the Monday though, Kevin Keegan called me into his office. Stuart Pearce, his assistant manager, was there, as well as Derek Fazackerley, who had always been on Keegan's coaching staff wherever he went. Kevin started off by telling me that my actions, in walking out on a game that was still being contested, were hugely disrespectful to the club, its supporters, my coaches, my teammates, but more than anything, to myself. He couldn't get his head around how a player with so much ability – me – was giving myself so little chance. It could have happened at any time, but that was the moment that the dam broke and all those years of frustration and under-achievement, probably going all the way back to Houllier and Thompson, came pouring out. I was angry and emotional, primarily at myself, and I gave Keegan and the coaches an honest account of where I was at.

I told them things I would never have imagined myself saying – that I felt like an imposter, sometimes – like I had no right to be turning up and putting on the kit and going through the motions of being a footballer. I told them that I was scared and unhappy, and that, more than anything, I just wanted to do myself justice on the field of play and start scoring goals again. I didn't blame anyone but myself and I think they could all see I'd reached my lowest ebb. Keegan told me that that was all he had wanted to hear – that I wanted to put things right and start scoring again. He told me that he was going to have to discipline me for walking out on my teammates. Other than that, he wanted me to take time out, get myself right and work on the psychological as well as the physical side of myself. There would be no time limit – I was to come and see him when I felt ready to do the job again. I was relieved and grateful, but I still left his office full of doubt.

Stuart Pearce followed me out down the corridor, put his arm around me and told me that every single one of them had every belief that I would turn this lousy spell around and come back fighting. Afterwards, I sat in my car and, for the first minute or two, felt like I was going to break down crying. But then, gradually, it began to sink in what they were saying. It was brilliant – it felt as though years of underperforming frustration had been blasted away and that, finally, I would come good again.

I'm terrifically thankful to Keegan and Pearce for the way they tackled that whole thing. They could see that I was near to breaking point and they chose to treat the situation – and treat me – with dignity and compassion. In football, there is often a time when the short, sharp shock approach is called for; we all need a bollocking every now and then. But Keegan and Pearce gave me my dignity back instead and paved the way for a second coming few would have foreseen at the time.

As someone who is about to embark upon a new adventure in management, I've been fortunate enough to play under some of the best coaches and motivators in recent times and I've been able to glean ideas and innovations from each and every one of them. And this whole episode taught me one of the fundamental basics of management – identifying when to put your arm around a struggling player and tell them it's all going to be okay. That might sound soppy, but it's a huge part of successful man management and it genuinely is so important to be able to talk about the way you feel.

I listened to the coaches and worked doggedly on a new fitness regime. In the past, I might have conned myself I was ready and rushed back into action. But, with my family there to remind me that, as much as I love it and am addicted to it, football is just a game (Kerrie and the girls would point and shout, 'Ah, I'm telling!' if I so much as ate a chip), I was feeling the benefits of a more patient approach. At the start of 2005, a combination of my new-found mental clarity, impetus and physical fitness, coupled with Nico's departure for Fenerbahce, finally led to me finding a bit of consistency with City. I've always been very clear that Nicolas Anelka is a wonderfully gifted player, but the basic fact is that me and him simply couldn't do it as a strike pair.

In the February, we went to Carrow Road for a thunderous game against Norwich. I'd started to build up a good rapport with Shaun Wright-Phillips and, when he was playing, Antoine Sibierski. With the game poised at 2–2 going into the last few minutes, I think both sides felt a draw would be a fair, honourable result. Right at the very end, Shaun pulled one back across goal and I hit it first time, left-footed: 3–2 to City! The merry band of fans who'd made it down there were over the moon, as was I.

It was my 150th Premier League goal, making me the third-highest scorer of the modern era. Only Alan Shearer and Andy Cole had scored more and, with Cole retired, he was now well in my sights! Kevin Keegan came out afterwards and gave this incredible, heartfelt interview, congratulating me on what I'd done and putting me up there with people like Jimmy Greaves and Rushy. I was almost in tears again, this time for the right reasons. We travelled home a much happier bunch than we'd been before Christmas, when we were losing to teams like Newcastle, Middlesbrough (my old partner in crime Mark Viduka netting two) and Everton.

Two weeks later, Keegan was sacked.

In those days, before the despised Europa League (why, by the way, why?), the UEFA Cup was still a prestigious competition. Qualifying for Europe was a bare minimum requirement for clubs that considered themselves to be among the elite and this year, you could finish as far down as seventh and still qualify. We were in a straight fight with Tottenham, Bolton and Middlesbrough for those positions that hadn't already been nabbed and, after the euphoria of the Norwich win, we were up against two of those rivals next – Bolton, then Spurs.

The Bolton game in March 2005 is the one where all the City fans were singing, 'We all live in a Robbie Fowler house …' It's true to say my agent George had cannily invested in quite a few terraced streets around Greater Manchester and Lancashire so there's a remote, though not impossible chance, that I was an enlightened absentee landlord to some of the City hardcore! With this affectionate, tongue-in-cheek ditty, the fans seemed to be warming to me – though that was as good as the day got. The guy Gérard Houllier, in all his Euro-wisdom, had brought in to replace me at Liverpool, scored the winner for Bolton and put a severe dent in our Cup hopes. Yep, the crucial goal couldn't have gone to a nicer chap... El Hadji Diouf.

In our next game, we went down to White Hart Lane, where another ex of mine, Robbie Keane, scored in their 2–1 win. So, in the space of a fortnight, both Spurs and Bolton had stolen a march on us. The City board clearly felt that a change was needed if we were going to dust ourselves down one last time and give it a big, final charge for Europe. They did what they felt they had to do and that was that, game over for Kevin Keegan.

Stuart Pearce came in as caretaker then full-time manager and straight away had a galvanising effect. We beat Liverpool, Portsmouth, Aston Villa and Birmingham, drew a few tricky away games and ended up with everything to play for on the last day of the season – our Cup rivals Middlesbrough, at home. Bolton had already claimed sixth spot and Spurs had, uncharacteristically, simply melted away after beating us back in March. Boro were the team in seventh with 54 points and we were a place behind with 51. However, with our marginally superior goal difference (we were +1 ahead of Middlesbrough), a win would see us leapfrog them into seventh place and guarantee us the final spot. That's what it came down to: Boro had to stop us beating them in order to qualify for Europe, we had to win.

It's a game I will never forget, for so many reasons. Midway through an understandably tense first half, Jimmy Floyd Hasselbaink put Middlesbrough ahead. They must have had a good 5,000 Boro fans inside the stadium that Sunday afternoon and at half-time, it was them doing all the singing. Kiki Musampa equalised for us with literally the first attack of the second half and after that, we just laid siege to their goal. A combination of bad luck (for us), nerves, bad finishing and good luck (for them) kept the game even-stevens into the 80th minute.

At that point, I glanced to my left to see our reserve keeper Nicky Weaver warming up and David James leaving his goal-mouth to be substituted. *What?* I hadn't seen Jamo take any kind of a knock! It would take a power drill to make any impact on his gargantuan frame, anyway. There was less than ten minutes left with Euro qualification at stake and Stuart Pearce's masterplan was to bring a new *goalkeeper* on? I couldn't fathom it – surely we needed another striker, if anything? But then, suddenly, it all made sense: Mr Pearce had reverted to the old reliable adage that desperate times required, well, innovative measures, let's say! In that moment, he produced a stroke of coaching genius that made dwarves of football philosophers like Cruyff and Rinus Michels. By taking off Claudio Reyna and sending Nicky Weaver on, the boss was freeing up Jamo ... to play up front. Seriously.

I don't know if I was more shocked, amused or terrified, but the Boro defenders soon knew Jamo was there. The boss had instructed him to get in the box and without actively fouling anybody, to rough them up a bit, charge right through them and let them know he was there every time the ball came into the box. The order came that everyone had to sling as many high balls into the mixer as possible. David James – all six foot six of him – was going to knock the ball down for me, or, if the opportunity arose, have a go at goal himself. Like so many keepers, he'd started out life as an outfield player and had a pretty nice touch on him, as well as a piledriver of a shot. It was like he was playing Whack-a-Mole – the Boro defenders were going down like roadkill as he steamrollered them out of his way like an American footballer, each opponent just an inconvenient obstacle between him and the ball.

With bodies strewn around the box, he nodded one down for me. I got a toe on it and it looked in all the way, when Mark Schwarzer somehow clawed it out. Shaun Wright-Phillips fizzed it back across goal, David James flung himself and it was flying into the net. We were already reeling around, ready to celebrate the most unlikely winning goal ever – until Frank Queudrue produced the kind of goal-line stop that Gordon Banks would have been proud of.

Penalty. The 93rd minute of the last game of the season, and we finally had the plum goal-scoring opportunity that would, if taken, irreversibly deliver European football to the City of Manchester Stadium. Here was my opportunity, at last, to win those long-suffering fans over; to stitch my name indelibly into Manchester City folklore. With 45,000 fans holding their breath and the other 5,000 whistling and screaming to take me off, I settled myself, decided where I was going to put the ball, stepped up and hit it absolutely perfectly. Didn't stop Mark Schwarzer flinging himself to his left and stopping it, though. Unbelievable! Nearly the Hero Syndrome had followed me to City, now, and I wanted the goalmouth to swallow me up. Moments later, the ref blew for time and that was that: Middlesbrough qualified (and went on an incredible run, all the way to the final), while we stayed exactly where we were – in seventh place, out of the action, looking on from the sidelines.

I went around apologising to the players and staff from the club, but there was an overwhelming sense of despair enveloping everyone. As soon as I could, I took myself off the pitch and just sat there in the dressing room, head between my knees, absolutely gutted. I'd let everybody down and I felt horrible. Suddenly, I could hear this huge, sustained cheering coming down from outside. Stuart Pearce appeared in the door and basically said: 'Come on, Robbie, these things happen in football. The fans here know the score – they've seen you boys have given it all you can... go on up. Honestly, you'll feel better for it.'

I dragged myself out of the dressing room and went up to join the other players on the pitch and, to a degree, Stuart was right. The City faithful who'd stayed behind had picked themselves up and, disappointed as they obviously were, were giving the team a rousing send-off. I put on a brave face and applauded them back but, inside, I was leaden. For me, football is all about results; winning, achieving your goals. And the pen would have – or could have – changed everything. Everyone knows how much Liverpool means to me, but I would have loved to have delivered that result for City.

Amid the disappointment, though, came a ray of hope – several, in fact. Firstly, and completely unexpectedly, the City fans voted me third in their Player of the Season awards. Now, third place in a club award might sound like small beer but, honestly, it meant the world to me. I'd only really been a regular since the turn of the year, after which I produced a consistent run of form and plenty of goals. Scoring that pen with the last kick of the last game of the season would have been the icing on the cake but, sadly, it was not to be. More than anything, though, it was what the award symbolised: I may only have got third place but to me, it felt like I'd actually won the thing, it meant so much. Those fans had, with some justification, *detested* me for over two years. To them I was an overpaid, disinterested has-been who'd been put out to pasture and was now barely going through the motions in their beloved sky-blue shirt, picking up a big fat wage just for turning up and shuffling around the pitch.

That perception of me, every bit of it, but especially, the not-giving-a-toss part, stung like mad. Anybody who knows me will understand how competitive I am. There is nobody who challenges me more or sets me tougher targets than I do myself. There were times at Manchester City when I let my frustration and disappointment get the better of me – there really were times when I just wanted to turn around, walk away and finish with football altogether. Yet, after that incredible vote of confidence, firstly from Kevin Keegan, then Stuart Pearce, I convinced myself I still had something to offer.

19

GOD'S SECOND COMING

There was a ray of light shining over Liverpool 4. After replacing me with Milan Baros, El Hadji Diouf, Antony Le Tallec and Sean Dundee, Gérard Houllier had still not managed to find the elusive formula that would bring the Premier League back to Anfield. Inevitably, in the summer of 2004, there was a parting of ways and Liverpool brought in Rafa Benítez from Valencia to try something new. Benítez inherited Houllier's final signing, Djibril Cissé, but not his luck.

At different times during a difficult first season, Benítez lost Cissé, Harry Kewell, Jamie Carragher, Steven Gerrard and Xabi Alonso to sustained periods of injury. Somehow, however, his makeshift squad of juniors, reserves and foot soldiers made it to the final of the Champions League, more as a result of sheer collective resilience and willpower than any great skill. If ever a team was more than the sum of its parts, it was that Liverpool side of 2004–05 – their strength as a unit overcoming all and any technical inferiority.

Not that they were lacking in individual brilliance – this was a team that boasted Luis Garcia, Harry Kewell, Xabi Alonso and the inspirational captain, Steven Gerrard, in their ranks. Like I say, though, Benítez rarely had the chance to put all four of them on the same pitch at the same time. At different times during crucial ties against the likes of Juventus, Bayer 04 Leverkusen (who had Michael Ballack, Dimitar Berbatov and Roque Junior in their ranks) and the all-powerful Chelsea, Rafa had to field Scott Carson, David Raven, Igor Biscan, Antonio Nunez and Josemi to make up the numbers. It was an incredible feat by Benítez, managing to drive this team on all the way to Istanbul. With my season's duties over with Man City, I was only too happy to accept the invitation to join a small bunch of former players travelling with the club to watch the final.

Nothing that I can say will add to the legend of Istanbul – it was simply incredible. There was no way anyone would have forecast that that Liverpool team, dead on its feet, dead in their hearts as they trudged off the Ataturk pitch at half-time, would come back out and, within 15 minutes, turn the entire game on its head. Not even our chaotic, brilliant win in Dortmund came close – it was football at its mad, unpredictable, remarkable best. I was cheering and screaming as loudly as anybody when Jerzy Dudek saved that penalty from Shevchenko and I was lucky enough to join in the celebrations with Stevie, Carra and the squad back at the team hotel.

I saw Rafa in a corner, watching everyone enjoying themselves – a big, contented smile on his face. Yet, knowing him as I do now, he would already have been thinking ahead to the next stage: 'How do I build on this? How do I take this team to the next level?' I went over and congratulated him and gave him a cheeky wink: 'All you need is a proper goalscorer, now.' I was half-joking with him – in fact, I was pretty much completely having a laugh with him – but the glaring truth was that the end-of-season stats showed with nine goals in all competitions, Milan Baros was Liverpool's top scorer. That was that – the party continued, and the team went back to Liverpool to an unbelievable hero's welcome.

With Andy Cole and Darius Vassell arriving at City in the summer of 2005, my playing time was becoming even more limited – but there was to be one last, glorious cameo and one hell of a twist in the story before I said my goodbyes. I'm led to understand that the first led directly to the second ...

It was the middle of January, 2006, and we were playing Man United at The City of Manchester Stadium – remember, this was before Thaksin Shinawatra's ownership, let alone the turbo-powered Sheikh Mansour era. I was on the bench, but City came out of the traps all guns blazing. Joey Barton was winning all his duels in midfield, Cristiano Ronaldo was continually complaining to the ref about this tackle and that challenge, but City ran into a 2–0 lead and, by half-time, it could easily have been 4–0.

Talk about a game of two halves! Ronaldo decided he'd give a bit of needle back and received a straight red for a nasty challenge on Andy Cole with about 25 minutes of the game left to go. As so often happens in football though, instead of this making the game easier for City, we didn't seem to know whether to stick or twist. Ruud Van Nistelrooy pulled a goal back and Wayne Rooney went close. The boss pulled Andy Cole off on 75 minutes, put his arm around me and said, 'Go out and nick us one, Robbie.' But the goal that settled the game wasn't so much a pickpocket as a complete smash and grab. In the 94th minute, with nerves jangling and the ball ricocheting around the Man United box, like pass-the-parcel, I ran in and smashed it high into the net for what turned out to be my last goal for City. A 3–1 derby win, and I was a Manchester City hero at long last – better late than never, and the goal was an absolute pearler, too!

Rafa Benítez must have agreed. Stuart Pearce had given us the Monday off. It's almost an unwritten rule that foot-ballers take up golf, snooker or both – and I've never been one to disappoint my audience – so I was about to tee off at Caldy Golf Club when my phone went. I was actually going to ignore it, but when you have kids, there's always one emergency or another, so I whipped it out of my pocket just to make sure. I didn't recognise the number, so I let it ring out. Again, I was about to tee off, but this niggling voice in my head wouldn't let me relax: 'Play back your voicemail!' it insisted. 'Robert, I repeat, play that message!' So I did, and it was the unmistakable voice of Rafa Benítez asking me if I'd come in for a chat – well, that was the golf done with for the day.

I found myself shaking with excitement and trying to temper my expectations, but no matter what I told myself, I just couldn't imagine that Rafa wanted me to come in for an idle natter about football. Maybe he wanted my advice on some investments? What was for sure was that, as much I was hoping that this was The Call, I jumped back in my car and tried to keep my mind occupied with anything other than Playing For Liverpool Again. The irony is that I can jog from my house to Rafa's in about five minutes yet there I was, belting back through the tunnel for a meeting which might – just might – be about to deliver all my dreams, all at once.

I went into his office and he just came out with it: nice goal yesterday, Robbie – how do you feel about coming back here and maybe scoring a few more for Liverpool? We have Crouch, Morientes and Cissé, but we feel we need a different sort of option. It might be that you don't start every week, but we'd love to have you back here. Would you be interested?

What? Yes! The answer is yes!

Rick Parry came in, a big smile on his face. He wanted to know whether he should call my agent George, fax him the offer, talk over the details of the contract and so on. All I was bothered about was signing that contract, getting my medical done and getting changed into that red shirt before anyone changed their mind!

Liverpool, in common with all football hotbeds, is rife with transfer gossip, rumours and speculation to the point where it has almost become a cottage industry. The rule of thumb is that unless and until your photo appears on the back page of the *Liverpool Echo* with a big daft grin on your kite, your arm around the manager and a scarf above your head, a signing hasn't happened. I wanted to get to that moment as quickly as possible – so much so that I didn't bother reading the terms they placed in front of me. All I could think was: Where do I sign? How quickly can we get this done?

I didn't even know how much money I was going to be on – I honestly would have walked from Manchester to Liverpool and played for nothing. As it turned out, the deal was only until the end of the season, but I was determined to savour every minute of it. In the press conference to announce the signing, Rafa said:

We have signed a player with so much passion for this football club that it can only rub off on everybody else. This is a boost for the team, a boost for the supporters and of course, a boost for Robbie himself. I don't think I've ever seen a player so happy at joining a club before!

And he was right: I was beyond elated. Sitting in my car after it was all done was like a religious epiphany. The transformation in my fortunes, from the despair of being sat in the City of Manchester Stadium car park on the verge of a breakdown to this unbelievable high, it was almost too much to take on board. I felt this overpowering emotion surge through me, as though what had just happened was of huge spiritual significance.

The Liverpool fans certainly seemed to think so. I was given the Number 11 shirt – Djibril Cissé was 9 – but, in all truth, I would have worn Number 109 just to play for Liverpool again! I signed my contract on 27th January and five days later I was warming up, ready to pick up where I'd left off. Talk about unfinished business – when I came on as a substitute on the hour mark against Birmingham City, the Anfield crowd gave me the most thunderous standing ovation. All four sides of the ground rose to their feet to cheer me onto the pitch again. The hairs on the back of my neck were standing up and I honestly didn't know how to respond.

There was a flag on The Kop that read:

FOWLER, GOD – 11
WELCOME BACK TO HEAVEN

20

HEAVEN ELEVEN

To complete the religious theme, the flag had a liver bird with a halo around its head, too! And I very nearly had a miraculous impact on the game. We were drawing 1–1 with less than ten minutes remaining when a long throw came in from the Kemlyn Road side of the ground. It bounced up and, with my back to goal, I volleyed a perfect bicycle kick high into the roof of the net. Oh, my word! The roar from The Kop was off the scale – everyone was going mad with joy that the returning Son had delivered the perfect postscript.

Yet it was not to be. The moment I turned to run towards the crowd in celebration, the first thing I saw was the linesman, his back ramrod straight, flag in the air, staring upwards and over the players' heads in that 'I am correct and my decision is absolute!' way that they have. I was gutted – absolutely sick. It was a bit of a downer, too, that I was cup-tied that season. Just the week before the Man City v United farewell game, I scored an FA Cup hat-trick against a tenacious Scunthorpe side. That ruled me out of what turned out to be a glorious campaign for Liverpool, culminating in another tense but ultimately victorious final against West Ham.

I'll never forget the date – 15th March 2006 – or the relief when the first goal of my second coming finally came. And guess what? It was against Fulham – again – in another five-goal win for the Reds. Harry Kewell sent a wicked, bendy corner across, Fernando Morientes headed it on and, somehow – because the ball had already gone beyond me and, by rights, I shouldn't have been able to get any kind of purchase on it – I strained every sinew in my neck and managed to head it back beyond Mark Crossley and into the opposite corner.

What a moment!

This time there was no doubting the goal would stand and the entire team mobbed me. I was trying to shrug them off so I could run around the entire four sides of the ground, but Stevie Gerrard had other ideas, hauling me down, WWF-style and leading the pile-on. It was fabulous! I went on to score five in the final six games of the season, resulting in high praise – and a new, one-year contract – from Rafa.

'We are delighted that Robbie has agreed to sign for another year,' said Rafa. As if I was going to think twice! 'He has done really well and thoroughly deserves this.'

As end-of-term reports go, it was music to my ears. My second goal in that run took me above the great Kenny Dalglish in the ranks of all-time Liverpool goal-scorers. To complete my renaissance, Djibril left the club and I was able to go into the 2006–07 season as Liverpool's Number 9 – I was home!

As it turned out, Rafa brought in Dirk Kuyt and Craig Bellamy that season to play alongside Crouchy as his first-choice strike duo. We also added Daniel Agger, Momo Sissoko and Jan Kromkamp. There was a story – never verified, needless to say – that Everton were scouting Danny Agger for an entire season.

'Get us that elegant, ball-playing Danish centre-back,' said David Moyes. 'He's mustard!'

So, a deal was done, though it took Moyes a few games to realise he'd been given Per Kroldrup instead of Agger! Whatever the truth, it's fair to think that Liverpool got the better player.

* * *

We started the 2006–07 season at Bramall Lane and I started the season with a goal. It was a stiflingly hot day and, in all truth, neither side was particularly fluent. With an hour gone and his team a goal up, Neil Warnock seemed happy to shut up shop. They parked the bus and we were running out of ideas when Stevie Gerrard ran onto a pass, swerved a tackle and accelerated into the Sheffield United box. Both their keeper and central defender converged to close Stevie down. Morgan was about to lunge in for a tackle then seemed to change his mind and pull out. Stevie went down and the referee pointed to the spot.

In a press conference after the game, the ref said, while he realised that little or no contact had been made, it was within the letter of the law to award a penalty for 'intent', if the match officials believed a player meant to impede an opponent. A grey area, but one from which we were very happy to benefit! I have to say I stroked the pen home with great nonchalance and, fume as Neil Warnock might – and, boy, did he fume! – we were going home with a point we didn't look like we were going to get for much of the game.

Oddly, and for me, disappointingly, penalties against Sheffield United were the only goals I scored for Liverpool in that second season – three of them. There can be no way of knowing at the time, but my last goals for Liverpool came on 24th February, 2007. In a strange first half, we got two penalties at the Kop end in the opening 25 minutes. I took them both and scored them both – there was never a doubt in my mind. The second one, though … I don't know. I'm not saying I knew that this would turn out to be my last ever as a Liverpool player, but there was something eerie about it. I'm always very certain with my spot kicks – I make my mind up, take three or four steps back and whack it in. This one against the Blades, I took a longer run-up, then hesitated for a split second – which is something I never do. Was I making the moment last just a little bit longer? I honestly don't know. Paddy Kenny guessed the right way – I hit it low, to his left – but it was a nice one, right into the side netting so he had no chance. If there had been some magical way of knowing that that would be my last, I would have taken the inevitable booking and jumped into The Kop whirling my shirt above my head. We won the game 4–0.

But I was on top of the world, back where I wanted to be, playing for Liverpool in a team which was going places. And, to compound my new-found happiness, Kerrie gave birth to our fourth child – a boy, Jacob, born in May that year. I was besotted with my little tribe of girls, but the arrival of a son completed my family bliss. It would be a while until he could kick a football, but I was already marking out a little pitch in the back garden, ready to set the miniature goals up. Madison, Jaya and Mackenzie were my absolute pride and joy, though none of them showed even a token interest in the footy. Whether Jacob liked it or not, I had his card marked, right from birth. He was going to be my football buddy from that day forward!

Although Jacob and I have already created many a fantastic memory together – not least our trips to Spain to see Liverpool play Barcelona, that wonderful night in Madrid in June 2018 – he was too young to see his dad's last couple of games in a Liverpool shirt. On 1st May 2007 we found ourselves, once again, up against José Mourinho's Chelsea side in the return leg of the semi-final of the Champions League. They had won the first leg at Stamford Bridge 1–0, courtesy of a Joe Cole strike.

While it would have taken something very, very special to rival the atmosphere of the 2005 semi-final – which I'd gone to watch with Macca – there was still a spine-tingling sense of destiny as The Kop drowned out the UEFA anthem with 'You'll Never Walk Alone' as the two teams were led out. I've asked myself many, many times over the years what it is about Anfield that is so unbelievably special, especially on nights like this.

Many people will automatically assume I'm biased, that I'm just blowing smoke up the Liverpool fans' arses, but let's not forget that I started out life as a Blue. I'm a romantic – all footballers are – but I'm not delusional and when I say the Anfield crowd is unlike any other set of supporters anywhere else in the world, I'm saying so with a degree of perspective. Pep Guardiola recently came out and said the same thing – Anfield generates its own magical power, and it's very hard to combat. I've thought about it time and again, even when I'm just watching the game on the telly, and I've come to believe that a huge part of the witchcraft is the anthem itself: 'You'll Never Walk Alone'. Symbolically, and in terms of the message it sends and the spectacle it provides, it is the ultimate, perfect statement of intent about what the club stands for and what it is. As the teams came out for the Champions League semi in 2007, you could sense there was something in the air. José Mourinho seemed to feel it, too. I caught him staring at The Kop – if not in awe then in admiration – and there was a sense that he was thinking how much he'd love to work for fans like these in an atmosphere like this.

I was on the bench, but obviously dreaming of coming on at some point and, hopefully, making a difference. In a well-worked routine from a Stevie G free-kick, Danny Agger struck a beautiful left-footed equaliser after 20 minutes. Game on! If the atmosphere hadn't been quite up to the mega decibels of 2005, then it was now. The entire stadium was shaking as the crowd sang 'We Shall Not Be Moved'! After Dirk Kuyt rattled the crossbar with a bullet header, there weren't too many cut-and-dried chances and as the game staggered through extra time towards a penalty shootout, Rafa Benítez brought me on. Was this to be my swansong? Was I, finally, going to notch the penalty that sent the crowd into raptures and sent my team to another final?

I immediately held my hand up to take our fifth penalty – hoping, hoping, hoping that things would go that far. The penalties were taken at the Anfield Road End, where the Chelsea fans were gathered, but there was still a brain-melting level of hissing, booing and whistling from the Anfield crowd as their players took their pens. I knew Arjen Robben was going to miss his from the moment he placed the ball. All the 'tells' were there – licking his lips, glancing at the ref in a way that seemed to say: 'Let's get this over and done with!'

The Kop got right inside the Chelsea players' heads and we went into a 3–1 lead. Their combative little Cameroonian midfielder Geremi stepped up to take Chelsea's third pen. If he scored, it would be down to Dirk Kuyt, then me ... But Geremi hit his penalty tamely and Pepe Reina saved. Now it was down to Dirk, not just to keep the shootout alive, but to win it for us. There is a bit of footage out there in YouTube land of all the Liverpool players in the centre circle, watching the penalties. If you were to focus solely on my face and my reaction, you might be forgiven for thinking we'd lost. What was going through my mind was all the memories flooding back – it only seemed like yesterday that I was scoring in front of The Kop on my Anfield debut. The four-and-a-half-minute hat-trick against Arsenal. The double against Everton – snorting the touchline. My 100th goal, in record time. In the blink of an eye, 14 years had flown by and I was standing here with a new set of teammates, willing us into another huge European final, yet wanting to deliver the magic moment, courtesy of my own trusty left boot.

Anyone looking at that YouTube footage will see a very brief look of resignation on my face as Dirk Kuyt slams the winning penalty home and Anfield goes berserk. Steven Gerrard seems to give me a little hug of consolation. Seconds later, I'm racing after Dirk with everyone else, celebrating another triumph over José's men, but for that split second, I truly hoped it would have been me rather than him that won the game for us.

My huge and lasting regret about my first spell at Liverpool was that I never got a chance to say a proper farewell to the crowd in what turned out to be my final game, when I was subbed at half-time against Sunderland. By the time we played Charlton in the last game of the 2006–07 season,

I knew that my contract wasn't going to be renewed – and I was pretty certain I wouldn't be featuring in the Champions League final in Athens, either. This time, though, I had the honour of leading the team out as captain for the day and staying on the pitch almost until the last kick. On 88 minutes, Rafa took me off and led the standing ovation as the entire ground – Charlton supporters, too – rose to their feet to clap me off. Was that a fleck of dust in my eye? I was bawling my heart out! And, in one of those bittersweet moments that tend to happen in football, just after I'd come off, Charlton gave away a penalty! Harry Kewell made a comical bid to the ref to let me come back on again, but rules is rules – even for God. Harry slotted the pen, we drew 2–2 and that was my long goodbye to Anfield, over and out.

21

HOLD YOUR HEAD
UP HIGH

My old man wrote an open letter to the club and the fans in the days after my last appearance – including a mention for the late, great Bobby Wilcox, a legend on The Kop and in The Albert for his generosity, his fabled Wilcox Tours away trips and his duets with fellow leg-end Lenny Woods. Here's what Dad wrote:

Words fail me but I'm going to try.

I had a lovely time on Sunday at the Liverpool v Charlton match. I cried much of the time, not because the dream was ending, but in gratitude that it had ever taken place. I am grateful for the highs, too many to recount, but also for the lows which gave friends and the extended Red army/family the chance to show how much they cared, keeping him going and hoping against hope for a miracle.

The miracle happened and the unfinished business of his first 'leaving' has been resolved. Robert got to say goodbye and thanks, receiving the same in double measure. To picture, even now, him standing at both ends of the ground with his family, on and off the pitch, is a memory which will never end. I can't thank all who deserve to be thanked, including Liverpool staff past and present – particularly the latter for making Sunday happen – but thanks to Bobby Wilcox and gang for their lasting support. Liverpool can rest assured they'll never walk alone. The club will always be in the Fowler hearts.

Well said, Bobby! I couldn't have put it better myself. But, me being me, I knew that I could still do a job at the highest level. Numerous clubs came in for me, including Portsmouth, now being managed by my old mate Jamie Redknapp's dad, Harry. I'd met Harry loads of times and always found him great company and genuinely innovative in the way he thought about the game. I'd been lucky in that respect – Roy Evans was at the time one of the pioneers of a three-man defence in the modern game and Harry was an advocate, too. He also talked a lot about a midfield diamond, which I hadn't heard before. Harry was in his second spell at Portsmouth who, this time around, were flush with cash, courtesy of a new owner, Alexandre Gaydamak. He talked about playing me at the tip of the diamond, effectively a third striker rather than a midfielder, but with the transfer deadline looming, our initial conversations hadn't translated into a firm offer. Maybe Harry was already working on his TV persona, where he drives to his office on transfer deadline day, his arm half out the car window, ready to tell the waiting media that he's still expecting 'one or two' to sign as the day goes on!

* * *

Meanwhile, Cardiff City made me a very good offer. I'd always really liked Dave Jones as a football fella, but there was also still a sense of 'once bitten' when I found myself on the receiving end of another Peter Ridsdale charm offensive. You have to hand it to Ridsdale, though – he genuinely loves the game and I do think he sincerely believes the vision (and the version) he is trying to sell to you. He'd recently taken over as Cardiff chairman and had already used his Leeds connections to bring Jimmy Floyd Hasselbaink and Stephen McPhail to the club.

With a promising crop of young Welsh lads like Aaron Ramsey and Joe Ledley, Cardiff City held high ambitions. Dave Jones laid out a three-year plan to move the club into a brand-new stadium and for the team to be playing in that arena, in the Premier League, within that time frame. To achieve that, like any team with ambition, they needed goals and Dave felt certain that, in tandem with Jimmy Floyd, I was the man to provide them. Walking around Cardiff to get a feel for the place, I found the people warm, hugely welcoming and passionate about their team. So, on 21st July 2007,

I signed a two-year contract and went away honoured and excited to be joining this great club.

I'd missed the start of pre-season with Dave Jones and the squad and was keen to get myself up to speed as soon as possible. Once again this was my undoing as, almost from my first flat-out sprints, I tore my quad – so, essentially, I injured myself trying to get match fit! That didn't keep me out for long, though. I got back down to training and, little by little, built up my fitness once again – then I started to feel these shooting pains in my back. The pain would subside for a while and I'd convince myself that it was all just a reaction to pre-season training and re-acclimatising myself to the intensity of our routines. Anyone would think I might have learned my lesson by now, but I did the worst thing possible, which was to stay quiet and push on through the pain. Seeing my lack of sharpness, Dave Jones drew the conclusion that I was way behind on my fitness. I wasn't even on the bench for the first couple of games and, at that point, I really should have said something to the club doctor rather than taking it upon myself to step up my training.

Towards the end of September – mainly, I think, to give me some much-needed match fitness rather than any sense that I was tearing up trees in training – I was handed a start against Preston. I got myself on the end of two crosses, scored two goals and, just like that, I was back – except I'd go back to the hotel where I was based during the week and barely be able to sleep, my back pain was that bad. Driving back to

Merseyside to see Kerrie and the kids was such agony that, increasingly, it was literally becoming a labour of love.

But the goals against Preston kept me in the team. I probably knew this subconsciously but, in effect, every sprint I made, every game I played, I was making the injury worse and prolonging the recovery time. Yet I carried on scoring. I got two more in a League Cup tie against West Brom, setting us up for a fourth round tie at Anfield, where the entire ground seemed to be willing me to score! That was an odd night for me – so much love from both sets of fans, yet I came off the pitch knowing that I was letting everyone down, including myself. It was time to face the music: I got medical examinations done.

The outcome of the tests was a recommendation that I be seen by one of the top specialists in Europe, Hans Mueller-Wohlfahrt, based in Hamburg. He was brilliant! Straight away, he told me that he could see from my stance that I was 'carrying' on my left side – in other words, I was listing to the left. His first impression was that this was a chronic injury – a deep-lying, historic issue that has developed and got worse over time. Once again, those thoughts popped into my head that perhaps my problems could be traced back to the 'clicky' hip I was born with.

Mueller-Wohlfahrt started telling me about a specialist in Colorado, who might be able to address the condition with micro-surgery to the other hip (which was over-compensating for the weaker, left hip). Before he had time to finish his sentence, I knew who he was about to recommend – Dr Richard Steadman, the sports fractures guy who had got Jamie Redknapp playing again. I was keen to get the problem sorted once and for all, but it was late November, the 'new' season at my new club was well underway and I just wanted to play and give a good account of myself. I asked the doctor whether there was any way I could delay my operation until the summer so that I could get back out on the pitch and play some football. Was it within the realms of possibility that I could take anti-inflammatory drugs to help me 'play through the pain' or would I just be making the injury worse? His solution was a course of injections – 28 of them, in fact, which I had to administer before training and before matches. It was a massive pain in the arse – the sheer amount of jabs became a saga – but I got back in the team and was managing to move without pain, when my old pal Darren Purse, a colleague at Cardiff by now, whacked me in training! This time it was the old ankle again. It was sore and swollen, but didn't need anything more radical than elevation, ice and rest to fix itself – but still, the specialist was projecting at least a month before I could run freely again.

Rather than sit around waiting for the swelling to subside, the Cardiff management and I decided to use this 'dead' time to take a leap of faith and head out to Colorado for corrective surgery on my hip. I was under a hip specialist called Dr Marc Philippon, who initially thought keyhole surgery and a little clean around the joint would clear up the issue. It was only when he had me under the knife, though, that the surgeon realised the full extent of my hip problem and how that, in turn, was contributing to my ongoing back pain. He decided that micro-fracture was the only way of curing the problem long-term, so in effect, broke my hip and reset it. The theory was that, once the bones knitted together properly, I would have a regular, pain-free gait and hips that would last me into my dotage – and I was all for it.

The op was done in the January of 2008. Cardiff issued a statement saying I would be back flying for the start of the 2008–09 season in August, but for the time being, we wouldn't be seeing any more of Robbie Fowler in the Bluebirds shirt. As soon as I could walk again though, I started my rehab programme – physio, stretches, manipulation, gentle jogging and so on. I kept expecting to feel a twinge or worse, but the hip stood up to everything. I was made up! Cardiff, meanwhile, went on a mad FA Cup run, beating Middlesbrough 2–0 at The Riverside to set up a semi-final against mighty Barnsley. Wembley Stadium was newly reopened and – much in the same way as Harry Kane must have had his eye on Madrid as he worked his way back to fitness for Tottenham – I was starting to harbour dreams of an unlikely return in front of 90,000 at New Wembley for a Cup Final against Portsmouth or West Brom.

Cardiff beat Barnsley 1–0, Harry Redknapp's Pompey beat West Brom by the same score and, for the first time since 1927, Cardiff were contesting an FA Cup final. The atmosphere in the city was incredible, almost as though they'd been given a month-long bank holiday as the big day drew near. There were flags and blue bunting everywhere and there was almost daily speculation around the game. Would Wembley play the Welsh National Anthem alongside God Save The Queen? In the event of a Cardiff City win, would the FA put us forward as one of the English qualifiers for the UEFA Cup – and would they accept us as participants?

In the week leading up to the final, I felt good enough to fast-track my rehab. Myself and the physio team upped the intensity, putting me through sprints, turns, all sorts of joint-intensive pressure training, trying to get me match-fit for the final. The thinking was, even if I could go on from the bench for the last 20-odd minutes, I might be able to make a telling contribution. This time, though, we all recognised that I was pushing myself too hard, too fast, and that it was best all round if I sat this final out. It was a fabulous day though, with both sets of fans providing an unbelievable spectacle of noise and colour. Kanu put Portsmouth ahead and Cardiff desperately searched for an equaliser in the closing minutes, but it wasn't to be. Because I'd been out injured since the turn of the year, I hadn't played in any of the earlier rounds of the competition, either. So, with zero minutes on the clock and no real case for me gazumping one of the other 18, I missed out on a – admittedly unexpected – finalist's medal, too.

Things changed over the summer. I can't quite put my finger on it and I really don't want to rake it all up again, but

Peter Ridsdale called me in and asked if I'd help the club out by signing a pay-as-you-play contract. It wasn't stingy – the rewards would be there if I put together a decent run of games. But my issue with it was that I already had a contract, I was happy enough with things as they were, and if I laid myself open to the whims of selection by signing this new proposal, I might go an entire season without being picked, played or paid. It was hardly pistols at dawn, but it's fair to say the club and I had a bit of a falling-out over it. On reflection, I wish I'd just signed the revised contract; not doing so is easily my biggest mistake and biggest regret in football. Cardiff is a brilliant city, a great club, and looking back, I would have loved to have done something for those fantastic fans – given them something to remember me by. But the family was by now firmly and happily ensconced in West Kirby and I began to think a move nearer home might be best all round.

Enter my old comrade Paul Ince, now manager of Blackburn – and enter the embers of my career as a top-flight player in the English Leagues. In September 2008 I signed a short-term agreement with Blackburn, primarily on the basis that Incey was there, Ewood Park was a 45-minute drive away from our house and I'd get to see much, much more of my family. But the move turned out to be one of those that you just consign to the 'didn't quite work out' folder. Blackburn in those days were still very ambitious. They'd won the League not so very long before, had enjoyed semi-regular incursions into European football, and with lads like David Dunn,

Ryan Nelson, Brett Emerton, Benni McCarthy and my old teammates Stephen Warnock in defence and Paul Robinson between the sticks, had genuine Top Six aspirations. They'd sacked Mark Hughes – who'd done a decent job – over the summer, so Paul Ince was under the spotlight, right from the start. But, for whatever reason, Blackburn were stop-start under Incey, winning difficult away games then fluffing the ones that looked easiest on paper. I wasn't getting much of a look-in anyway, but when local rivals Wigan Athletic won the derby game 3–0 (including a goal for one Emile Ivanhoe Heskey), I knew that the writing would be on the wall. A run of six consecutive defeats saw him getting an early Christmas present. The sack. I knew the writing would be on the wall for me, too, and I don't think I came back in after that to formally receive my P45. I can summarise my highlights in a Blackburn shirt as follows:

24th September 2008: Everton (League Cup, home), Won 1–0

Have that, drug rumourmongers!

* * *

Over the years, I'd had no shortage of enquiries from emerging football nations – Japan, USA, Thailand – but the one that appealed to Kerrie and I was Australia. We'd spoken quite a lot about the possibility of sampling a whole new life-style in a completely new country and The Land of Oz was one we particularly fancied. As a family we're into the Great Outdoors – even if that's just a walk around Marine Lake in

West Kirby, these days – and there was something about the simplicity of the Australian lifestyle that appealed to us at that point in our lives.

In a similar way that our old Division One became the Premier League, Australia's big-league football was re-branded as A-League in 2007. Part of the new set-up allowed for each team to sign a 'marquee' player, the idea being that they'd bring in a player of international standing who, first and foremost, could still play to a high standard but, secondly, would raise the profile of football, locally and nationally. In short, they hoped we would put bums on seats! I actually received an offer from Sydney FC before I went to Cardiff, but Jacob was still only a baby and I needed to be as close to Kerrie and the kids as possible.

Towards the beginning of December 2008, I started to receive serious interest from North Queensland Fury, based in Townsville, right up on the North East coast of Australia, between Brisbane and Cairns. If Kerrie and I were serious about a new culture in a new world, then the opportunity to play my football on Australia's Gold Coast was definitely one to consider. Big Sam Allardyce came in at Blackburn to stave off the looming threat of a relegation dogfight. Neither Sam nor myself are fools, we both knew how this was going to play. Before the week was out, Blackburn and I tore up my contract, allowing me to leave as a free agent.

I had two firm offers from the States, but the North Queensland opportunity was intriguing. The club had only been founded earlier in 2008, but had made swift progress to Australia's top division, the A-League. Anyone who has followed A-League football on the telly will know the standard is very high. The League has a commitment to developing Australian football, so there are strict budgetary rules as well as limits on the number of 'marquee' players a club can sign. So, for example, if a club's annual budget was $2 million (that's a decent amount in the A-League), the challenge is to use that money to build a balanced, homegrown squad that can punch its weight but also win enough games and play with a style that will bring the crowds through the turnstiles. This is where the marquee signings come into it. A lot of clubs will look to keep a portion of their budget aside to lure the kind of big, international star that could attract more fans to the game. There was a huge catchment area around Townsville and the Fury had big ambitions of growing the club and its supporter base. Their coach Ian Ferguson was continually on the phone, selling the area and the lifestyle, as well as the club itself. It's difficult for people who have never been there to appreciate how vast Queensland is, but let's just say you could hide the entire United Kingdom in it, many times over. It's *yowge*! And within that region, there is so much history, variety and culture.

Townsville itself is an old port, originally founded to transport gold, silver, copper and zinc from the Queensland mines, all around the world. There was also a major sugar industry, as well as farming and, in more recent times, tourism – the Great Barrier Reef runs right alongside the Queensland coast. The 2009–10 season was to be North Queensland Fury's first in the A-League. Ian, and the Fury chairman Don Matheson, were passionate about building this new club for a new generation of supporters. So, as soon as Christmas and New Year were out of the way, I jumped on a plane and spent a week out there – mainly to check out the club, the ground and the training facilities – all of which were top-notch. I also really liked the kit – a nice, green and white design, almost like a cyclist's shirt. I could definitely see myself wowing the A-League fans in a shirt like that – Queensland's next Tommy Hilfiger model (or, in my case, Tommy Full Figure).

But if I was going to make this move, then the family would be coming with me, and I wanted to be sure this was a place I could see us settling. Over the course of the week, I was hoping to get a real sense of North Queensland as somewhere Kerrie would be happy and the kids would thrive, and in that respect I couldn't have asked for more. If your image of Australia is based on *Neighbours* and *Home & Away* – a friendly, outdoorsy community centred on family, barbecues, surfing and sport – then you're not far wrong! I could see my family settling very nicely in Townsville so, in February 2009, I signed for an initial two years.

Ian made me club captain and, as irony would have it, I scored on my debut – against the first club in Oz to come in for me, Sydney! On an individual, professional level, the season went well. I found that the climate and the lifestyle suited me. I was fit, scoring regularly and won Player of the Year as voted for by the fans, Players' Player of the Year and, as top scorer, The Golden Boot. On a club level, though, I started to see some of those same ominous signs that began to creep to the surface at Leeds. The common denominator was two clubs with huge ambition, both of them in a hurry to be the biggest and the best.

With Fury, based in a vibrant but remote little city, while everyone's heart was in the right place, perhaps the dream was more lucid than the reality. Almost inevitably, there were cash flow problems, to the extent that Football Federation Australia had to intervene towards the end of the 2009–10 season. As the club's marquee player, I was simultaneously its most valuable asset and the biggest financial commitment – and there's the rub. The marquee player's contract is treated as an entirely separate entity that falls outside of the general cashflow and accounts of the football club. So, when North Queensland Fury hit financial problems, the FFA stepped in to cover all the players' wages – except mine!

From that point until the end of the season, it was actually costing me money to continue playing in Australia. Still, I found out a lot about the way sports franchises work in the A-League, as well as the kind of first-hand experience that will serve me well as I forge my way in management. The upshot was that I left NQF in May 2010 and signed for Perth Glory for the following season. Fury subsequently went into administration, eventually being removed from the A-League in 2011. But I was on my way to the other side of that vast continent, continuing a love affair with Australia that was to be rekindled in years to come.

22

ONE LAST JOB

As a kid and as a younger player, you look at fellas in their thirties struggling to get around the pitch – struggling to get into their kit – and you think to yourself, why do they do it? Why not just quit while you're on top, leave the fans (and yourself) with only the most brilliant memories rather than a huffing, puffing husk of what you were in your prime? Yet it's only once you start edging towards that point that you fully realise just how much the game means to you, and how much you're going to miss it once it's taken away. Part of the fallacy is that you don't see yourself as any different to the player you've always been. But the even bigger part is your absolute love of and addiction to the game.

I recently saw *Diego Maradona*, the brilliant new feature documentary about his life (fun fact – I bumped into Maradona at the Tottenham v Liverpool game at Wembley in 2018 and was made up that he knew who I was and that I'd scored a few goals!). Though a lot of people see Maradona's story as the ultimate sporting tragedy, I found it inspiring. There was so much I could relate to. An ordinary, working-class kid with an outrageous talent for kicking a football is, almost overnight, anointed as a football god. His life is turned upside down. From the age of 17 onwards, he almost never has a moment to himself. Wherever he goes – Buenos Aires, Barcelona, Naples, airports, car parks, supermarkets, even his own home – there are crowds of people thronging all around him, just wanting to be in his orbit. They shove pieces of paper in front of him, touch his clothes, breathe his air, shout his name: 'Diego, Diego, Diego …' All through it he smiles and tries to give his best – signing autographs, posing for photos, kissing babies. He is bigger than the Pope himself. Huge murals of his face cover the sides of entire housing blocks. He can't get away from himself – except on the football pitch:

'When I'm on the pitch, life goes away. Problems go away. Everything goes away.'

That line in particular struck a chord. Even when you've done it all your life and you've become well known for it, it takes you by surprise, sometimes, just how much you fucking love football! The idea of it not being there anymore – just the sheer satisfaction you get, every time, from thrashing a ball into the back of the net – is scary. There's so much about the game that you would miss – the camaraderie, the laughter, the joy of winning – but the biggest thing you would miss is the absolute joy of playing. That's the reason

I went to Thailand, plain and simple – I wanted to carry on playing.

After Perth, I started on the long and arduous road of taking my coaching badges. As I might have mentioned once or twice, I'm addicted to football and I had not the slightest flake of doubt that, once my playing days were done, I would go into coaching and management. It's not just a matter of staying in the game, it was always a key part of my long-term plan. But my last few playing contracts had not worked out in the way I hoped for when I signed them, and there's always this little voice in your head, saying:

'One last crack at it, Robbie. This is the one!'

Peter Reid had just taken over at Plymouth Argyle and, in the summer of 2011, we started talking about a possible player-coach role for me down in Devon. But when the invitation to sign for the current champions of Thailand came, that little voice was shouting louder than ever. Still only 36, I figured the Thai league, though competitive, would be less of a physical challenge than Division Two, where Plymouth were currently plying their trade. And, even if the standard wasn't exactly top notch, the Thailand offer presented a real chance for me to carry on scoring goals at a meaningful level. Muangthong United played in the Siam Cement Arena (formerly, The Thunderdrome) in North Bangkok and they wanted me to be their new Number 9. And so it was that, in July 2009, I headed out to Thailand to find the back of the net again.

It was, in every sense, a culture clash. MTUTD (as they were known) fans turned out in their hundreds to greet my arrival at Suvarnabhumi Airport, but instead of mass hysteria as Robbie Mania gripped Thailand, they applauded politely and bowed quite a lot. I bowed back, signed a few shirts and headed off with Muangthong's general manager, Ronarit Seu-Vaga, to commence my press tour.

Ronarit was an absolute diamond who I just got on with, right from that first meeting. Like so many people in that part of the world, he knew more about football than most of us have forgotten; he could describe goals from unimportant midweek games from years ago against Stoke or Sunderland as though they'd happened last night – a complete football nut. Our first port of call was to meet the Prime Minister, Yingluck Shinawatra. Name sounds familiar? Yep, she's the younger sister of the former Manchester City owner, Thaksin Shinawatra. Prime Ministers, presidents, sheiks, oligarchs, world rulers and all sorts of rich and powerful figures, all over the globe, have got wise to the pulling power football has – not just as a crowd-pleasing attraction but as a force for unity in restless nations.

I remember during the time I was at City, Rick Parry and a couple of the LFC directors flew to Bangkok to hold talks with Shinawatra, who was interested in buying a controlling stake in Liverpool. You can see the appeal for Shinawatra – Liverpool, even in 2004, were a huge global brand and it would have been a major coup for him to acquire one of the biggest clubs in the world, essentially using the club as an official ambassador for Thailand. This has been happening more and more over recent times – entire nations like China or Qatar investing mega millions in a sport that has the whole world under its spell. In that respect, Shinawatra was way ahead of the curve, even though the Liverpool deal didn't materialise. First off, there was a huge backlash locally over the Thai Prime Minister setting up a National Lottery to help cashflow the deal – effectively asking the general public to buy the club with their own hard-earned dosh! I think the Liverpool delegation was also rightly concerned about Shinawatra's human rights record. For all these reasons, having arrived in Bangkok and taken a closer look at the proposition and the set-up, Liverpool decided to pass on that particular opportunity. The rest is history.

Shinawatra's loving gaze then fell upon Man City, who had no such qualms about completing a deal. He purchased a sleeping giant that had just moved into a brand-new stadium, so whereas Anfield desperately needed expanding, City didn't need major investment in a new ground. Shinawatra's money helped spruce the squad up and improve the club to a level that made City an attractive investment for Sheik Mansour. From that point, obviously, Man City have never looked back, improving on every imaginable level, year on year. It took Liverpool a little longer to wake up and catch up, but I believe that, in FSG, the club now has the ideal owner custodians.

My next big appointment in Bangkok was with the MTUTD manager, Henrique Calisto, where more culture shocks were waiting. The first and oddest of these was the sight of elephants wandering along the high street, swinging their trunks without a care in the world. That was clearly going to take a bit of getting used to! The other surprise was that, in a vaguely worrying turn of events, Calisto seemed unaware the club had signed me. He wasn't happy at all that MTUTD had gone behind his back, as he saw it, and brought in a player he hadn't sanctioned. Once he recovered from the shock, Calisto and I had a slightly forced chat about football, The Kop, Cristiano Ronaldo and Calisto's homeland, Portugal. It wasn't the ideal start to a brand-new manager-player relationship and, as I was to discover, Calisto was never really able to move on from the fact that I'd been signed without his say-so. But Ronarit's sheer enthusiasm was infectious, we all shook hands and, for the time being, everything seemed okay. The fans followed me everywhere on little mopeds, beeping their horns and shouting 'Robbie!' and 'God!' In my first week in Thailand, the club sold over 10,000 'Fowler 9' shirts – incredible!

I hadn't played competitive football for four months by this point, so I brought my own personal trainer over to get me match-fit as the season drew near. But Calisto mustn't have thought I was up to the rigours of Asian Federation Cup football because he left me out of the team to play the crunch game against Al-Kuwaiti in September 2011 – which MTUTD went on to lose. I wasn't exactly crying myself to sleep when Ronarit sacked Henrique Calisto soon afterwards and asked me to take over as player-coach. So, there I was, nearly 10,000 miles away from home, inheriting a squad of players I didn't know and, without remotely planning to, taking my first fledgling steps as a manager way ahead of schedule.

My ambitions of becoming a coach were being fast-tracked far quicker than I'd anticipated, but the best way of learning to swim is to throw yourself in at the deep end. Having accepted the player-manager challenge, I dived on in!

And I loved it, too. The Muangthong crowd was brilliant. It seemed as though every one of them brought a flag and the noise they made was fantastic. It wasn't like an English crowd, which tends to respond to the action on the pitch – if you're creating chances, the crowd roars you on. If there's a placid patch where not much happens, the crowd tends to go quiet. In Thailand, there was an almost perpetual din, which only grew louder when we scored.

By the time I took over from Calisto we'd lost a couple of games. I won my first two games, during the second of which I scored my first goal for MTUTD – a straightfor-ward poacher's nod-in from point-blank range, but they all count! We had an okay season after that and finished third in the League. We also made the final of the Chang Cup – the Thai equivalent of the FA Cup, which was every bit as hard-fought and prestigious as our own. We got to the final after an epic semi-final against Songkhla that went to extra time

– and it was a similar story in the final that December against reigning champions Buriram, the strongest team in Thailand. We gave as good as we got and ran them close, with the match still goalless at full-time. In extra time, we tired a little and, in spite of incredible backing from the MTUTD fans, Buriram snuck a goal to beat us 1–0. So, we finished third in the League and got to the Cup Final in my first season.

Just after New Year 2012, I received the terrible news that the much-loved former Liverpool and Everton star Gary Ablett had died at the age of 46. Even though it was widely known that Gary was being treated for a rare form of blood cancer, his death at such a young age shocked me to the core. I made immediate arrangements to get back home for his funeral at Liverpool Cathedral.

Standing there in the cathedral among so many fellow players, I had all sorts of different thoughts – so much to be thankful for in my football career and family life. Madison and Jaya were both christened in the cathedral, only a few hundred yards from the streets where I grew up and more than anything, I felt a renewed connection with my city. I came away from Gary's funeral feeling philosophical about life and certain that I wanted to stay right here, in Liverpool.

For a long time, I'd been giving serious thought to ways I could use my experience and my contacts to make a meaningful contribution to the lives of young people in the city and, if we got it right, create a valuable, lasting legacy. One thing that continually played on my mind was, 'How would my life have turned out if I'd had one of those horrible, serious injuries when I was still on schoolboy terms at Liverpool?' Or, 'What would life look like if LFC took the same view as the England Schoolboys set-up?' Too small. Not good enough. Won't make the grade. Things would obviously have worked out very, very differently. I always felt particularly badly, too, for the kids that the big clubs let go when they're 16. Not just the big clubs, either – a kid can be training with a club and go through their Academy system from age 6, 7, 8 – basically growing up believing that they're going to be a professional footballer. Then, when it comes to signing full-time, the club tells them that they haven't quite made the grade. It must be devastating for them.

Our Scott and I had been talking about this, with the idea of setting up a specialist college along similar lines to the sports campus schools they have in the States. There's a major emphasis on the education side – every single student splits their time between the classroom and the sports field. I'd been thinking for a long time that we could do some-thing like that in Liverpool, initially aiming it at 16–19 year olds who had recently been released by their clubs. That is basically how Scott and I came up with FEFA – The Fowler Education and Football Academy. Fittingly, we found a location in Wavertree, not far from the site of my boyhood college, Nugent. Scott, as Operations Manager, brought in Brian McGorry as Principal and the academy has gone from strength to strength. FEFA is the current holder of English

Colleges FA national championship, Dubai Cup winners (beating Ronaldo's Brazilian academy in the final) and is about to open a second site in Warrington. It's great to know that something that started as the seed of an idea has developed into a physical entity with lasting value to so many young people.

So, having decided that my immediate future was here in Liverpool, I informed MTUTD that I wouldn't be returning to Thailand. The club was initially a little shocked and obviously disappointed but once again, Ronarit showed his class. He straight away asked me if there was anything he could do at his end to make me change my mind, but I was just honest with him; coming home had made me realise just how much I missed my family, my home and my city. Liverpool. And Ronarit was completely sympathetic about that – something I will always respect him for. He brought in Slavisa Jokanovic – the same Jokanovic who took Fulham from the Championship into the Premier League – as head coach, and I stayed in Liverpool. But I'd had my first taste of management, and I wanted more.

23

GETTING MY BADGES

Right back to when I was playing schoolboy football, I had thoughts of one day becoming a coach. It was something that took shape in my plans during those long and arduous periods in rehabilitation from serious injury. Having now had my first brief taste of this new, different, but equally addictive aspect of football, I was left in no doubt that this was how I saw my future.

Before I took the Muangthong job, I'd already started the groundwork into getting my UEFA coaching badges – now I could fully concentrate on completing that process. There are five levels to the European coaching model – Level 1, Level 2, B Licence, A Licence and UEFA Pro Licence, all administered by a country's National Football Association.

An experienced professional or former pro doesn't have to do the Level 1 and 2 stage, we can be fast-tracked to the B Licence. This takes nine to twelve months to complete, taking in roughly 120 hours of work, most often at County FA level.

Typically, you start dealing with things like the development of possession, transitions of play, movement to create space and other tactical issues. But the school side of it is intensive: there's a lot of classroom work and background reading. A lot of theory too: football, food and fitness, injury identification, sports science, psychology, in-depth player analysis. We're also given monitored, observed coaching sessions. If you're applying for a coaching job in the professional game these days, the B Licence is the minimum standard expected.

The A Licence is serious, sustained hard work and study. The best way of explaining it is that it's a bit like getting a degree in coaching. It's a two-year, tailored course, devised specifically for professionals or ambitious football coaches who want to go for the prime jobs in the game. You can only get it by working with your national FA, but once you get it, the A Licence radically increases your prospects. It's divided into two parts, based around two-week summer sessions, with distance learning and support sessions the rest of the year.

The UEFA Pro Licence is the very top tier, a qualification you need to have if you want to manage a team in either of the two big European competitions. This is a much more intimate pathway, with smaller classes targeted at the unique situations you can expect to come up against as a top-level football manager. There'll be modules in all sorts of management skills, like handling top-class players, sports psychology and mental preparation, contracts and agents, handling the media, commitments to club sponsors and tours, using the latest technology, analysing opponents' strengths and weaknesses and different ways of dealing with a player's problems, on and off the pitch. Like I say, it's all heavily geared towards the actual day-to-day realities of football club management. To pass, the coach has to prove that he or she is competent in a whole host of areas, including:

- How to plan and evaluate your team's strategic season programme;
- How to succeed in one key fixture during the season;
- Improving the performance of one key player;
- Improving your own interpersonal skills;
- Building upon your existing coaching skills with specific emphasis.

There'll be visits to centres of excellence, like Ajax or Juventus, along with regular masterclasses from absolute world leaders in sports management – Carlo Ancelotti, Sir Clive Woodward, Fabio Capello, people of that calibre – and regular assessments, too. Interesting fact, here, fact-lovers: neither Alex Ferguson nor Harry Redknapp holds a UEFA Pro Licence! Not that they would struggle to get one, of course – I just don't think it was such a big deal having one when they were in their prime.

If there's a controversy surrounding coaching badges, especially the UEFA Pro, it's the cost. The same course – admittedly delivered to varying specifications, country to country – can cost as little as €535 in Germany and all the way up to almost £8,000 in England. For me, it's money well spent and money I can afford to spend. But for someone who hasn't been in the game for a few years or who missed out on the big TV money or whatever, it could be a real stretch.

I found the whole thing stimulating and challenging in the best possible way, culminating in my *Nature vs Nurture* thesis. But, as tailored and comprehensive as the various courses and modules are, I do think experience as a former pro gives an ex-player an added advantage – a context, if you like – that the pure theorists and academics don't have. If you have personally been through the scenarios you're being schooled in, you can process that experience in a way that is relevant and useful to the players under your charge as a manager. For example, when we did our module on mental health, I was immediately able to relate the case studies back to players I knew and had played with. You recognise some of the individual circumstances and that, in turn, focuses you on what you would do today if one of your players displayed similar signs of depression. Equally, you look at different forms and methods of motivation and apply those theories to the real-life managers you've worked under and played for. What was it about X that made you want to run through a brick wall for him? Why did you find Y's training regime such a chore? How would you freshen things up and keep the squad motivated, energetic and competitive?

One fascinating module was all about in-game psychology, including how different players respond to the unique pressures and circumstances of a big match. A classic recent example (more of which in a mo!) is the way Barcelona threw in the towel at Anfield in 2018's Champions League semi. I was there to see it and I've experienced similar capitulations as a player, so it was interesting looking at the phenomenon of a whole team's mental collapse from an academic standpoint. This is an area where I'm convinced former players like myself, Frank Lampard, Ole Solskjaer and Stevie Gerrard have a distinct advantage. With all the respect in the world, there is no substitute for actual relevant experience. We have played in the biggest games for the highest stakes – major finals and internationals, all over the world. There is no scenario we haven't faced. Drawing upon that wealth and variety of experience, from Schoolboy Football all the way to the big European finals gave me, I believe, an edge when it came to my coaching badges – and there'll never be a player who can come up to me and say: 'Show us yer medals, Fowler!'

At the end of it all, I walked away as fully qualified UEFA Pro Licence coach and waited for the stampede for my services.

24

LIVERPOOL – THE
THIRD COMING

After I finished in Thailand, the big thing I missed more than anything was playing. You miss the laughs, the piss-taking and the friendship, too – but you really miss playing the game itself. When I did ITV's *Harry's Heroes: The Full English* in 2018, the common agreement was every one of us players immediately said yes to the invitation because we wanted to revel in the buzz of the camaraderie one more time.

It's hard to explain if you've never played a team sport week in, week out, all your life, but the kind of witty, cruel, cutting and often hilarious repartee you get, in and around the training ground, is strangely addictive. Just through being there and being part of it, it sharpens your own act and, honestly, the back and forth, ripping and ribbing off each other is just brilliant *craic*! I sometimes wish I'd installed CCTV cameras in the Liverpool changing rooms at the height of the mid-90s badinage. Neil Ruddock and John Barnes could have done stand up – they were so quick-witted, nothing but nothing was off-limits! It was a joy when I was reunited with the pair of them for *Harry's Heroes* and along with Merse, Matt Le Tissier and the gang, we immediately tore into one another's clothes, hair (or lack of it), paunches, teeth and breasts. Needless to say, the svelte, athletic recruits like myself and Lee Sharpe were continually reminding the less disciplined chaps about their expanding waistbands, but this was nothing compared to how Ruddock and Barnes would wind each other up.

John is known for his love of fried chicken so, one afternoon, Razor had a massive order of KFC delivered to JB's house. Seriously, there was enough to feed an entire squad! I still don't know whether Digger knew it was a prank. He just shrugged, brought the chicken in and set about demolishing it, then, when the TV crew revealed themselves, he just said, 'Spicier, next time, please.'

But, even more than the repartee, we all agreed that it's the actual pulling on kit and lacing your boots and playing a proper, competitive game that you miss most of all. Just as, first time round, I didn't get the chance to say a proper farewell to the Anfield fans, I never really had a moment where I thought, okay, that's it, my work here is done. There was no official announcement, no press statement to a heart-broken nation, I just stopped getting realistic offers and therefore didn't have a choice to make.

Once it dawned on me that I'd retired at the tender age of 37, I jumped at any and every opportunity to play again.

Since Sky TV instituted its own version of veterans' five-a-side with their *Masters Football* in the early 2000s, Liverpool had been, well – Masters of the Masters. With a talent pool of recently retired players like John Barnes, Jan Molby, Steve McManaman and John Aldridge at our disposal, along with LFC's long-standing infatuation with the short-form game, it's no surprise that Liverpool became the team to beat. I jumped at the chance of turning up in the red shirt again and, from the Masters, that whole Liverpool Legends scene grew. It's quite a huge thing these days, with the Legends travelling the globe to play exhibition games and charity fund-raisers against equivalent veteran teams from Real Madrid (Leyendas) and AC Milan (Glorie). Modesty prevents me from listing some of the TRULY OUTSTANDING GOALS I've notched in that ridiculously snug-fitting shirt.

Oi, Liverpool Legends kit manufacturer! Why the snug kits?

It seemed like a logical progression from the Legends when I became an official Liverpool Ambassador over the summer of 2014. Straight away, I was off to Chicago for the pre-season match against Olympiakos at Soldier Field. Working as an ambassador has been something of a Libero role for me. The best part is that you get to travel the world in your LFC blazer and meet thousands and thousands of diehard Liverpool fans from far-flung places. These fans are sometimes a little snottily referred to as 'tourists' or 'OOTs' (Out of Towners), as though their support is somehow less valid than that of someone from, say, Bootle, who goes to every game. Don't get me wrong, that Bootle fan is, it goes without saying, a proper, committed Red – but I often think, especially after having met so many brilliant overseas fans face-to-face, that we're a bit spoilt, getting to see the team we love, week in, week out. Try being that Liverpool-mad kid in Lapland trying to follow the game on a dodgy stream, or the hardy supporters' groups who set their alarms at some godforsaken hour every week so they can meet up with their fellow Reds in a downtown bar in Perth, San Diego or Bandung to cheer the team on.

That's not to mention the time, dosh and dedication those fans who travel hundreds, thousands, sometimes tens of thousands of miles devoted to the love of their lives – following Liverpool. Some might only come once a season, but whether we're playing Burnley on a rainy Sunday or Barcelona in a Champions League showdown, that trip to Anfield means the world to them. And that's why the ambassador job is so brilliant. Not to sound cheesy, but it means the world to me, wherever I go, being reminded that, even though I hung my boots up a while ago now, my time as Liverpool's Number 9 (and 23, and 11!) has meant something special to all these people – I'll never get blasé about that.

Over my five years as an ambassador I've also taken some specialist striker training and academy masterclasses, helping the forwards with little things to work on, some ideas and techniques I've picked up over the years. I love being around the club and, more than anything, I love being on the training pitch. But, being out there, working with the players, organising routines and drills and presentations only whetted my appetite to put my coaching badges to full use. Every time I would get in from one of those striker sessions at Melwood or The Academy, I'd bang off a text or an email to my agents, saying, please get me a coaching job!

* * *

Brisbane Roar is a club steeped in tradition. The team's orange shirts can be traced back to the Dutch community in Brizzy, who founded the club as Hollandia FC, back in the 50s. Footy was mainly played by Australian immigrant communities like the Italians, Slavs and Greeks, but, in 1973, there was a big move to popularise football all over Australia and clubs were encouraged to name themselves after their home towns and cities. Hollandia became Brisbane Lions, but the orange strip stayed. The new name of Brisbane Roar came with the launch of the A-League in 2005. In 2011 and 2012, the club won back-to-back A-League titles and went on a record-breaking unbeaten run of 36 games – which still stands today. But, over recent times, things have not been so great at this historic football club. The 2018–19 season saw the Roar hit rock bottom, winning only four games all season and conceding 71 goals.

I already had a modest profile in Australia after my stints at Perth and North Queensland – some might say, if I'd stood sideways on, the profile would have been even bigger … Since then I'd got my Pro Licence and I'd made my first tentative steps as a coach, but I know that my travels and my work as an LFC Ambassador played a huge part in persuading Brisbane Roar to approach me, too. We began to discuss the idea of my becoming the Roar's manager around the start of the New Year, 2019 and those initial conversations quite quickly developed into something much more focused. It was clearly from an early stage that the Liverpool philosophy is one that has spanned the globe. For Brisbane Roar, it's not just my ideas and methods the club is buying into, it's also that pedigree of a near lifelong association with LFC.

We tied up the basics – coaching staff, budget, refreshing the squad and so on and, not long after my birthday in the April, the club formally invited me to become their new manager. Before flying out there, though, I had one last mission to complete as a Liverpool employee ...

25

BEATING THE ODDS
(PART TWO)

In so many ways, mine has been a story of fathers and sons. I started out by kicking a ball about with my dad, Bobby – admittedly to a repetitive, almost obsessive extent. For all those youth games, trials, trips to Melwood, Anfield, home and away, Dad was by my side. His health slowly but inexorably declined after he suffered a stroke in 2004 and I was devastated beyond words when he was finally taken from us in April 2017. There are landmarks in your life, professional and personal, that compel you to take stock of what you've done and where you are: the loss of your father is a time for reflection.

My lad Jacob is on Liverpool's books, a huge source of pride for me, Kerrie and the whole family. It might sound an odd way to describe a team game, but a footballer's life can be lonely at times. For all the undoubted highs, you have to expect some pretty crushing lows as well – injuries, loss of form, getting dropped, losing key games. You don't just simply take those things on the chin and move on, it's tough. So, as his father and his mate, I'm grateful that I've earned that perspective and I've been able to guide Jacob through the game's ups and downs. He's a brilliant footballer, two-footed, instinctive, creative – completely his own player (but with a definitive Fowler knack for finding the net!). He lives and breathes Liverpool as much as I do and there are few things I love more than the times we spend together, going to games. We may get to travel with the team sometimes (and we might get the best seats!), but we are no different to any other fans, hoping against hope, longing for glory, dreaming in Red.

On the afternoon of the Champions League semi-final against Barcelona, I was sitting in a plaza with Jacob, watching all the fans coming and going, hundreds of them, thousands, enjoying a sunny afternoon in a beautiful European city, wearing their shirts with pride. And that was a thing that hit me, big time – the way Jürgen Klopp has given the Liverpool fans their pride back. I was sitting there outside a street café with my little lad before one of the elite fixtures in world football and I said to him: 'What a brilliant time this is to be a Liverpool fan.'

He said, 'I know, Dad. But this is just the start.'

In spite of how well we played against Barca that night, we somehow came away on the wrong end of a 3–0 defeat. I found myself in the strange position of – supposedly – being the grown-up, being consoled by my kid.

'It's not over. We've done it before, Dad. Loads of times. We can do it again.'

I've got to be honest, I wasn't feeling it at all. Even with Liverpool's great history of turning these sorts of setbacks around, I honestly could not see a way this was going to be one of them. Beating Barcelona by a clear four-goal margin was not looking likely to me at all.

In the run-up to the return leg, I started to feel more positive. All season we had been scoring late goals and winning tricky games, just as they seemed to be slipping away from us. There was Divock Origi's goal in the 96th minute against Everton, guaranteeing them a Blue Christmas. The late show at Southampton, where Mo Salah scored an absolute beauty right at the end. Then Salah got that nasty head injury that saw him stretchered off at Newcastle. Liverpool were still neck and neck with Man City in the race for the title so it was critical that we take all three points to keep the pressure on them. But, all of a sudden, luck was beginning to conspire against us. We already knew that Bobby Firmino was out of action for the Barca game and now our talisman Mo Salah looked like he was going to be out, too. It was still 2–2 at Newcastle with a few minutes left of the time the ref had added on for Salah's treatment. I was glancing over at Jacob, thinking, *Poor kid! We've had a good go in the League, but we're not quite gonna make it, now. And we've got to score four against Barcelona without Salah and Firmino. And without them scoring …*

I was getting this big speech ready for him about how you draw strength from adversity; how Jürgen Klopp had transformed LFC and how next season was *definitely* going to be our year – when up popped Origi to nod a header in at the far post: 3–2 to Liverpool! Delirium in the Fowlers' front room!

Liverpool were once more two points clear of City at the top of the Premier League. If Leicester could get a draw, or somehow win the game, then we would have to beat Wolves' last game of the season to be sure of being Champions. Leicester gave as good as they got for over an hour and City were launching attack after attack, but it was Filbert The Fox's team who created the two best chances. Just as me and Jacob were starting to think this might be on, Vincent Kompany – who, I've got to say, is a phenomenal player and a born leader – crashed in that bastard of a shot from about 35 yards. It was one of those shots where you just have to nod your head and say, okay, that was absolute quality. And if your team is going toe-to-toe with Man City, amassing 97 points and only getting beaten once over the entire season and City *still* end up as Champions, then maybe you just say fair do's. You give City the credit they deserve and come back next year, ready to go again.

My overriding fear was that, after the euphoria of the win at Newcastle on the Saturday night, the disappointment of City's own late show on the Monday would burst our bubble heading into the return game against Barcelona the next day.

No chance! If my own household was anything to go by, these young Reds had no intention of lying down and dying. If they were to go down and go out, they'd go down fighting. Jacob said to me, 'Dad, it's the biggest game in Europe. We're 3–0 down at half-time. Ring any bells?'

I'm writing this many weeks after the season ended and I still get a shiver down my spine, thinking about that night at Anfield on 7th May 2019. I've known some stupendous nights there, including a semi-final of my own against Barcelona, back in 2001. The roof nearly came off The Kop that night and the game against Roma on that same UEFA Cup run to Dortmund was special, too.

My dad's pal Bobby Wilcox always used to talk about the European Cup semi-final against Inter Milan, back in 1965, as being the loudest and scariest he'd ever heard Anfield, while the entire ground was shaking for that first semi against Chelsea in 2005. The old stadium manager, Ged Poynton, once told me that they have the equivalent of a Richter Scale to measure what would be considered a safe level of 'trembling' in The Kop's structure but he added that, for the 2005 Chelsea game, all four stands were shaking way above any level they had ever recorded!

These are all fantastic memories, and all go towards the folklore of Liverpool Football Club, but I swear the noise as Jordan Henderson led the Liverpool team out against Barcelona that night was something else. You know when people say 'There's something in the air'? Well, that was it.

It was phenomenal, one of those unique and magical nights where the team, the fans and the occasion all come together to create an unstoppable force. When it happens like that at Anfield, it goes beyond anything you can explain – it's witchcraft. I was in the commentary box with Michael Owen, Rio Ferdinand and Gary Lineker and, honestly, they just stopped speaking and turned around in their seats in a stunned kind of disbelief. I know Rio wouldn't want to admit it, but he knew he was witnessing something very, very special.

From the moment Origi slotted in the rebound from Jordan Henderson's effort at six minutes, you could see Barca knew they were up against a higher power, too. They kept on going, and did create the odd chance, but for me, it looked as though they were going through the motions. It was as though they were hoping that just by turning up and being Barca, it would be enough to get the job done.

I went down to find Jacob at half-time, buzzing. Honestly, there was an electric current running through you, this absolute, heightened anticipation that something crazy was about to happen. You could sense it. And yet there was still the realist in me thinking all they had to do was break away and score one goal and that would be the tie, dead. Looking down at their attacking trio, Coutinho, Messi and Suárez, were we really going to keep them out for another 45–50 minutes and still score three more ourselves? Surely, the more we had to push forward for those goals, the more we'd leave ourselves open at the back? And then Jacob nudged me and said, 'Listen to that!'

We were down in the bowels on the Main Stand, but the noise rising up from the crowd ... You could feel it throbbing through the soles of your feet! There must have been whole miles of analysis and reflection written about that second half, but here's mine: The fact that the third goal came so quickly after the second is what finished Barcelona. From the moment Gini Wijnaldum scores our second, wrestles the ball from their keeper, runs back to the centre circle and plants the ball on the spot, Liverpool are like boxers who can smell blood. Barcelona are rocking on their heels, their eyes wild and scared as they hang on the ropes, trying to buy a bit of time to recover. They're thinking, 'If I can just survive these next few rounds, we can see this out and take it on points.' Then Liverpool go down the other end and score again – from 1–0 to 3–0 in a minute – and Barca are dead on their feet.

I looked down onto the pitch and you could see it all over them – the world's best front three were just stunned. Clueless. Coutinho looked as though he wanted to be made invisible (which he had been all night, to be fair!), Suárez was shaking his head, unable to take it in. But Messi's face was the one that told the biggest story: he was in pain, psychological torment, because he knew at that point they were going out. It was only the 55th minute and a stronger team with a better collective will should have been able to galvanise themselves, regroup and come up with something between them to get that crucial goal. But Barcelona didn't lay a glove on us. They were literally petrified, turned to stone by the occasion. They'd thought that being 3–0 up and with Salah and Firmino out of the game, it was all over, yet the two lads who came in to replace them – Shaqiri and Origi – were not there to make up the numbers, they were killing them.

My view is that Liverpool were by far the better side in both games, it was just that Barcelona scored more goals than us in the first one. And as they stood there, waiting to kick off again after our third, all those side-stories came home to roost: Coutinho's backache in the lead-up to his departure to Barca, Suárez telling the world he had to leave Liverpool to fulfil his dreams. Well, now Liverpool were fuelling his worst nightmares, finally putting Barcelona out of their misery with that remarkable fourth goal from a brilliant, intelligent short corner.

Even from the commentary box, the scenes were ridiculous! Jubilant fans all around us were leaping on top of complete strangers in total ecstasy, a tangle of limbs, everyone dancing round, arms around each other. As a match pundit, I found it all very difficult to put into words at the end, but for once, my raw emotion said it much more powerfully. I was almost in tears, so proud of the team, the club, the supporters, the city.

I left the box to celebrate with Jacob – our faces were contorted with joy. I went to lift him up. By that time, I was in very advanced talks with Brisbane Roar about the manager's job. I hesitated for a second, thinking how many times my back and my hip had given me trouble over the years. Was I going to risk going into my first proper coaching job with a ricked back? Too right I was! The Fowler boys were up there with the best of 'em, giving it loads. That sight of the entire team stood in front of The Kop, arms linked, singing 'You'll Never Walk Alone', will live with me forever. Mo Salah in his 'Never Give Up' T-shirt, his big, radiant grin lighting up the night sky. Me and my lad were there to see all that and be a part of it – and now we were off to Madrid for the final!

26

THE MAGIC OF MADRID

Go to any big game in any city and the closer you get to the ground, you'll hear a muffled shout of: 'Any spares?' Well, from the moment we arrived in Madrid, the question me and Jacob were asking ourselves was: 'Any Spurs?' It was just red shirts, red scarves, Liverpool flags hanging from hotel windows, Liverpool songs in the air as you inched your way through the city centre. Jacob had done his bit, going out with his mum to get a sheet of red material and making his own banner: MADRED. I could see the pride on his face as he unfurled it next to all the other flags – his own little part of the story.

I did the interview with Sadio Mané – thanked him once again for being so kind as to shatter my fastest-ever hat-trick record – then we went on a little tour of the Wanda Metropolitano, Atlético's spanking new stadium where the final was to be held, then wandered the streets near our hotel, just taking in the atmosphere. A gang of lads we knew were all having a kickabout in the square and one of my most cherished memories is the way they railroaded me into a game of 'Bin Ball Challenge'.

We lined up in two rows of five, heading the ball from one to another without once letting it drop. Number One headed it across to Number Two, Two headed it on to Three, nice cushioned headers. The last two links of the chain were Fowler & Fowler – no pressure there then. Jacob nodded his up beautifully for me to finish the job and head it down into the bin – GOAL! One of my finest ever, without any doubt at all. We did a quick lap of honour and wandered off into the night, chuckling about Bin Ball and marvelling at the sheer numbers of Reds out and about.

There's an ever-shifting, never-ending debate about which is the biggest club in the world. You can make a big case for Real Madrid and Barcelona, but for me, it has always been a rotating balance of power between Liverpool and Manchester United. I've played and worked all over the world and, even since retiring, I've clocked up the air miles. That's where you really get a sense of the global reach football has. Nelson Mandela asking you to sign his Liverpool shirt. Kids in Thailand running around the backstreets in Liverpool kits. And then 95,000 Liverpool fans packed into the Melbourne Cricket Ground giving as great a rendition of our anthem as you'll ever hear, anywhere.

Being completely honest about it, there was a long period when all you'd see was Man United shirts, everywhere. You used to see a lot more Arsenal shirts than Liverpool ones in Africa, too. But, since Istanbul and obviously, in more recent times, since Liverpool began reaching European finals on a regular basis again, and Mo Salah, Bobby Firmino and Sadio Mané started weaving their magic (I'm a striker, okay? I'm biased!), I've got no doubt that Liverpool are the biggest club in the world right now.

If Madrid was anything to go by over the weekend of the 2019 Champions League final, Liverpool were about ten times bigger than Tottenham Hotspur. It was phenomenal – oceans of red, all over the city, wherever you looked. One thing that Liverpool supporters do brilliantly is fan culture. Banners, flags, songs, parties, pyro ... our fans are innovators and originators. For starters, there are a whole load of brilliant little independent retailers and manufacturers like Transalpino and Hat Scarf Or A Badge who come up with the best T-shirts and matchday merchandise. In the run-up to Madrid, there were so many great designs – a personal favourite would have to be one that Transalpino released, based on Jacob's 'MADRED' flag (okay, it's a fair cop – I helped design it!).

The songs and banners are legendary and going back to the days of Brendan Rodgers' side, the way the fans started turning out in their thousands to greet the team bus was brand new for the Premier League back then – clouds of smoke from their flares and pyro turning the Anfield sky crimson. Best of all for me, though, is the way the club itself recognises the huge role the Liverpool fans play in making LFC special. They've always listened to the fans and co-operated with different groups, like Spion Kop 1906, who co-ordinate the flags and banners on The Kop, and Spirit of Shankly, who speak to the club regularly about ticketing policy, policing, stewarding and so on.

One of the lesser-known figures behind the scenes at Anfield is a guy called Tom Cassidy, who is in charge of the LFC stadium tours and marketing. Tom's brief has also, by default, taken on what is effectively Liverpool's party planning responsibilities. We'll talk about the sheer joy of the homecoming bus parade in a minute but one of the great things that Tom has identified is the way a younger generation of fans has been celebrating the club. There's The Anfield Wrap, probably the best footy fan podcast out there. Then there's Redmen TV, up there with the very best subscription TV channels. And there's Boss Night – the exuberant, grassroots Liverpool fan parties that grew from the popular (and sadly, now, no more) *Boss Mag* street fanzine. Boss Night is a heads-down, no-nonsense celebration of LFC fan culture – basically, a massed ranks, boozy singalong with Liverpool bands and singers leading the Kop karaoke.

A quick observation here – if the dozens and hundreds of bands that have poured out of this city are anything to go by, from The Bunnymen, Elvis Costello, Pete Wylie and The Lightning Seeds to The Las, The Farm and The Zutons, then Liverpool is about 90 per cent Red! Boss Night cottoned on to a new breed of Liverpool performers, like Jamie Webster and

Kieran Molyneux, and started running party nights after big games or Christmas fixtures. I remember our Jacob showing me a YouTube clip of hundreds of them celebrating the win against Man United just before Christmas and saying how he wished he was old enough to go to one of those nights. Tom Cassidy and Tony Barrett, LFC's fan liaison officer, had joined up with Boss Night to put on a fantastic party in Shevchenko Park, ahead of the previous year's Champions League final in Kiev. (Another quick observation – look at the way I just said 'Last year's Champions League final' as though it's an occasion that Liverpool just pop in the diary and turn up for, year on year. I'm not being smug at all, but what did I say to Jacob in that square in Barcelona? 'How good is it, being a Liverpool fan right now?') in 2019, for Madrid, the LFC/Boss Night union wanted to go one better.

From breakfast time, the square began to fill up with happy, noisy Liverpool fans. Plaza de Felipe II will go down in Kop folklore for time ever more, but at first glance, it was an odd choice of venue for a Liverpool fan zone. It's a long, narrow, inner-city plaza – more of an oblong than a square, with a strange kind of Stonehenge obelisk structure at one end. Maybe the Madrid authorities thought the allocation of 16,500 tickets for each team would mean that Liverpool and Spurs would have perhaps 10,000–15,000 supporters congregating in their designated fan parks, maximum.

We ambled down to take a look and soak up the pre-match atmosphere. By the time the compère Ben Burke started warming up the crowd at 10:30, there must have been 30,000 Liverpool fans there already. And by the time the DJ whipped them into a mad, joyous, tumult of red, bouncing along to 'Bohemian Rhapsody', there were well over 50,000 (some estimates said 80,000) packed in. Speaking of 'Bohemian Rhapsody', one thing I'll never quite be able to get my head around is the mad array of old-time classics the Liverpool fans seem to love. 'A Horse With No Name', 'Ring Of Fire', 'Sweet Caroline', 'American Pie' … and that's before you get into all the old Floyd, Genesis and Frank Zappa stuff they seem to buzz off. 'Solsbury Hill'? Oh, okay then! It's one of those where you just smile to yourself, shake your head and get right on it. The highlight of these parties is always Jamie Webster's set, where he gets the entire crowd singing along to all the players' songs and club anthems. I think Tom Cassidy, the Boss Night team and everyone else involved thought they'd never top Shevchenko Park, but the sight of all those tens of thousands of Liverpool fans going nuts in that square is an absolute lifetime highlight for both Jacob and myself.

Even though the stadium reflected what we'd seen in the city centre over the past couple of days, you've got to give the Spurs fans their due. Heavily outnumbered, they didn't half make a racket in that end away! I've always thought of Tottenham as being a 'proper' football club, steeped in their own north London community, their history and their traditions. One of those traditions that I love is the way they sing that slowed-down version of 'When The Spurs Go Marching

In'. The whole build-up to the final and the day itself was a real celebration – two great old clubs going toe-to-toe, with the greatest prize in club football at stake. The game itself wasn't a classic, but who cares? I think that both Tottenham and Liverpool had enough credit in the bank after those incredible semi-finals to justify an element of After the Lord Mayor's Show when it came to the big one. And, as I've made pretty abundantly clear, it's the Cups that you count; your medals are your memories. The history books record the result, you sit at home long after you've packed in playing the game and you look at your medals.

So, when the final turned into an edgy game of cat and mouse after Mo Salah banged that penalty in, it didn't bother me one little bit. I was all for a cagey, boring 1–0 win – so long as we ended up lifting that beautiful big cup! For once, I was supremely confident. Knowing how badly it hurts, losing in a big, big game like this, I was sure that the lads would use the bitter experience of that Kiev final last year to see them through this one – and going ahead so early only made me even more certain. My poor lad was living every stray pass, every missed chance, every Spurs attack, but I kept saying, 'We've got this, pal! We'll be fine.'

But I've got to say, when Divock Origi wrote himself into the LFC history books for all time with that winner, the relief that gushed from us both was something else! I don't think I've hugged Jacob so much since he was born.

What a moment! What an occasion! What a feeling!

If I could crystallise an all-time high as a supporter, it would have to be that – the moment my lad and I knew for sure that Liverpool were six-times European Cup Winners (how good does *that* sound?). I think the joy, the relief and the sheer emotion of Origi's goal wiped Jacob out. As Jordan Henderson went up for the Cup and the team started going through their celebration 'rain dance' on the podium, Jacob just stood there, wide-eyed, absolutely spellbound. Captain Henderson cavorted in front of the team for a moment, prolonging the climax for as long as he could before lifting that beautiful cup sky-high. The stadium erupted – and so did the biggest smile on my lad's face. A day, a night and a moment in time that neither of us will ever forget.

And if it was a joy to be there in Madrid to see the Reds lift the Big One, it was a total privilege to be on the bus for the celebratory homecoming parade on the Sunday. How we made it back to Liverpool in time is a mystery, because the party back at the team hotel was something to behold! I've got to say, if Jürgen Klopp should ever become bored of the repetition of winning cups and leagues with Liverpool, he has a very promising future on *Strictly Come Dancing*! What a mover! He was gliding around that hotel bar like he was on coasters.

I'm not averse to a modest celebration when the occasion demands it, but those players – the whole entourage, in fact – let rip with mighty abandon. The last cameo I witnessed before we toddled up to our room was Alex Oxlade-Chamberlain leading the entire room in a gloriously off-key version of the Virgil Van Dijk song. Talk about cats' chorus! Yet there they all were, bright-eyed and bushy-tailed, posing on the plane with Big Ears, already looking forward to the homecoming parade. The team of players, club officials, staff and extended LFC family is so sizeable now, they had to lay on two fully re-decorated 'Liver Bus' double-deckers to accommodate everybody.

The last time I was on the bus like this for the great LFC homecoming party was after the treble-winning 2000–01 season. It's funny when you look back on times gone by – you remember what you were thinking and how you were feeling just as clearly (sometimes even more so) as you remember the games and the cups themselves. As Jacob and I sat there waiting for the parade to start, I found myself looking back on that 2001 homecoming with fondness, and a little bit of regret. That season was spectacular, but it came back to me that, on the open-top bus last time around, among all the smiles and cheers, I was very worried about my future.

I didn't start the FA Cup final and I'd come on against Deportivo Alavés as a substitute. I scored the goals that helped us win the League Cup; got us to the FA Cup final; kept us in the UEFA Cup final and qualified us for the Champions League. Yet it was becoming clear to me, even then, that I was no longer an automatic pick for Gérard Houllier. A day of joyous celebration was tinged with anxiety.

Sitting on the bus all these years later, with my son next to me and new challenges just around the corner, I found myself just profoundly grateful for the incredible career I've had – and grateful to still be a part of this fantastic club, if only for a few days longer. But what a way to go out! I knew, by then, that this would be one of my final duties (though 'duty' is hardly the word for such an honour) as an official LFC ambassador and I was determined to make the most of the day. The players and the boss went ahead on the first bus, with club officials, guests and ambassadors following on in the second Liver Bus. In every way imaginable, it was emotional. With Jacob alongside me, I had a sense of déjà vu – I, too, was viewing the whole thing through a young boy's eyes.

This was where the journey started out for me – watching triumphant teams coming back home, parading the cups they'd won. I'd gone on to experience those highs myself as a player, and now here I was, a dad and a Liverpool Legend, living the whole thing one more glorious time and lapping it up like never before. As the tour started off in the outskirts, the streets were jam-packed with flag-waving fanatics and their families. There's a funny, long-running burn that the Evertonians like to cling to, that all Liverpool's support comes from Scandinavia and beyond. If that's the case, there must have been a good few thousand planes landing in Liverpool overnight, because there was something like a million fans lining the streets on 2nd June 2019 – not to mention the 100,000 still in Madrid! Seriously, if John Henry, Tom Werner and the rest of the team at FSG still harboured any doubts about the size of LFC and the potential to go ballistic, the homecoming parade would have blown their minds! Every now and then I would catch sight of John Henry shaking his head and nudging his wife, Linda, as though to say: 'This is insane!' I wanted to lean over and whisper, 'About that new Anfield Road stand ... we might want to make it a little bigger ...'

There was one brilliant moment where a fella stripped naked to attract the team's attention, stood on a rooftop wearing just his socks, clinging to a chimney pot! It was mental – a moment so off its head that Jürgen Klopp almost fell off the bus, he was laughing and pointing so much. This was all in and around the suburbs, by the way. When we got to the periphery of town – oh my word, it was like you'd imagine VE Day to have been like, added to the Millennium New Year's Eve, added to a free-festival reunion of The Beatles – just the biggest outpouring of love, joy and red smoke the city has ever seen.

The fact that I lived that entire unbelievable weekend with my son by my side will remain a lifetime joy.

FOOTNOTE:
WALKING ON

By the time you read this, A-League will be well under way and we'll all have a much better idea as to how my first serious foray into management is progressing. I'm out in Brisbane with my own equivalent of The Brain – my very good pal, the brilliant football thinker, Tony Grant, who is my trusted Number 2 at The Roar. We haven't gone down the 'marquee signing' route, instead allocating the bigger part of our budget to creating a good mix of gifted and experienced Australian players with some canny recruits from the UK leagues.

Like I say, last season was an all-time low for the Roar, finishing second from bottom with 74 goals conceded and only four games won. Granty and I had to take a root-and-branch approach, and that's never nice – essentially telling 15 players they're going to have to find a new club. It's all part and parcel of management, though – it can't all be accolades and laps of honour. We've brought in a whole new bunch of players and just enjoyed an excellent pre-season, winning eight out of nine games (and only losing the other one on penalties – so technically a draw!) We're doing okay. There's a fantastic buzz about the place and you can genuinely feel the optimism and the energy, going into the new season proper.

It's one hell of an exciting challenge being a proper manager, with calls, concerns, camera crews, players, plans and priorities coming at you, one after another after another. I love it! One or two of the UK newspapers have leapt to the inevitable conclusion that my time over here is merely a 'stepping stone' to bigger and better things. That's what they think. My mind is fully and solely focused on returning this great club to its former glory, bringing the crowds back in their thousands and giving them something to shout about. Look no further than the great Bill Shankly if you want a touchstone for my ambitions – I want to make the fans happy.

Everyone has their dreams, though. After our Barcelona Bin Ball Challenge, one of the lads we were with asked me if I ever saw myself managing Liverpool one day. Here's my answer in full:

> '*Well, Liverpool already have a brilliant manager and I don't think Jürgen has any plans of going anywhere else, any time soon. Anyway, I've got a brilliant job at a fantastic club and I'm completely committed to … Fuck it! Yes!*'

Walk on, people.

ACKNOWLEDGEMENTS

Lifelong thanks to Jim Aspinall, Steve Heighway, Hughie McAuley and Dave Shannon for nurturing me on and off the pitch.

To Ste Calvey for being there, through the bad times as well as the good – the best mate a man could wish for.

And to Alex Inglethorpe for believing in me.

IMAGE CREDITS

INDEX